PERSPECTIVES ON ENGLISH

W Wilbur Hatfield

Secretary-Treasurer
National Council of Teachers of English
1920 to 1953

Perspectives on

English

ESSAYS TO HONOR

W. WILBUR HATFIELD

EDITED BY

Robert C. Pooley

A PUBLICATION OF THE

*National Council
of Teachers of English*

NEW YORK

APPLETON-CENTURY-CROFTS, Inc.

PRINTED IN THE UNITED STATES OF AMERICA

EDITOR'S NOTE

THE ESSAYS in this volume were written in response to an invitation by the editor. Each contributor chose his own subject and developed it as he wished. The views and opinions expressed, therefore, are those of the authors themselves. Nothing in this volume may be considered an official or unofficial pronouncement of the National Council of Teachers of English.

ROBERT C. POOLEY

CONTENTS

vii

1

ROBERT C. POOLEY

Introduction

W. Wilbur Hatfield

NOT OFTEN does one man encompass in his lifetime the foundation, the development, and the flowering of a professional organization of teachers. It was the opportunity and privilege of W. Wilbur Hatfield to be associated with the handful of English teachers who founded the National Council of Teachers of English, to serve for thirty-three years as its secretary-treasurer, and to see it attain a membership exceeding 60,000. When he retired from office but not from active interest in the Council, it had become the largest and most influential subject-matter association of teachers. This organization offered Wilbur opportunity, but it was his ability, his wisdom, and his personality which made the opportunity a privilege and a career.

"If I were to choose a single word to describe Wilbur Hatfield, it would be *dedicated*," Professor J. N. Hook, successor to Hatfield as secretary-treasurer of the NCTE, wrote me recently. "And whenever I think that the working capacity of a man is limited, I recall Wilbur and wonder whether we do not underestimate human capacity. How did one man accomplish so much? He edited two magazines, part of the time with almost no assistance . . . he simultaneously managed an office with a steadily increasing business staff, and helped in various ways with two other magazines. He served as secretary-treasurer of the NCTE and treasurer of the CCCC. He kept informed about what was going on in the Council's many affiliates, and encouraged their formation, activities, and growth. He attended countless conferences . . . he wrote extensively . . . He carried heavy personal responsibilities known to very few. How did he accomplish so much? I come back to the word *dedicated*. Wilbur Hatfield makes

ROBERT C. POOLEY Professor of English and Chairman, Department of Integrated Liberal Studies, University of Wisconsin. Formerly Assistant Professor of English, Colorado State College of Education. Granted first W. Wilbur Hatfield Award for "extraordinary contributions to the teaching of English," and honorary life membership, 1952. Currently member of the Curriculum Commission, NCTE, and appointed liaison between it and the Board of Editors of the forthcoming college volume in the curriculum series. Author of *Teaching English Usage*, 1946; *Teaching English in Wisconsin*, 1948; *Teaching English Grammar*, 1957. Editor of numerous high school anthologies of literature. President of NCTE, 1940-1941. Director of Publications for NCTE from 1942 to 1951.

3

me believe that the truly dedicated man can do more than we normally believe to be possible for anyone."

W. Wilbur Hatfield (the W. stands for Walter, his father's name) was born in Pittsfield, Illinois, April 1, 1882. His father, Walter R. Hatfield, a small town school superintendent and later a Chicago school principal, was instrumental in bringing together the various regional teachers' associations to form the present powerful Illinois State association. After receiving a B.A. degree from Illinois College, Jacksonville, Illinois, Wilbur worked for the YMCA, did some graduate work and teaching in a Kansas college, and gained three years of high school teaching experience. At twenty-seven, he came to Chicago to teach in a high school and was assigned to what was then a brand-new school—Farragut. In fact, the school was so new, the staff so small, and the student body so limited that Wilbur was the only teacher of English and his students were exclusively freshmen.

The young teacher of English soon found himself engaged in a city-wide endeavor to revise the curriculum in high school English, in which undertaking he was the official representative of Farragut High School. This gathering was important to Wilbur and subsequently to the whole profession of teaching English, for it brought him to the attention of Dr. James Fleming Hosic, who was present as representative of the Chicago Teachers College (then Chicago Normal School). Of this meeting, James Mason reports from conversation with Dr. Hosic: "the discussion grew warm and young Hatfield was vocal. [Hosic] was attracted to Wilbur and was impressed by his brief but sane and well-expressed comments." (Hosic's words, quoted by Mason, to whom I am indebted for many details.)

Wilbur Hatfield's father and President Owen of Chicago Normal were good friends; this led to Wilbur's employment in 1912 as a teacher of English at Parker High School, connected with the Normal College. When he was tempted, shortly thereafter, to resign this position to enter college teaching, he was persuaded by Dr. Hosic to remain inasmuch as Hosic was planning to leave. Hosic did leave, and, in 1915, Wilbur was appointed to Hosic's position in the college. Thus began a teaching assignment which lasted for thirty-two years, until Wilbur's retirement from the college at sixty-five. In 1921, he was appointed head of the English Department, which administrative post he held, in addition to his teaching, editing, publishing, and secretary-treasurer duties in the Council, until his retirement.

In 1907, Wilbur married Grace Harriet Chamberlain. Mrs. Hatfield gave her husband a lifetime of affectionate understanding and companionship in facing all his responsibilities, and her keen mind and cultivated taste were of constant assistance to Wilbur in his task of keeping abreast of general and professional literature for review in the *English Journal*. Mrs. Hatfield, after a bravely endured long illness, died in 1958; two daughters survive.

At the charter meeting of the National Council of Teachers of English in Chicago in 1911, Wilbur was not present. It was an invitational meeting to which a limited number of representative teachers were called. But his ideas were sought, and were expressed in the first volume of the *English Journal* under the title, "What Can and Should the Council Do?" Impressed by this article, and recalling the vigorous young teacher at the earlier curriculum meeting, Dr. Hosic invited Wilbur to assist him in editing the *Journal,* and, in time, Wilbur took over the entire responsibility when Dr. Hosic was in New York and in Europe. From 1917 to 1921 Wilbur was officially the associate editor, and in 1921 he made arrangements to purchase the *English Journal* on a plan of amortized payments. His editorship of the *English Journal* continued until 1955, although the *Journal* was purchased by the Council in 1953, along with *College English* which Wilbur founded in 1939 (earlier there had been a college edition of the *English Journal.*) Wilbur continued to edit *College English* until 1955, also.

Ten years after the founding of the National Council of Teachers of English Wilbur became its secretary-treasurer, an office he held without salary or honorarium for thirty-three years. His first meeting with the Council took place in 1912; he was active in membership and attendance after 1912, missing only one or two meetings in over forty years. Oddly enough, the meeting at which Wilbur was elected secretary-treasurer (Boston, 1919) he was unable to attend for personal reasons. James Fleming Hosic, who had been secretary-treasurer, was that year elected president, and no doubt had a part in nominating his protégé for the office he was vacating.

In 1929, Wilbur purchased a building at 211 West 68 Street in

Chicago as the headquarters for his editorial activities, which became the official headquarters of the Council in the same year. A
disastrous fire in this building in 1953 destroyed much valuable
property: Council records were lost, and many publications stored
in the building were ruined by water. "The morning after the fire,"
writes Dr. Hook, "Mr. Hatfield, always eyes on the future, was already seeking new quarters. Aided by Business Manager Frank
Ross, he quickly found something usable and the move was made."
In the meanwhile, however, Wilbur was distressed by the polite or
angry letters which came to his desk from teachers who did not
know about the fire: What happened to my order? Where are the
books, pamphlets, recordings that I ordered? Dr. Hook adds, "By
the summer of 1953, the Council office was again functioning
smoothly, the complaints were all answered, and the NCTE was
once more on its feet." It was in November of this year that Wilbur
relinquished his office of secretary-treasurer and was made an honorary life member of the Council he had served so long.

How does one appraise the services of such a man? It is difficult
to do so without sounding absurdly eulogistic. This would annoy
Wilbur, who is, of all the men I know of notable achievement, the
most modest, unassuming, retiring. To the best of my knowledge this
is the first biographical sketch of Wilbur officially written for the
NCTE, and this comes seven years after his retirement from an
office he performed faithfully and gratuitously for thirty-three years!

I first met Wilbur in November, 1929, at the convention of the
NCTE in Kansas City. Arriving early, I was permitted to attend
the meeting of the Board of Directors on Thanksgiving afternoon. It
was a dramatic meeting; after formal preliminaries a sharp controversy
arose over administrative matters between the late C. C. Certain
and Wilbur Hatfield. From acrimonious debate they threatened to
proceed toward physical encounter before quieted by the officers
and delegates. Whatever the rights and wrongs, Wilbur was firm
in his position, and in the end victorious, for Certain withdrew from
the Council to found the National Conference on Research in English. It is characteristic of Wilbur that he became an active member
of the new organization.

"In a lifetime of an unusual number of notable achievements,"

I asked Wilbur, "what stands out as the most interesting task, the most satisfying accomplishment?" He thought a few moments, then replied that so far as he could recall, the editing of *An Experience Curriculum* was his most interesting task. This influential curriculum study of 1935 took more than the usual editing of a compilation. Wilbur had to complete many sections prepared by committees and to supply the grammar treatment and the illustrative expanded units. To this Mr. Hatfield gave much of his time: then, a semester's leave of absence from Chicago Teacher's College; finally, a summer. But the task was well done and earned for the Council a new level of respect and leadership. As to identifying his greatest accomplishment Wilbur said, perhaps a little wryly, "Getting the executive committee to keep the CCCC within the Council. "For once," he added, "I used my influence to sway the committee." It is a source of pride to Wilbur that this growing and vital college organization is a part of the National Council of Teachers of English.

One of the chief characteristics of Wilbur is his ability to guide and direct others without self-assertion or importunity. I became first aware of this quality during 1932 and 1933, having been elected second vice-president of the Council, and, thereby, becoming a member of the executive committee. At this time, Wilbur had been secretary-treasurer for thirteen years; presidents and other officers had come and gone; the new officers whom I joined were freshly elected, and except for the retiring president, were inexperienced. It would have been natural for the continuing secretary, with the whole history and tradition of the Council at his finger-tips, to direct the officers toward the performance of their duties, and, indeed, to set forth the problems then facing the Council. On the contrary, Wilbur joined the group, and, alert and silent, awaited events as though he were the most recently elected officer. When appealed to for background, he would state the facts objectively, briefly, and without expressing his opinion. It was his clear intention that policy should evolve from the executive committee undirected by the continuing secretary-treasurer. When I became president later, and, as a consequence, chairman of the executive committee, Wilbur's quality of self-effacement struck me afresh. When I deliberately asked for background or policy, I got it. But I never once felt, in all my flounderings and errors, that I was nudged, even ever so gently, in any direction by Wilbur. Other presidents, observing this quality, have expressed wonder and admiration which equals mine.

This withholding of direction did not indicate any lack of enthusiasm for the advancement of the Council. The Council—its growth, its members, its affiliates, its journals, its publications—were the center of Wilbur's professional life. To these he gave himself unreservedly with a constant eye toward the future. Nor did this eager anticipation diminish with the years; rather, it increased. Dr. Hook relates, "The first time I was in Wilbur Hatfield's office was in the summer of 1953, although I had known him for a number of years, as most English teachers do. After we had talked for awhile, he pulled a very fat folder from a drawer of his desk. I saw that it was labeled 'Ideas.' He scratched a few lines on a sheet of yellow paper which he inserted in the folder. This small act impressed me more than anything else in our day-long conference. Here he was, a man of seventy-one, about to relinquish a difficult job at which he had worked effectively for years, but still facing the future, still noting new ideas, still searching for ways to help the Council and improve the teaching of English." Current readers of the *English Journal* and *College English* know that this alertness to the latest advances and developments in English has not waned. One of the clearest, sanest articles on that newest of Council concerns, "Structural Linguistics," appeared under Wilbur's name in the *English Journal,* December, 1958.

In what manner is Wilbur now "retired" at age 78? He has retired to a job as consultant to teachers of the language arts at an elementary school near his home where he is helping retarded readers gain pleasure and knowledge from books. Nor is his intellectual curiosity the least diminished. Last week, when he walked nearly a mile with me in a cold wind to see me off at a railway station, his last query was, "How can we identify the signals by which we know in English that a statement is completed? How can I teach these children to recognize sentences?"

As Dr. Hook says: this is dedication. All who have known Wilbur, and they are thousands, have been enriched by his life. What more can be said of anyone?

2

RUTH MARY WEEKS

Prologue

Common Bond

When Arthur ruled in England battling back the Saxon hordes,
His native tongue was Gaelic, which has left the lovely words
That name her lakes and mountains, her rivers and her dales
And lend a lilting melody to British hills and vales.
The Saxons brought a sturdy speech of duties daily done,
Of farmstead and of folkmoot that made the village one.
Then came a blended language to unite all English folk,
That hardy Saxon freemen and Norman noble spoke;
The Saxon words of house and home, the generalities
Of Norman art and thought and rule that spell our liberties—
All these in one great warp and woof of simpler grammar wove
To fabricate man's noblest tongue, and endless treasure trove
Of words from every land and time, from every race of man,
Which borrows still as always since the English speech began—
The Greek of all her sciences, the Latin of her law,
The richest rhythms any verse of any people saw;
The tongue in which the grandest bard of all the nations wrote
The shining lines which down the years the lips of all men quote;
Great offspring of the ages, bright flag of thought unfurled,
New common bond of man to man—the language of the world!

RUTH MARY WEEKS   Now retired, formerly teacher of English in the high
schools and junior college of Kansas City, Missouri. Teacher in summer sessions in many colleges and universities. President of NCTE, 1929-1930. Chairman of the local committee for the NCTE convention in Kansas City. Editor
of NCTE English Monographs: *Current English Usage* and *A Correlated
Curriculum in English*. Author of books in the field of education including
The People's School, and numerous articles and poems in magazines and
newspapers.

3

HELEN K. MACKINTOSH

Let Them All Read

J ANUS-LIKE, writers of this volume and their readers will be taking both a backward and a forward look while they attempt to pause in 1960 to put their many and varied ideas of English into perspective. Rather, there will be a series of perspectives that may more nearly resemble the old-fashioned kaleidoscope than a mirror of past, present, and future, as one writer after another focuses on that aspect of English which is most significant in his own experience.

Usually to any person, whether teacher or parent, child or adolescent, literature, both old and new, is one of the basic elements in his experience. Those young children are fortunate whose parents can quote nursery rhymes which by their very rhythm may induce sleep, serve as an introduction to literature, and at the same time develop a common bond between child and adult. Early contact with verse is a form of communication that will never be forgotten, will always have meaning.

IMPORTANCE OF INTERESTS AND ATTITUDES

What a teacher of literature can do with and for children in the elementary school depends upon the experiences and attitudes that children bring with them when they come to school from home for the first time. If parents have quoted or read poetry to children, read aloud to each other, or to the family group, the child will pick up an interest in books and reading quite readily. Even more can be done to stimulate such interest if the young child has books of his own; first, cloth books, and, later, books of tough paper not easily torn; not an occasional book, but books at certain regular intervals such as on birthdays and at Christmas. As he builds a collection

HELEN K. MACKINTOSH Chief, Elementary Schools Section, U. S. Office of Education, Washington, D. C. Formerly Assistant Professor of Elementary Education, University of Pittsburgh; Associate Professor and Head of Department of English, School of Education, Miami University, Ohio. President of NCTE, 1956-1957. Associate Director, Curriculum Commission, NCTE; Co-chairman, Language Arts for Today's Children, 1954. Author of *A Critical Study of Children's Choices in Poetry* and bulletins of the U. S. Office of Education.

between bookends, then graduates to a bookshelf, and eventually to a bookcase of his own, the child establishes a feeling of ownership and interest which can ultimately become a lifelong habit.

In this aerospace age such advice may seem to be unrealistic; actually, the development of a feeling of the importance of a book to an individual is timeless. Furthermore, such an attitude represents the first step in the teaching of literature in the sense that a book and a child are brought together at the right time and in an appropriate way—one that is informal, yet highly personalized. To the extent that this approach can be preserved throughout the elementary school years, love of poetry and delight in reading can be fostered and at some point transmuted into a confirmed attitude of interest in books and a habit of turning to a book as the highest form of enjoyment. Such a situation can be brought about provided that no teacher applies pressure in the form of questioning or forced memorizing.

Marguerite Wilkinson, writing in 1925, quotes Sara Teasdale as saying: "I do not think a child should have to analyze poetry at all. It is likely to turn him against it forever. A love of poetry is too valuable a possession to jeopardize it by turning poetry into a task." [1] The same poet is quoted further: "A child should enjoy a poem just as he enjoys going out in an automobile, without understanding the mechanism of it, and without needing to know what was in the inventor's mind when he made it." [2]

This point of view is no less true of prose than of poetry for the child of elementary school age. These are the years when a child must be saturated with good literature, both that which has been time-tested as having permanent interest for any child, and the new in books for each successive year of the child's life. Whether old or new, the poem, the story, the book should possess that elusive characteristic, *literary quality*. There may well be a debatable issue here, as concerns the old and the new, the classic and the modern, but the thesis of this chapter follows Peoria in saying, "A little of both if you please."

One of the greatest hurdles that face the teacher of young chil-

---

[1] Marguerite Wilkinson, *Contemporary Poetry* (New York, The Macmillan Co., 1925), p. 5.
[2] *Ibid.*, p. 5.

dren is the insistence of some parents that, for children, the acquisition of the learning-to-read skills is the ultimate in reading. But a sober second thought should cause parents and teachers alike to remind themselves that the basic purpose in acquiring skills is to be able to read for one's own pleasure and enjoyment. Reading for pleasure and enjoyment, and to give pleasure to others, is a highly personalized experience, not to be confused with reading for study purposes. No value should be attached to skill for skill's sake. Overemphasis on the mechanics of reading has led keen observers of children to admonish the teacher with the caution, "Lose not the nightingale."

The adult takes a nostalgic look at the past, his own past, and the part books and reading played in his childhood. To each, his personal recollections are of most worth. To this writer, putting thoughts on paper on a cold winter evening, comes the memory of a bitter winter day, of the snow-crunching journey home from school, of sitting in the twilight as close as possible against the glassy red eyes of the coal stove, to be intrigued by the imaginary figures of Una and the Red Cross Knight silhouetted in the growing dusk of the room. Their story had been told and read so often that a glimpse of the figures gave wings to the imagination. The story was one of many that shared the stage with "A Dream of Fair Women," Chaucer's "Prologue," the Psalms, and Andersen's as well as Grimm's fairy tales. Since every child does not have this heritage, the teacher must begin where children are as they arrive at school for the first time, at the beginning of a new school year, or as they enter a new school. They may bring with them much or little mental baggage in the form of experiences with literature.

BEGINNING WITH CHILDREN WHERE THEY ARE

Nearly forty years ago Sterling Andrus Leonard enunciated a basic principle in teaching when he stated: "First, we must begin where pupils actually are, in experience, knowledge, and skill, if we would get them anywhere." [3] Teachers in this period were reminded of the studies of the previous century which emphasized the

[3] Sterling Andrus Leonard, *Essential Principles of Teaching Reading and Literature* (Philadelphia, J. B. Lippincott Co., 1922), p. 75.

importance of interest in the selection of materials for use with children by researchers such as Dunn [4] and Jordan. [5] They carried on experimental studies designed to discover, on the one hand, selections of greatest interest to children in grades one to three and, on the other hand, the actual books chosen by children who made voluntary withdrawals from public libraries. The findings of such studies were used by authors of so-called literary readers, who selected material not by guess work or personal opinion, but in terms of what children were known to choose.

The same soundness of point of view expressed by Leonard was brought out in a book sponsored by the National Council of Teachers of English and put into print twenty-five years ago. It was a volume [6] designed to encourage teachers to look at the continuity of English, including literature, from kindergarten to college. Set forth were principles and illustrations designed for the guidance of readers which were in no sense a prescription.

It is interesting to read the headings used at that time as organizing centers for literature experiences in kindergarten through grade six. These included (1) enjoying action and suspense, (2) enjoying humor of various kinds, (3) enjoying the world of the senses, (4) exploring the social world, and (5) enjoying fantasy and whimsy. Of particular interest was a special unit entitled "Sifting the Radio Programs," which was used to summarize the literature section of the volume. For each of the categories of experience there were materials listed ranging from easy to difficult, but there was no attempt to assign them to a grade level. Some of the poems, stories, and books are as usable in 1960 as they were a quarter of a century ago. Other titles would be eliminated because material of greater value is now available, or because children's interests have shifted. The teacher had a great deal of leeway in determining the way in which she would bring children and books together. Descriptions of practices in that period follow.

[4] Fannie W. Dunn, *Interest Factors in Primary Reading Material.* Teachers College, Columbia University Contributions to Education, No. 113 (New York, 1921).

[5] A. M. Jordan, *Children's Interests in Reading.* Teachers College, Columbia University Contributions to Education, No. 107 (New York, 1921).

[6] W. Wilbur Hatfield, Chairman, *An Experience Curriculum in English.* A Report of the Curriculum Commission of the National Council of Teachers of English (New York, Appleton-Century-Crofts, Inc., 1935).

LITERATURE PROGRAMS IN ACTION

Good teachers were reading aloud with comment by themselves and by children. Children were reading "around the group" for sharing purposes. Children were divided into small groups, not in terms of ability, but in terms of reading a book which interested them. They were motivated to prepare the material for reading aloud to the whole class, or children had opportunities to choose their favorite poems for reading aloud, or to use them for choral speaking. The most effective use of choral speaking came about when children had heard and read a poem so often that they had memorized it painlessly. The form of choral speaking was such that children practiced enough to get personal satisfaction from participation, but not so much that a polished production became the goal.

Good teachers recognized that questions should not emphasize definitions or details, but should stress central idea, situations, and characters. In order to bring out these aspects of a story, a book, or a story-telling poem, teachers made interesting use of various forms of dramatization.

Pantomimes, impersonations, dramatic play, informal dramatizations, movies, peep shows, puppet shows, converting a story into a play by having one child read the narrative and others the character parts, and developing a play in written form—these were all ways of accomplishing the purpose of having children appreciate the significance of the story through experiencing the thoughts and emotions of the characters. Such forms of participation as those mentioned called for discussion, expression of opinion, exchange of ideas, re-reading to clarify, identifying periods in history, or re-creating a mood. Naturally the maturity of the children and their previous experiences determined the teacher's plan for bringing children and books together.

It was usually true that the teacher developed a lesson within the limits of a daily period. The writer, however, recalls a teacher who in the 1920's used a visit of Vachel Lindsay to a university community to stimulate the reading and study over a period of several weeks of his poems that were appropriate for fifth grade children. The result came after Lindsay made his appearance. The children enthusiastically organized an assembly program based on his life and the poems they had especially enjoyed. In another instance, a group of second grade children became so absorbed in the stories told and illustrated by Beatrix Potter that they read and compared *The Tale of Peter Rabbit, The Tale of Squirrel Nutkin, Town-Mouse, The Tale of Jemima Piddle-Duck,* and *Tom Kitten,* and spent several weeks enjoying these books. But these examples were probably exceptions rather than the rule.

RE-EMPHASIS ON LITERATURE FOR CHILDREN

In 1954, Volume II [7] of the series produced by the Commission on the English Curriculum highlighted the place and importance of literature in children's experience. In the section describing the integration of the language arts, there is a detailed account telling of the way in which in Norfolk, Virginia, primary grade children write and illustrate their own stories in book form. In early stages children may dictate the story to the teacher. Beginning in the latter part of second grade and continuing in grade three, children do the writing as individuals, or collaborate in small groups. (They learn the use of the word *collaborate.*) The written stories develop after illustrated books for children are read aloud to them; they then reread the books themselves. Such books, made by children, are dignified by being given a place on the library shelf in the classroom where they were produced. Beginning with the fourth grade in the Maury School, Richmond, Virginia, children may type their stories or dictate them to the teacher or to an older pupil who types. Children go through the process of illustrating, binding with hard covers, and giving the volume every appearance of being a valued addition to the room library. Later, the book is taken home, and may be the only book which the child owns. The influence of good books in these situations makes a deep impression upon boys and girls, an impression which teachers recognize as a permanent influence in encouraging children to enjoy the reading of books, and most of all to own books, as a part of their daily living.

[7] Commission on the English Curriculum, *Language Arts for Today's Children* (New York, Appleton-Century-Crofts, Inc., 1954).

RESOURCES FOR THE TEACHING OF LITERATURE

A constant resource for teachers in the elementary school is found in the files, as well as the current issues, of *Elementary English*, the official magazine of the Elementary Section of the National Council of Teachers of English. Scarcely an issue appears that does not contain an article or articles rich in suggestions for making literature come alive in classrooms at all levels of the elementary school. Such articles are written primarily by classroom teachers who are close to children and can, for that reason, give practical help.

Take, for example, the article which appeared in the March, 1956, issue of *Elementary English* entitled "The Process of Creative Writing," [8] which reflects the fact that the children studied had been exposed to many poems which they had heard and no doubt reread for their own pleasure. Six children were willing to share their thought processes aloud with their teacher as they wrote original poems. In the one case which is reported in detail, the first column gives the child's sequence of thought, and a corresponding column gives the teacher's interpretation of what is happening. The final result, an eight-line poem entitled "A Day at the Beach," reflects the accumulation of a child's impressions, influenced by his exposure to poetry. Children frequently choose poetry as the form of creative expression they will attempt.

Behind all such products is the experience with many poems brought about in a wide variety of ways. The teacher reads poems aloud, rereads favorite poems by request, and makes poetry books easily available for children to read for themselves, especially those including poems they have enjoyed listening to. He encourages informal choral reading of poems which often results in memorization, or children taking character parts while one of their number reads the narrative, as in A. A. Milne's "The King's Breakfast." [9] Children should be encouraged to tape record their reading of poems in preparation for sharing a favorite poem with the group.

[8] Kathleen McEnroe, "The Process of Creative Writing," *Elementary English*, XXXV (March, 1958), No. 3, pp. 159-162.

[9] A. A. Milne, *When We Were Very Young* (New York, E. P. Dutton & Co., Inc., 1924).

Two third-grade children themselves initiated the play that follows [10] as a result of having read many of the poems of A. A. Milne.

A DAY WITH CHRISTOPHER

ACT I

Place: In a palace. KING *and* QUEEN *are sitting on their thrones.*

(CHRISTOPHER ROBIN *walks in*)

C.R.: Have you seen my mouse? I opened his box for a half a minute just to make sure he was really in it and while I wasn't looking he jumped out. Has anybody seen my mouse?

KING: Excuse me, but I'm waiting for my butter for my bread.

(EMMELINE *walks in*)

EMMELINE: Dear Queen, I am Emmeline. Are my hands clean?

QUEEN: Yes.

KING: (*to C.R.*) I haven't seen your mouse.

(C.R. and EMMELINE *walk out*)

ACT II

Place: The Market Square.

(C.R. *comes in and says to the* LAVENDER LADY)

C.R.: Have you seen my mouse?

LAVENDER LADY: No.

(C.R. *walks over to* MARY JANE'S *house*)

C.R.: Is Mary Jane in?

NURSE: I don't know what's wrong with Mary Jane. She won't eat her rice pudding.

(C.R. *walks out and goes home*)

ACT III

Place: In CHRISTOPHER ROBIN'S *home.*

(C.R. *is playing "Round-about"*)

C.R.: Round-about and Round-about and Round-about I go! I think I am a postman.

C.R.'s MOTHER: Come in for lunch.

(C.R. *goes in to lunch. After lunch,* C.R. *says*)

[10] Original play by Peggy Ableman and Cathy Hatch. Grade 3, Highlands School, Wilmington, Delaware, 1959.

C.R.: I will play with Binker.

MOTHER: Who in this silly world is "Binker"?

C.R.: Binker is my imaginary playmate.

MOTHER: Don't mess things up.

(C.R. *goes to his room*)

ACT IV

Place: In CHRISTOPHER ROBIN'S *room.*

(C.R. *starts to play and falls asleep. After his nap* C.R. *wakes up and has the sneezles*)

(DOCTOR *comes in.* DOCTOR *examines* C.R.)

DOCTOR: It might turn into measles.

ACT V

Time: That night.

(C.R. *is ready for bed and says his prayers*)

C.R.: God Bless Mommy! I know that's right. Oh! God bless Daddy! I quite forgot. Oh! God Bless Nanny and make her good. Oh! Thank you, God, for a lovely day and what was the other thing I had to say? God bless me!

What children think and do as a result of their experiences with poetry or with other forms of literature is the measure of the effectiveness of teaching.

In 1957 a subcommittee of the Elementary Section Committee of the Council brought out a portfolio [11] in loose-leaf form consisting largely of articles reprinted from *Elementary English*. A number of these articles, such as "Eight-Year-Olds Tangled in *Charlotte's Web*," give a firsthand account of how a book and its author became a permanent possession of a group of third-grade children. Other titles in the portfolio to be explored are "Pupils, Teachers, and Creative Dramatics," and "Reading about Emotions in the Primary Classroom." These are guidelines, not prescriptions or recipes. The teacher with ingenuity and creative imagination will use them as springboards for adventures with books.

The resources are available to teachers for continuous improve-

[11] The National Council of Teachers of English, *Creative Ways in Teaching the Language Arts*. A Portfolio of Elementary Classroom Procedures (Champaign, Ill., 1957).

ment of the teaching of literature old and new. To the extent that teachers familiarize themselves with books of all types that children of today enjoy, they will be able to find the right book for the right child at the teachable moment. What more can be said? The value of literature is far-reaching. The impact of real or imaginary characters and situations on a child's own attitudes and behavior is one of the intangibles. Even so, in the fast-moving and ever-changing world of today each individual needs moral and spiritual support that must come from inner resources. These, he himself, his teacher, and his parents have developed together throughout his elementary and later school life, perhaps to a greater degree through literature than as a result of any other one influence. And so once again be it said—"Let them all read!"

4

MARION C. SHERIDAN

The Teaching of Literature
in Secondary Schools

> Cool'd a long age in the deep-delved earth,
> Tasting of Flora and the country green,
> Dance, and Provençal song, and sunburnt mirth!

He may smell the perfume of all Arabia, or "steaks in passageways," when, in Eliot's [3] "Preludes"—

> The winter evening settles down. . . .

Archibald MacLeish [4] would measure time through odors in *Land of the Free*—

> It was two hundred years from the smell of the tidewater
> Up through the Piedmont: on through the piney woods.

Responsiveness to literature, whether fiction or nonfiction, involves mood and emotion: happiness, gaiety, mirth, depression, anger, sadness, pity, and fear; it involves objectivity, the development of power to think. If the student develops a rapport with literature emotionally and intellectually, he is likely to have what is of supreme importance—a literary experience. With that may come vision.

Speaking to writers at the tenth annual National Book Awards ceremony, Dr. Arthur H. Compton, [5] a Nobel Prize scientist, indicated well the possibilities of literature:

But now it is not the vision of the scientists which is needed. It is the vision of you whose concern is first of all with what is in the hearts and minds of men. How can we open the way for the fullest growth of the spirit of men? Here is the question that is in our hearts.

Out of the teacher's firm belief in the power of literature "to open the way for the fullest growth of the spirit of men" comes conviction. The teaching of literature has a purpose, and that purpose determines the method.

A literary experience is not likely to result from the teaching of literature by centering in parroting. Memorizing facts about autho' or about literary periods, lists of characters or of vocabulary, defi tions of types of literature is not likely to lead to a literary experie Nor is a literary experience the outcome of drawing two sides

[3] *Ibid.*
[4] From *Land of the Free* (Copyright, 1938, by Archibald MacL printed by permission of Harcourt, Brace and Co., Inc.).
[5] *New York Times*, Wednesday, March 4, 1959, p. 23, col. 1.

triangle to represent a plot, labelling the angles and putting a finger on a spot called *climax*.

The literary experience comes rather from the impact of a book which has something vital to offer a particular student at a particular time, some revelation of breathing, feeling, thinking human beings. Whether or not a student has a literary experience is a severe test of the teaching of literature.

Since our literary heritage is a massive one, embracing widespread places, generations, and cultures; reflecting the aspirations, failures, and achievements of mankind, the teaching of literature is not a simple matter. It involves innumerable choices in books and in methods. Where there are no choices, where all the choices have been made, the teaching is likely to be perfunctory and ineffective, instead of lively, searching, creative, and satisfying. All books are possible choices. Which of all the books in the world should be presented? When and to whom should they be presented? How can each best be presented? These questions cannot be answered in a few words, nor can they be answered for all teachers of literature in secondary schools, nor for any one teacher for all time. They are questions requiring constant reflection.

Choices of books and methods are contingent in part upon a teacher's knowledge of his students: their abilities, their stages of development, their interests, and their needs. In a comprehensive high school the range of abilities is very wide. It is, therefore, easy to go to extremes, thinking of the simplest material and the most difficult. Chatting recently with a tenth-grade student in an independent school, I learned that she had spent the morning reading for her English class an interlinear version of Ovid's *Metamorphoses*. Her group had been studying ancient history and Greek and Roman literature. Is Ovid's account a wise choice? This question is not so easy to answer as one in regard to the use of books rewritten with a view to simplification. For the most part, the answer to the latter point is a vehement "No!" Rewritten books, if · used, should be chosen deliberately and with the greatest caution. What can their place be in "literature"?

The teaching of literature should be subtle and artistic, concerned with the whole student—his senses, his emotions, his imagination, and his intellect. It should make his mind receptive. Without being bewildering, the teaching should do many things at one time, the kind of teaching that Miss Lucia Mirrielees so wisely called "*oblique.*" If the teacher has a clearcut philosophy and a deep knowledge of literature, oblique teaching makes implicit in every lesson ways to approach and to penetrate literature. With a definite end in view, the teacher will not waste time. His goal will be a long-range goal towards which he will strive patiently day by day. Perhaps literature is a mosaic into which little pieces are fitted each day. Eventually the pattern will be defined and will be discovered, oftentimes with genuine excitement.

An undercurrent in the teaching of literature—no matter how able the class—is the teaching of reading skills. For the most part this teaching will be implicit; from time to time it may be explicit. The teacher of literature must be acquainted with research in reading techniques and should incorporate them in his teaching. He must be aware of eye span; vocalization; pace, or speed; the comprehension of words, sentences, paragraphs; and, most important of all, wholes. Involved with the literary work as a whole—long or short—are the parts and their relationship to the whole. And that whole is greater than the sum of its parts. It is obvious that in a society with books, literature cannot possibly be revealed to those who cannot read.

Closely allied to the need for reading skills is the need for the recognition of various types of literature. For each type, an adjustment must be made, for each type has its own conventions with which it achieves communication; each offers material in its unique way. Different types—poetry, plays, biographies, essays, novels, short stories—call for different approaches. Recognition of type may give a clue to getting at the author's point. The study of poetry is extremely important, not that students will be poets, but that the methods of poetic communication are especially helpful as a basis for the interpretation of all literature.

Flexible definitions of type are important, for classifications are not rigid and unchanging. The dividing line between short story and essay or even tragedy and comedy may be shadowy. Critical and biographical accounts, factual and fictional biographies need to be distinguished. Exactly what a novel is, has not been agreed upon.

Comments such as Edith Wharton's in her "Introduction" to *Ethan Frome* reveal an author's concern about the way to present a story. Some poetry is prosaic; some prose is poetical.

At the recent presentation of Charles Laughton's stage adaptation of *John Brown's Body*, by Stephen Vincent Benét, at the Yale School of Drama, the program note by Dean F. Curtis Canfield, [6] illustrates the flexibility of a type of literature:

The flexibility of the theatre as an avenue of communication with few stop signs has been demonstrated recently by several successful "dramatic readings" of various works of literature not originally intended for presentation on the stage. . . .

There is no question in my mind that productions of this kind are capable of stretching the boundaries of the theatre medium. They also make us aware of the folly and confusion which ensue when we try to arrive at a rigid definition of what a play is. In fact, if it does nothing else *John Brown's Body* should give weight to the liberal notion that a play is anything which is presented by actors on a stage before an audience.

There must be a place in our modern theatre for such productions, if only to remind us that even the Homeric Epic was probably meant to be spoken or sung rather than read in silence.

Whether *John Brown's Body* is a play or not is a much less important question than whether or not you are moved and stirred by it. And naturally we hope that you will be.

Audio-visual approaches often aid in the teaching of literature; they may stimulate the imagination and suggest what is to be found on the pages of books. Motion pictures, filmstrips, radio and TV programs, and pictures are resource materials which may contribute to a realization of the implications of print. Often the result of their use is to impress the students with the superiority of communication by words in books.

Commercial films in motion-picture theaters have been difficult to use with classes because they cannot be shown when they are needed. But excerpts from commercial films—cut to fit into class periods, often with time for discussion or cut to offer a dilemma or a situation for discussion or to whet interest for the full story—may incite a desire to read further. Among such excerpts are "David Copperfield: the Boy"; "Kipling's India," based on Kipling's *Kim*;

[6] January 20-24, 1960.

"Washington Square," based on Henry James's story; and "Meet the Forsytes," based on Galsworthy's *The Forsyte Saga.* "Dickens: Characters in Action" gives glimpses into characters in several of Dickens's works, with a view to stimulating wide reading of Dickens. Excerpts of such recent films as *The Doctor's Dilemma* and *The Devil's Disciple* have stimulated attendance at the showing of the entire films, have encouraged reading, and have prompted the purchase of books, especially paperbacks.

Films such as the twelve carefully prepared thirty-minute lessons on *Our Town, Hamlet,* and *Oedipus,* filmed in color in the pilot project carried on by the Council for a Television Course in the Humanities for Secondary Schools, Inc., indicate further opportunities for the use of films in the teaching of literature.

Radio programs of a literary nature may be discerning and provocative. They may be taped and repeated for a class or for individuals.

Some students may not have an opportunity to see TV programs at home. During school hours few literary programs have been available. A number of TV programs have served, as have paperbacks, to make old books seem recent. At their best, they show, as do motion pictures, what can be created from an author's words: imaginatively, in the spirit of the original. Unfortunately words may be distorted when filmed—and the vision of the author destroyed.

Recordings of literary works by their authors or by excellent readers may be stimulating. The number of such recordings is multiplying rapidly due to improved recording devices and increased interest in the spoken word. The National Council of Teachers of English pioneered in making literary recordings. In a recent issue of the Sunday *Herald-Tribune,* a critic, Herbert Kupferberg, had high praise for recent London recordings of performances of uncut Shakespearean plays in the John Dover Wilson edition. Instead of trying to present a theater performance, the Marlowe Society of Cambridge focused on home listening. The recording of *Othello* was praised especially. The reviewer wrote that the only word to describe the seven recordings is "stunning." [7]

Attendance at an actual play is really an audio-visual aid in the teaching of drama. It supplements stage directions that may seem

[7] Sunday, January 24, 1960, Section 4, p. 8.

stark and unimaginative. A stage production forcibly brings to life
words, the significance of which may be overlooked in silent reading.
Words become alive when they interpret, reveal tone, control gesture;
when they are enhanced by lighting, setting, sound, and, sometimes,
even silence.

The teacher of literature should be something of an actor. George
Sokolsky, who when he was younger resented Leonard Bernstein's
"hamming," recently watching it on television with children in the
audience, realized that "hamming is a great art, the art of making
the mind receptive, the art of teaching." [8] Students, too, need a
chance to act.

Audio-visual aids help readers to "translate" the printed page. The
appreciation of literature is a form of translation, not from a European or Asiatic tongue, but from more or less familiar English words
set in type on a page. They may be glanced at and read in rote
fashion, perfunctorily, without emotion and without analysis. To
some students, these letters are as inscrutable as the Rosetta stone
was to scholars before it was deciphered. Translation turns symbols
into human thought and into the actions of human beings with ten-
sions, satisfactions, problems, and joys; into space and strange worlds,
near and distant.

Sometimes students are unable to translate a printed page of
fiction because they do not identify the narrator. This is true in the
reading of Browning's dramatic monologues, of *Ethan Frome,* and,
even, of *Treasure Island.* In their translation they must be sensitive
to time and place. Knowing only here and now, they may be satisfied thoughtlessly with a vague "during this time." Time must take
on meaning, whether the passage of time is from day to day or year
to year. Words such as *Crusades, Elizabeth, Shakespeare, Milton,
Johnson, Franklin, Victoria,* and *Melville* should bring to mind a
wealth of associations with various eras.

Though the settings of *My Ántonia, Death Comes for the Arch-
bishop, Arrowsmith, Ethan Frome,* and *Washington Square* are all in
the United States, the backgrounds are by no means identical. They
must be distinguished from each other and from Lafcadio Hearn's
Louisiana, Mark Twain's Mississippi, and Carl Sandburg's Chicago.

[8] "These Days," "Some Thoughts on Leonard Bernstein and the Art of
Teaching," *New Haven Evening Register,* Friday, March 6, 1959.

Part of the attraction that Benét's *John Brown's Body* has for students is its vivid creation of the personality of places in the United States. Naturally, actual travel contributes to the implications of time and place. A surprisingly large number of students today have lived in or traveled to places away from home including distant lands. Visits to libraries and to literary shrines wherever they may be—the home of Longfellow in Cambridge, of Stevenson in Monterey, of Carlyle in London, of Keats in Rome—ordinarily induce reflections on writers and their influence. In Finland, for example, it is striking to note respect and a kind of dependence upon and gratitude to their writers, such as the poet Runeberg; the novelist, playwright, and poet Kivi; the prose writers, Sillanpää and Pekkanen; and Lönnrot, the compiler of the *Kalevala.*

Although great writers present universal truths far more important than local scenes, travel, actual or vicarious, gives valuable insight into authors and their works, into national characteristics, sympathies, and antipathies. Travelers find new meanings in accounts written of their lands by natives: Mike Waltari writing of Finland, Hans Christian Andersen and Isak Dinesen writing of Denmark. Countries and sections may be presented well by those who are not natives. In *Two Years Before the Mast,* Dana has been said to present California more successfully than natives have done. E. M. Forster succeeded with India; Maugham and Michener, with far-off islands; Henry James, with Italy; and Lawrence Durrell, with Cyprus.

The international nature of literature is emphasized by the increase in foreign-language books in the United States and by books in English in book stores on the Continent. Pasternak's *Safe Conduct,* purchased in Bergen, Norway, leads to reflections. H. E. Bates presents Switzerland, Burma, and India. The plays of Ibsen, Shakespeare, O'Neill, Tennessee Williams, Maxwell Anderson, Arthur Miller, and others have been presented in Finland. Stockholm has had priorities on the presentation of O'Neill.

Even though the main issue is not the presentation of place, place may be inextricably woven into unforgettable stories, as in Pearl Buck's *The Good Earth,* Joseph Conrad's *The Rover,* Alan Paton's *Cry the Beloved Country,* and Albert Camus's "The Guest."

Authors may be indifferent to place, as Shakespeare was in writing *As You Like It.* To focus on actual geographical places in *Macbeth* or in *Hamlet* is to miss the effect the genius of Shakespeare created, even though few sight-seers in Denmark would wish to miss Kronberg Castle.

It is important to distinguish between *place* as an environment for human beings, as in the writing of Hardy, and *place* as the end, as it is in stories of local color. Universality transcends mere location. Robert Frost cannot be confined to California, to Vermont, or to New England, nor can Thoreau's *Walden* be localized as stereotyped descriptions of the book sometimes suggest. Thoreau was certain there was nothing in the world that could not be found at Walden; his book had implications for mankind in many far places, including Great Britain and India.

Often it is valuable for students to read more than one book or one poem by an author. Identical elements in the novels of Hardy—setting, peasants, music, style—reveal patterns; each book makes another more clear. The works of an author may provide interesting contrasts and range, as in the works of Hemingway, of Milton, of Shakespeare. Students should be introduced to collections of poems by one poet or to collections of short stories by one writer.

Authors may advantageously be compared: Mark Twain, Henry James, Edith Wharton; Jane Austen, Charlotte Brontë, Emily Brontë; Dickens, Thackeray; Longfellow, Wordsworth, Whitman, and MacLeish.

Teaching literature by theme may throw into relief different points of view, different visions. Literature of any type may be used to illuminate the theme. Themes are innumerable; those chosen should be worthy of deep consideration. The aim of the author should not be distorted in order to fit a work into a category, nor should focusing on a theme distract from literature as literature by placing an emphasis on information or minor points.

Among themes of interest may be those concerned with families and family relationships, as in *The Human Comedy, Pride and Prejudice, The Forsyte Saga.* Man and the earth may be of interest in Mildred Davis's *Winter Wheat,* Pearl Buck's *The Good Earth,* Ernest Poole's "'The Mother Everlasting,'" and Knut Hamsen's *The Growth of the Soil.* Literature can help in distinguishing between courage and fear, as in *Profiles in Courage,* Browning's "Clive," and *The Red Badge of Courage.* With mature students, the nature of tragedy may be of interest as a theme. Such studies as *Tragic Themes in Western Literature* and *The Vision of Tragedy* give significance to aspects of tragedy in literature.

The fact that discussion is stimulating in interpreting and appreciating literature is evident in panels on the radio, the discussion of Great Books, and reviews, for example, in the *Saturday Review,* the *New Yorker,* the *Atlantic Monthly,* and Sunday book supplements of the *New York Herald Tribune* and of the *New York Times.*

In English classes discussion should be informal, human, but still searching. It requires and promotes thoughtful, critical reading and reflection. Questions, provocative ones, should not avoid cold logic. Discussion may be about one book or parts of a book read intensively by a group; discussion may be about extensive reading. Students have a chance to test their reading, to realize how much they have failed to grasp or how well they have read. Discussion gives students a chance to share experiences with others and to test their own conclusions.

Through the discussion of complete literary works the architectonics may become apparent. Details, apparently casual, may become significant. The connotations of words may be realized. Irony may be recognized through concern for tone and mood. The purposes of metaphors and symbols may be clarified. Discussion is excellent for penetrating the author's method: the order in which he presents events, his way of juggling items in an attempt to communicate effectively. Discussion provides an opportunity for enrichment, especially of aesthetic aspects in the movement of the lines, and by noting parallels in art, sculpture, and music—all aspects of the imaginative.

Analysis is not incompatible with appreciation; it is more likely to be the source of appreciation. It is by analyzing, weighing, and evaluating that the reader develops appreciation of the artist who has pondered and planned, struggled to communicate his vision,—and succeeded.

The teaching of literature must always have as an end the stimulation of independent reading. Students must choose books carefully, for books are numberless and time is limited and precious. Independent reading must be encouraged by every possible means. The teaching of literature must provide an audience for excursions into libraries and discoveries of books that have meaning for individual students. Books should be available in the classroom. Teachers and students should bring in books. Students should be at home in the library, school and local, and in bookstores. Ultimately, probably, students will not read literature unless they read independently.

At the beginning of a school year, students may plan independent reading for the year ahead. This is not too far in advance if the list is regarded as flexible. Choosing books requires a study of book lists, book reviews, and catalogues, conversations with friends and librarians, attendance at lectures on books, browsing in the library. It means more than a subscription to a book club, for it asks for individual initiative in choosing from books of all types, all countries, all times.

A student should keep a record of his reading, giving at least the names of the books, the authors, original comments, and possibly brief quotations from the book. Cumulative Reading Records, forms published by the National Council of Teachers of English, are helpful in presenting brief accounts which give clues to a student's interests in reading and to his growth in reading.

The successful teaching of literature should make lovers of books, sensitive to fine editions, to plates, sketches, introductions, and the presence or absence of notes. These booklovers would cherish books and reread them, would be curious about books and eager and impatient to read. They would have a fondness for libraries and for browsing. They would respect all kinds of good books, delighting at times in paperbacks, in which they could underline, question, and make notes.

The teaching of literature would involve reading but also listening and speaking. It would be concerned with writing, suggesting content and method, and contributing to what has been called *power* in writing.

How can the teaching of literature be evaluated? The answer is not known. A literary experience is intangible. Essay-type tests have probably been more successful than short-answer tests in which it is difficult to avoid questions calling for facts. Essay questions to appraise numerically or alphabetically the literary experiences of students have been difficult, if not impossible, to phrase. Reading skills are believed to be measurable, but not the reading of literature.

A student's penetration into literature is more likely to be revealed indirectly than through tests, which should, however, be attempted. One inarticulate but sensitive student revealed his response to *Quentin Durward* by voluntarily modeling in clay figures and scenes that were imaginative yet true in interpretation. Another seemed to have developed a sense of values about books when he spontaneously regretted spending all his time reading *African Queen* and *Captain from Connecticut*. He was not criticizing those books, but with sincerity and enthusiasm he was considering other issues. A literary experience may have no connection with some so-called literary projects, which are actually carpentry, gadgetry, sewing, cutting, or pasting. The lighting up of a face, the repetition of a line, allusions, comparisons, chuckling, honest talks about books, curiosity about books, the purchase of books, incidental revelations may be the chief indications that something has happened as a result of the teaching of literature.

Interesting experiments are being carried on to utilize the potentialities of master teachers. They are concerned with flexible class size, modified from day to day. For what aspects of the teaching of literature should there be large classes? medium? small? How much time should classes in literature spend in the library? How should they spend that time? Which students should be in small classes? which larger ones? Within recent years a rush of students to high school tended to lower the teaching of literature. Now the desire to accelerate the "academically talented" and to make possible admission to college in spite of spectacular increases in the number of college applicants is pushing the teaching of literature upward. The teacher of literature will have many choices to make to adjust his teaching to the individuals in his groups. He may have an opportunity to concentrate on a type of literature or a period or a theme.

Literature, international and universal, is civilizing. It extends the scope of an individual through his senses, his emotions, and his mind. Literature makes it possible for him to see beyond himself into other lands, into other times, and into the minds and hearts of all kinds of people. If particular works of literature have survived, they are likely to reveal truths recognized and accepted by one or more generations. It is well for young people to know many of those works;

through them they may achieve some humility and a perspective. Even though the idiom of youth is the idiom of recent writers, secondary school students must not be limited to the contemporary.

In the secondary school, the teacher of literature with a deep love of books and a deep and wide knowledge of books may find this love and knowledge useless unless he also has, for one thing, a genuine interest in individuals and in their growth. For another thing, the teacher must be able to bring students and books together in such a way that the experience is mutually exciting and that it opens "the way for the fullest growth" of the human spirit. It can be hoped that, as a result of the teaching of literature in the secondary school, many students will find literature as indispensable as Arnold believed it to be when he wrote in "The Study of Poetry," "Even if good literature entirely lost currency with the world, it would still be abundantly worthwhile to continue to enjoy it by oneself."

5

THOMAS CLARK POLLOCK

Shall They Inherit the Realms of Gold?

There was a child went forth everyday;
And the first object he looked upon, that object he became;
And that object became part of him for the day, or a certain part of the
day, or for many years, or stretching cycles of years.

WALT WHITMAN, "There Was a Child Went Forth"

I F WE WERE ASKED, "Do we have a literary heritage?" the answer
would, of course, be *yes*.
If we were asked, "Should we transmit our literary heritage?" the
answer would, of course, again be *yes*.

If we were asked, "Are our schools now doing all they should to
help boys and girls grow into possession of their literary heritage?"
we might, if we know what is going on, become uneasy.

In the last generation, we have, I believe, made real progress in
many phases of the teaching of reading and the teaching of literature. But at the same time, I suggest that we have done less than we
should, less than we can, to help students not merely to read something, but to come, year by year, into possession of their literary
heritage.

In the 1920's, most educated Americans had common knowledge
of the English Bible, the major plays of Shakespeare, and Lincoln's
Gettysburg Address. What literature of lasting value do we have in
common now?

In this article, I am going to assume (and not try to argue or prove)
that its literary heritage is of inestimable value to a civilized society
and that the transmission of this birthright should be a normal and
fundamental part of the process of education. If I may not assume this
within the family of the National Council of Teachers of English,
we are more lost than I have suspected, and the sons and daughters
of the American people are in even greater danger of never becoming acquainted with their literary heritage than I think they
are. But with readers who are seriously concerned about improving
the teaching of English, I think I can assume that our literary heritage is important and that our generation should try to transmit a
recognition and love of it to the next generation.

THOMAS CLARK POLLOCK Dean and Professor of English, Washington
Square College of Arts and Sciences, New York University. Formerly Chairman, Department of English Education, New York University. President of
NCTE, 1947-1948. Member of Curriculum Commission, NCTE. Representative to Basic Issues Conference, 1958. Author of *The Philadelphia
Theater in the Eighteenth Century*, 1933; *The Nature of Literature*, 1942;
The English Language in American Education, 1945. Coauthor of *The Correspondence of Thomas Wolfe and Horner Andrew Watt*, 1954. Contributor
to learned journals.

In this article, I wish to call attention briefly to some of the developments in American society and American education during the last generation which have turned the attention of the schools away from our literary heritage; then, I want to suggest one or two things we can do about the scope and sequence of introducing the student to his literary heritage.

I

One difficulty has been that year by year we have become an increasingly large, complex, and pluralistic society. In the nation as a whole and in the cities in which most of us live, we are not one community, but several.

A small, "tight" community, even if it lacks the comunicative paraphernalia of printing press, phonograph, radio, and television, may have an easier task in communicating our literary heritage.

John Collier, [1] in *The Indians of the Americas*, comments on the process in a simpler form of society, in describing the life art of the Indian peoples:

Hence was built and sustained the life art. The elements of this life art were language, song, dance, ceremonial, craftsmanship, ascetic discipline, fighting, and the chase. All of these, including language, were sustained by unwritten tradition, and the tradition was communicated through the generations by systematized education. . . .

Their laws and languages, their racial bibles and folklores and poetic literatures, are carried in memory alone. . . .

Saturated with imagination, formed by imagination, the language enters into its fullness when it is sung, when it is danced, when the visual symbolism of craftwork and of ceremonial drama construe and expand its intent. Then great and ample speech takes form, and every member of the group joins in the amplitude of speech. "They of the earth-grown cities know what Homer knew."

In the ancient small-community civilization of the Pueblo Indians, for example, the month-by-month activities of the community gave normal occasion to transmit orally the literary heritage to the younger generation. In our more complex civilization, however, the occasions for transmitting this heritage do not occur day-by-day or year-by-year

[1] (New York, New American Library, 1947), pp. 21-22.

for our young people as a whole as a matter of course. (Some such occasions may occur for the members of particular religious groups.) On the contrary, today, a young person may live for years in the same apartment house with, say, a Shakespearean actor, a literary scholar, a poet, and a housewife who is an avid reader, and, not only never meet them, but never even suspect that traveling in "the realms of gold" is a regular and sustaining part of their lives.

Another difficulty arises because in Western civilization the public schools alone never have had the whole responsibility for transmitting the literary heritage. This responsibility was shared by the home, the church, and the school. In a more homogeneous social organization, which may still be found in some communities in the United States, the division of responsibility was less important. The children grew up in homes with much the same cultural backgrounds, went to the same kinds of churches, and carried with them to the school a common cultural experience. As our communities have grown more heterogeneous and pluralistic, however, the children have carried with them to school an increasingly diverse variety of cultural backgrounds. At the same time, our society has tended to assume that the public school was taking over from the home and the church the whole responsibility of educating the children. But the public school has not taken over frequently enough anything like the full responsibility for giving students, year by year, the rich background of literary understanding which should be their birthright. An American child today may gradually claim this heritage if he comes from a literate home with a well-stocked library, or if he is a member of a religious community which puts a strong emphasis on a Biblical tradition. He is much less likely to have this opportunity, however, if he comes from an illiterate home, is not a member of an actively literate religious community, and has to depend on the public school for his literary heritage.

Ironically enough, the strong emphasis on the division between church and state in our pluralistic society leads to an insistence in some communities that the public schools must not teach part of our literary heritage, such as the English Bible, which is also part of the religious heritage of many of the pupils in the school.

Another development in our society which has led to difficulty is the increasing vastness of our knowledge and the increasing tendency toward specialized knowledge. Man knows so much today that no-body can learn everything; indeed, no ten people can learn everything even if they parcel all knowledge out among them. As our knowledge has increased, we have, ironically, come to know less in common. This situation has become so serious in Western culture that Sir Charles Snow has recently called attention (in the Rede Lecture at Cambridge University) to the fact that even on the highest cultural levels, we are no longer one culture, but two. In "The Two Cultures"[2] he points out that even in our most highly educated groups we are split into two cultures—one literary, and one, scientific—with little common understanding or communication between them. People in the scientific culture have very little contact with their literary heritage.

As one would expect, some of the very best scientists had and have plenty of energy and interest to spare, and we came across several who had read almost everything that literary people talk about. But that is rare. Most of the rest (when one tried to probe for what books they had read) would modestly confess, "Well, I've *tried* a bit of Dickens," rather as though Dickens were an extraordinarily esoteric, tangled, and dubiously-rewarding writer, something like Rainer Maria Rilke. . . .

. . . It is not that they lack the interests. It is much more that the whole literature of the traditional culture does not seem to them relevant to those interests. They are, of course, dead wrong, and, as a result, their imaginative understanding is less than it could be. They are self-impoverished.[3]

There have also been developments in American education itself and especially in the teaching of English during the last few decades which have diverted the attention of the schools away from problems of transmitting the literary heritage. We are so close to some of them that it is a little hard to see them objectively.

The problem of developing an understanding of a large body of material in children and adolescents (not to mention adults) involves the questions of what we call, in technical jargon, *scope* and *sequence*.

[2] C. P. Snow, "The Two Cultures and the Scientific Revolution," *Encounter,* XII (June, 1959), No. 6, 17-24 and XIII (July, 1959), No. 1, 22-27.

[3] *Ibid.,* XII, No. 6, 20. He properly points out that those who have been educated only in a literary culture, without scientific understanding, "are impoverished too—perhaps more seriously because they are vainer about it. They still like to pretend that the traditional culture is the whole of 'culture,' as though the natural world didn't exist."

Of scope: What is the body of material we want pupils to understand? When this question has been answered, we face the problem
of sequence: In what order should the various parts of this material
be presented? The whole of literature in the English language is, of
course, too vast to ask any student to master, and most of it is of
peripheral value. So another question of scope is: Of all existent
literature in English, what are the parts which we believe children
and adolescents should be helped to learn?

This question had not been answered in American education when
the great numerical increase in the population of elementary and
secondary schools began in the twentieth century. It has not been
answered to this day. It would take us too far afield to analyze all
of the reasons for this discrepancy here, but one or two may be noted.
The literary tradition originally taught in our schools, as in our
colleges, was for a long time not English but Latin. As this tradition
—the tradition of the Latin Grammar School—died away in the
nineteenth century, no clear-cut understanding of the responsibility
of the schools to teach the English literary tradition was formulated
and generally accepted. The colleges themselves were just beginning
to accept the responsibility for teaching the heritage of English
literature as distinct from Latin and Greek and had little guidance to
give the secondary schools except at the point of college entrance
examinations. A list of "high school classics" to be used as a basis
for the annual College Entrance Board Examination was about all
the schools had to go on by 1920; and it was quite inadequate to
define the scope of the literary heritage to be presented in the
schools.

The colleges were preoccupied with their own problems of scope
and sequence in regard to the literary tradition to be taught to college
students and had little time or knowledge to help the secondary
schools with their comparable problems, though some professors did
find the leisure to berate them. Now that classical literature was no
longer the center of the curriculum, should the colleges teach their
students the history of English literature? This seemed logical. But
wait! What about American literature? *Was* there any American literature? Yes, certainly! And our college students should learn the
history of American literature. But—is our literary heritage really
the detailed history of either British or American literature? Is it not

rather the "Great Books" of Western Culture, whether originally written in English or not? And why leave out the Orient? Should we not be concerned with World Literature? Whatever the values of this confused debate, it did not enable the colleges to help the secondary schools with their problems of scope and sequence in the literary heritage.

The elementary and secondary schools, meantime, were concerned with taking care of a greatly increased number of students—tens of millions—many of whom came from nonliterary homes. The home often—usually—could not be expected to interest the student in reading after he had learned his *ABC's*. The problem of getting students to read anything intelligently and with interest took much of the teacher's time and the educator's research.

The psychology of learning was developing and we were understanding more about the relation between the interests, needs, and motivations of children. Hence, much attention was devoted to finding reading which would be related to particular needs and interests of particular kinds of children. This also helped to divert attention that might otherwise have been directed toward problems of scope and sequence in teaching the literary heritage.

Two more distracting interests, among many others, should be noted. The first, I believe to have been valuable, the second less so. First, in the absence of an analyzed scope of the literary heritage which was to be taught, efforts were made to define the values which students should gain from the literary heritage. [4]

In Dr. Dora V. Smith's phrasing, the question was: "What experiences should all young people have in common through contact with literature?" I suggest that this approach will be very helpful when we proceed, as I hope we soon will, to face more directly problems of scope and sequence in teaching the literary heritage.

Far more time has been spent in the last generation on another problem which distracted attention from the literary heritage. If teachers of English had not worked out their own problems of scope and sequence, other teachers and curriculum-makers had been working out theirs. The teaching of literature could be correlated with— the list is endless. I call it the "Literature for . . ." movement: Litera-

[4] See, for example, author's article, "Transmitting Our Literary Heritage," in *The English Journal*, XXXI (1942), 200-210.

ture for Social Studies. Literature for Mental Health. Literature for World Peace. Literature for Geography. Literature for Human Relations. "Literature for. . . ." If our civilization survives, I imagine that the "Literature for . . ." movement of the second half of the twentieth century will provide one of the most curious chapters in educational history. And, together with many other factors, only a few of which I have mentioned, it helped to distract the attention of teachers and students of education from the basic problems of defining scope and sequence in teaching the literary tradition.

II

What can we do about teaching the literary tradition?

First, we must recognize the problem and realize that it is very important. It is stated in the *Basic Issues in the Teaching of English*. Note, for example, Basic Issue 2: "Can basic programs in English be devised that are sequential and cumulative from the kindergarten through the graduate school?" And Basic Issue 3: "Should certain literary works be required at each of the various levels in a basic program?" [5]

Second, we should support with sympathetic interest the attempts of teachers of English to think through the problems of scope and sequence in transmitting the literary heritage. See, for example, "An Articulated English Program: A Hypothesis to Test." [6] This article was written by a number of members of the Conference on Basic Issues in the Teaching of English. Though a member of the Conference, I was not one of the authors of this article. But I applaud the authors, many whom are college teachers, for the active interest they are taking in the teaching of English at all levels and their initiative in encouraging experimentation in relation to what I am calling *scope* and *sequence* in transmitting the literary heritage. They propose this as an hypothesis which is worth testing:

[5] *The Basic Issues in the Teaching of English* was printed as a supplement to the *English Journal* of September, 1959, and in various other places. Copies are available at 25 cents each from the Executive Secretaries of the American Studies Association, the College English Association, the Modern Language Association, and the National Council of Teachers of English.

[6] *PMLA*, LXXIV (September, 1959), No. 4, 13-19.

The values of the literary component of English are sequential and incremental. They reside in enlargement of the mind by an experience of discovery and recognition, new discovery and association based upon increased recognition. The process is founded upon a continuous furnishing of the mind, first with such basic matter as mythology, folklore and fairy tale, Biblical lore, and national legends, which, interwoven inextricably into the moving pieces of our literary heritage, form the texture of allusion and symbol. Recognized in new combinations and different surroundings, these give a sense of depth and penetration—striking root into a far foretime, at once exciting and illuminating.

Finally, we should suggest two or three works of literature which should be included in the scope of the literary heritage of children or adolescents and decide in what sequence they should appear. For example, should Lincoln's Gettysburg Address be included? If so, how early or late? Should the Book of Ruth be included? If so, how early or late? Should *Hamlet* be included? If so, when?

There are two ways of playing this game, which should be fun and which may make a serious contribution. One is to start as I have above, with works of literature which have long been part of your own heritage and which you would feel much poorer without. Another, is to think of a kind of literary experience you want the children you love to have, and then try to think of a poem or novel or essay or play that has given it to you. ("O World, I cannot hold thee close enough!—Let fall/No burning leaf—").

6

JOHN C. GERBER

Teaching the
Introductory College Course
in Literature

TYPICALLY, about five per cent of the students enrolled in the introductory college course in literature plan to become English majors. Few of the students in the course are interested in the instructor's special field of competence. Few are interested in literary scholarship, or even know what it is. Indeed, if the truth is faced, few are greatly interested in literature. Yet for about 90 per cent of the students the so-called introductory course is also the concluding course. Clearly, then, teaching such a course confronts the instructor with a special set of problems. Clearly, too, the objectives and approaches for this course must be worked out in terms of the special conditions that obtain.

To get at the heart of the matter immediately, I should like to argue for three objectives as being peculiarly appropriate for the introductory college course in literature: (1) to create an interest in good literature, (2) to develop skill in the reading of literary works, and (3) to develop some understanding of certain acknowledged literary masterpieces. Since these objectives in one form or another have been discussed in professional meetings and appear in various course syllabi, I can hardly claim any originality for them. My concern, however, is not with their originality but with their validity and with the means best calculated to help us attain them.

Note two things about these objectives as a group. First, there is no mention of coverage, that shibboleth of so many teachers of literature. While these objectives suggest experience with the various literary genres, they do not suggest exposure to all the acknowledged masterpieces or even to all the major writers. Second, there is no mention of mastery of historical continuity. In the past, the introductory course all too frequently ran from Chaucer to Eliot, with emphasis on dates, titles, and the authors' residences, prejudices, diseases, and mistresses. These were courses in history, and not very

JOHN C. GERBER Professor of English, University of Iowa. Formerly Instructor in English, University of Pittsburgh and University of Chicago. President of NCTE, 1954-1955. Cofounder and Chairman of CCCC, 1949. Member of the Curriculum Commission, NCTE. Member of the Conference on Basic Issues in the Teaching of English. Author of *The Writer's Resource Book*. Articles on Emerson, Twain, Hawthorne, and Henry James. Coauthor of several texts in literature.

good history at that, for they isolated literary events and facts from the causal stream of which they were a part. There is a place for the historically oriented course in literature which shows literature as both a cause and a result of the social, intellectual, political, and economic stream. But the introductory course is not this place. It would be gratifying, naturally, not to have a student think that Wordsworth was a contemporary of Shakespeare, but it would be better to have him live out his days cherishing even this gross misconception and like *Hamlet* and "Tintern Abbey" than to have him be able to date the works and dislike them. Surely we must have learned by now that our function is not to prepare students for TV quiz programs. Or, to paraphrase a well-known bit of advice, what profiteth it a student if he hear all about the major and minor works of English and American literature and not come to love any of them? Better that he be cast into a course in physical education and there learn to develop his muscles for some useful and remunerative purpose.

I

The fundamental objective for the introductory course in literature —or for any undergraduate literature course for that matter—is to have the students learn to like literature. Only by so doing can we possibly make the course a beginning rather than an ending. This is a hard task, and not one that can be approached directly. Obviously, we cannot walk into class on Monday morning at 8:30 and say brightly and effectively, "This morning we are going to learn to like literature." What, then, can we do?

First, we can see to it that, within reasonable limits, we teach what excites *us*. Enthusiasm for literature, like enthusiasm for anything else, is caught rather than taught. Students may think *Paradise Lost* dull even though we find it exciting, but they are certainly going to find it dull if we think it dull. It would be well not to include any text in the course that fails in the given semester to seem live and fresh to us, even if the text happens to be *Hamlet* or *Tom Jones*. Staffs, like individuals, need to beware of creeping ennui. There are few novels better calculated to capture the interest of freshmen and sophomores than *Crime and Punishment*. Yet I have seen a staff, after using this novel for four or five years, grow so cold on it that they might better have been teaching *The Last of the Mohicans*. An incandescent interest in the works being taught is the first require-ment if we are to make literature interesting to the students.

Next, we can see to it that the course starts off on the right foot. Even though they make no attempt to be survey courses as such, many introductory courses for the sake of chronology begin with Chaucer. Now, delightful as Chaucer is, there is no gainsaying that the Chaucerian text confronts the student with special reading prob-lems. A course beginning with Chaucer makes literature seem more esoteric than even the engineering student has suspected it to be. To his mind and the minds of many others, it becomes something clearly for specialists. The introductory course should always lead from strength, not weakness, and the strength of the majority of freshmen and sophomores is in reading narratives in modern Eng-lish. Thus, it would seem that the introductory course might ap-propriately start with relatively simple narratives: ballads, or short prose fiction, or even Homer in a good modern translation. Once the average student finds that the college literature course is not some-thing for specialists, he can be challenged with more difficult reading —Chaucer, in due course, and Shakespeare, and Eliot. In short, the primary organizing principle for the introductory course should be psychological, not chronological.

In the third place, we can concentrate on developing in the student a sense of competence in reading literature. Most human beings do not warm up to things and persons that make them feel incom-petent or inadequate. And despite our darker notions to the contrary, students *are* human beings. Achieving the number one objective for the introductory course, therefore, is dependent upon achieving the number two objective: helping the student like good literature can be achieved only to the extent that we help him develop competence in reading it.

II

Every teacher of literature, I am sure, has heard those recurrent student plaints: "I don't know what I'm looking for," or "I see it when you point it out, but I didn't see it before." What the student is really saying in these instances is that he does not know how to read literature—and that probably he has not been taught how to read it. To put this figuratively, he is saying that he has not been shown what handles he can use in catching hold of a literary work.

This business of providing the student with "handles" is basic to our instruction. Effective reading, we tell students in remedial reading classes and even in composition classes, must be purposeful. Unfortunately, we too often forget to say the same thing in literature classes where such advice is even more essential. For if a student is to develop skill in reading literature he must learn to read it purposefully.

I would submit that the purposeful reading of literature is reading for the aspects or elements or characteristics of the work that contribute most prominently to the make-up and especial character of the whole: elements of craftsmanship as well as aspects of meaning. For example, purposeful reading, especially of fiction, might well be a matter in part of reading in order to discover how the author handles his *point of view*—that window, as Henry James suggests, from which the scene is viewed. The student needs not only to look for the type of viewpoint but to speculate upon its advantages and disadvantages. In *Huckleberry Finn,* for instance, it is easy enough to see that Twain is using Huck to reveal his point of view. But what does this commit him to? What can he see and not see? hear and not hear? think and not think? What effect does the point of view have on the structure? on the style? What would be the difference in the book if he had used Tom to represent his point of view? Or if he had used the authorial third person as he does in *Tom Sawyer?* These are not such profound questions that the answers are beyond the average freshman or sophomore. Yet the answers will lead to ever-widening circles of understanding. Point of view is clearly something to read for, a handle by which a literary work may be firmly grasped.

The same may be said for *conflicts.* Most students, if they read for anything, read for plot. Unfortunately, plot, though certainly important in fiction and drama, is a relatively inadequate handle for grasping these genres. Reading for conflict brings quicker perception of the inner, as well as the outer, issues; it enables the student to comprehend more adequately the complexity of the work and the

nature of the characters; it is a handle by which most poems, as well
as drama and fiction, can be grasped. The student reading *Huckleberry Finn* for plot comes up with a rather feeble story summary; in
reading for conflict he begins to grasp the amazing richness of the
book. He begins to discover the broad assortment of outer conflicts,
such as those between Huck and the Widow Douglas, Huck and
Tom, Huck and Pap, Huck and Jim, Huck and the King and the
Duke, the Widow Douglas and Miss Watson, and the King and
the Duke. More importantly, he becomes more quickly aware of
that great inner conflict of Huck's between his innate sense of goodness on the one hand and his acquired sense of goodness on the other,
the conflict that Twain had reflected upon ever since his reading of
Lecky.

Purposeful reading should certainly include reading for *style*. No
aspect of literature, I suspect, proves quite so baffling to most freshmen and sophomores as style. Even many graduate students, when
asked about style, come forth with nothing more than that old chest-
nut, "Style is the man." This is the kind of statement the student
loves; it sounds vaguely profound, yet it is not definite enough to
require any thinking.

Style, for the practical purposes of the introductory literature class,
need involve nothing more than the author's selection and arrangement of words. Thus defined, it is a handle that even the mediocre
students can grasp, not firmly, perhaps, but, nevertheless, grasp. They
can tell whether the sentences are long or short, whether they are
simple or complex, whether they move fast or slowly. They can also
tell whether the language is relatively formal or informal, bookish
or colloquial, abstract or concrete. And they can go on to make some
elementary observations about whether the words and sentences suit
the material.

The better students, of course, should do more. They should discriminate between such matters as dull and richly connotative diction,
clichés and fresh locutions, direct and ironic statements, illuminating
figures and useless ornamentation. They should be able to assess
dialogue for its fidelity to natural idioms. They should be able to comment perceptibly on tempo, rhythms, economy, coherence, and a
great many other aspects of style. These better students, reading
Huckleberry Finn purposefully for style, might well be expected to

discover such characteristics as the high degree of concreteness, the careful rendering of dialect, the drawling rhythms, the suiting of tempo to material, and the almost magical blend of the casual and the poetic. The very best students might be expected to demonstrate that certain elements push the style toward the poetic (the suggestive imagery, the richly connotative verbs, the economy of statement, the carefully molded parallelisms, the unobstrusive rhythms) and that other elements hold it to the colloquial (the semilocal idioms, the phonetic spellings, the mistakes in grammar, the lack of consistency in the use of personal pronouns, and such imprecise expressions as "awful pretty" and "except for frogs or something"). In short, I would argue that there are many specific matters that the average and certainly the better student can look for under the general heading of style, and that style therefore can be an element that lends itself well to purposeful reading.

Of the numerous other elements that can serve as useful handles in helping the student to grasp the literary work—setting, characterization, symbols, moods, tone, meaning, and the like—possibly only *meaning* deserves attention here. How can we help students to read purposefully for meaning?

First of all, the student must know how meaning is projected. Even the best occasionally need to be reminded that authors project meanings in a variety of ways, such as authorial statements, statements by characters, thoughts of characters, character description, symbols, conflicts, mood, and tone. To gain a strong sense of competence a student needs practice in discerning meaning conveyed in all such manners. Especially he needs practice in decoding symbols and in extracting the general meaning from the specific conflict. In too many introductory courses, however, the student is denied this necessary fingerwork because the instructor is so eager to exhibit his own overall interpretations—or ones that he has extracted from Dover Wilson or Brooks and Warren. The introductory course is no place for the compulsive lecturer. None of us learns how to swing a golf club well simply by watching the instructor show us how smoothly *he* can do it.

Besides knowing how meaning is projected, the student needs to know what meaning is—or what it is not. To point out that meaning is not a matter of an over-all moral or lesson seems, after all these years, to be flogging a horse that is not only dead but buried. Yet it is disquieting to see how many college students when asked for *meaning* still talk about "the lesson" to be learned. The results are often minor critical "classics": *The Scarlet Letter* shows us how true happiness can come only by leading a normal Christian life; *Hamlet* demonstrates that we must always act on our best impulses; Yeats's poetry teaches us that we cannot find happiness if we think that life is made up only of heredity and environment! This preoccupation with morals on the part of college students is, of course, gratifying. (It would be even more gratifying if they showed a similar preoccupation with the subject outside the literature classroom.) Moral chasing, however, they need to be shown once again, is likely to blind them to the real meanings of a work of literature, or at the very least, to oversimplify those meanings.

The same may well be true of the search for the over-all theme that is encouraged by many instructors and most introduction-to-literature texts. Certainly, many works have a controlling theme that must be recognized if the work is to be understood. But by no means does a controlling theme exhaust or even begin to exploit the meanings of most works. No student should be led to believe that it does. Can any statement of controlling theme, for example, however precise and provocative, suggest the rich and diverse meanings to be found in *King Lear*?

How can we best help the student read purposefully for meaning? To begin with, we need more frequently to think and talk in plurals —*meanings*—rather than in singulars—the *meaning* or the *theme*. Next, we need to use terms that suggest the illuminating power of literature: *perceptions, insights,* or even *ideas.* Such a simple change in vocabulary from *theme* to *perceptions* can create for freshmen and sophomores a wholly new orientation. They and the writer—and the instructor—now become students of literature and life. Their exploration is a joint one, and the matters they may discover are innumerable and inexhaustible.

Furthermore, it is useful to remind them that perceptions are of various natures: historical, psychological, sociological, ethical, metaphysical, and so on. Deliberately and purposefully looking for perceptions of varying kinds often helps students to become aware of insights that otherwise might elude them. The simple knowledge that

meaning can be found at these different levels—a matter that seems
so self-evident to the experienced reader—can, overnight, astonishingly improve the reading of the undergradute. *Huckleberry Finn* is
no longer a book in which one flounders rather helplessly looking
for a controlling theme, but a book in which one can perceive certain
aspects of the American past, certain truths of human behavior,
certain characteristics of organized society, certain ethical predicaments encountered by the person of good will, and certain sobering
facts about the nature of being that every thoughtful person must
inevitably face. Thus, the book becomes a work of ever-increasing
richness, one that can be read year after year with new pleasure and
insight.

I have been arguing that students in the introductory course should
be encouraged to read purposefully, and that this is a matter of
having them read for those elements or parts which most importantly
contribute to the nature and effectiveness of the whole. Frankly I
do not see how else we are to provide them with the reading skill
that will give them a sense of competence and a surer interest in
literature. Nevertheless, there are several criticisms of this recommendation that must be considered. One is that such an emphasis
on analytical reading will spoil the work for the student, just as
the rose is spoiled when it is pulled apart. This is the objection of
the sheer sentimentalist. In the first place, the analogy is a false
one. In analyzing the work of literature we are dealing with a rose
that can be pulled apart, yet which always stays together. More
importantly, the objection is based on a wholly false notion of
education. Education is a matter of learning, not titillating or quivering. If we don't believe that our appreciation of art grows with our
understanding of it, we should close our classroom doors, brush the
chalk off our jackets, and go home to watch TV.

A more cogent criticism of purposeful reading is that it is tedious
and may destroy, rather than enhance, the student's interest in
literature. The answer to this is that it can become tedious, but need
not. A student might well be encouraged to give each work a quick
first reading for whatever enjoyment he can get out of simply sur-
rending himself to its initial spell. Then a second reading can be
of the more purposeful variety. And this, at first, should not be too
difficult. He certainly should not be asked to read the work, at least

at the beginning of the school year, for more than one or two of its elements or aspects. During the course of the semester or year he should have practice reading for all of them but not necessarily reading any single work for all of them.

At least as an experiment, the triple-reading technique is useful. Have the student read the work once for whatever pleasure he can get out of it. Then have him read it a second time for particular elements or aspects: point of view, conflicts, meaning, or whatever. Finally, have him read it a third time again for pleasure—so that he can see for himself how his increased understanding of the form and content of the work augments his sense of competence and his enjoyment. Ordinarily, of course, this triple-reading technique is not feasible with novels or, possibly, plays. But it can be used frequently with stories and poems. Indeed, with a short poem the process can be gone through orally during part of a class hour. What ultimately happens, especially with the better students, is that the *first* reading inevitably becomes a more knowing and a more satisfying process. And this, of course, is what must happen if we are going to turn out students who will continue to read great literature once they have stopped reviewing for the final examination in the introductory course.

A third objection to the kind of purposeful reading I have suggested is that while it gets students acquainted with parts or aspects of works, it does not provide broad criteria for evaluating and comparing works as wholes. This may be true, but the loss, it seems to me, is not great. Broad criteria in the hands of freshmen and sophomores usually become either no criteria at all or such vague notions about literature and life that their evaluations become the flabbiest kind of impressionism. On the other hand, purposeful reading of the kind described equips the student with criteria for evaluation which are at once definite and manageable, criteria such as suitability of point of view, plausibility of conflict, consistency of characterization, usefulness of setting, adaptability of style to purpose and content, incisiveness and richness of perceptions, and so on. Such criteria as these would seem to provide the student with ample means for making judgments, not only about aspects of a work but about the work as a whole. Furthermore, they should result in critical comparisons of a high order of specificity.

A fourth objection still remains, and that is that purposeful reading of the kind described fails to demonstrate to the students the valuable kinds of understanding one gains by taking into account such matters as the relation between the work and the author, the relation between the work and the times it delineates, and the relation between the work and the aesthetic and philosophical movements of which it is a part and to which it contributes. It must be admitted that these are all valuable approaches to any piece of literature. And it must further be admitted that purposeful reading of the kind described does not in its purest form allow for the kinds of insight provided by these other approaches.

What seems clear, though, is that there is not time in the introductory course to give the student sustained practice in all of the important approaches to literature. One must choose the one that seems most likely to help the student to read with competence and pleasure, and reserve practice in other approaches for more advanced work. This is not say, however, that the students, even in the introductory course, should not be made aware of other approaches and the kinds of understandings they yield. Thus, after the students have read *Huckleberry Finn* with care, the instructor might well demonstrate the biographical approach, showing how a knowledge of Twain's life helps to explain such matters as the characters, conflicts, and tone of the book. He might demonstrate, too, the approach of the literary historian, showing how *Huckleberry Finn* can be identified in part with the local-color school, in part with the romantic tradition of the early ninetenth century, and in part with the realistic tradition of the later part of the century. The book could be examined as a landmark in American prose fiction, and Hemingway could be quoted to the effect that American literature really begins with *Huckleberry Finn*. Similarly, the students might be exposed briefly to other approaches that illuminate the work, for example, the sociological, the history-of-ideas, the impressionistic, the Freudian, and the Neo-Humanist. In short, the student might well be informed in the introductory course about the many approaches possible. Valuable as all of these may be, however, they do not especially help the student to read the work itself with the competence and pleasure we hope for. For this reason, if for no other, it would seem that no one of them or no combination of them should be made the basis for the day-to-day assignments in the introductory course.

III

Most introductory courses in literature include work in composition. Indeed the so-called literature course is often a kind of two-ring circus in composition and literature with the acts having little or no relation to each other. Papers are assigned for a variety of reasons, relevant and irrelevant: to improve the student's writing, to give him experience with scholarly techniques, to provide a basis for semester grades, to get him acquainted with the library, to keep him busy. In all candor, however, there is only one completely relevant purpose for assigning papers in a literature class, and that is to help the student understand and appreciate literature.

For a paper to serve this purpose it cannot be assigned *in vacuo*. It must be a part of a coherent series of papers geared to the reading program and designed to reinforce that program. Fortunately, a program of written assignments not only lends itself readily to the purposeful reading of literature but is almost essential to it. For nothing quite so compellingly requires the student to read purposefully as the need for writing a paper on what he has read. It seems important to this discussion, therefore, to explore the function of written assignments in what is primarily a reading course.

This is not the place for describing a particular set of assignments, for there is no set that is "good" in any absolute sense. But there may be point in suggesting four kinds of assignments that are especially useful in encouraging purposeful reading: the *explication*, the *interpretation*, the *evaluation*, and the *imitation*. Despite the fact that the operations signified by these terms overlap, certain distinctions between them can be observed.

The explication is simply a paper in which the student is asked to describe or explain the nature of one or more aspects of the work read. This type of paper has the distinct advantage of offering relevant topics on a broad scale of difficulty. For example, the poorest students can be asked to describe a major conflict, the use of setting, or the major divisions of the organization. Better students can be asked to explain the point of view in detail or to indicate the ways in which meaning is projected. The best students can be asked to explicate such matters as the over-all organization, symbol patterns, characteristics of style, the nuances of tone. This is the type of paper which should precede the more demanding papers requiring interpretation and critical judgment.

Second, there is the *interpretation*. This is a somewhat more difficult paper for the student because it requires him not only to recognize what is present in the literary work but also to explain what he makes of it. If done well, such papers require not only purposeful reading but considerable personal reflection. As batting practice, short papers involving interpretations of characters are often useful. To get the student started, such questions as these can be posed: How do you explain Huck's great admiration for Tom? Is Hamlet a victim of indecision or a decisive man caught in events beyond his control? Would the Duke in "My Last Duchess" have been considered heartless or immoral by Renaissance standards? From questions involving character, students can move to questions involving organization. They can be invited to enter the controversy over what is added by the last ten chapters of *Huckleberry Finn*. Or they can be asked to explain the movement, as they see it, in such works as "Song of Myself," *Walden, Moby-Dick*, or an Emerson essay. Indeed, any work in which the organization or movement is not obvious is a fit subject for an interpretative paper. Finally, of course, all kinds of papers can be assigned asking students to interpret the meaning of works. These can be as simple as asking the student to decide whether "Stopping by a Woods on a Snowy Evening" is a report of a concrete experience or a poem about death or both. More difficult questions might be similar to these: Is *Billy Budd* a defense of Christianity or an attack on it? Is "The Open Boat" unrelieved determinism? Is Tennyson attacking science in *In Memoriam?* With experience, the best students do not need the crutch of a specific question. They can be asked to explore such topics as the moral values in *Tom Jones,* the social philosophy evident in Shakespeare's historical plays, the metaphysical issues raised by *Moby Dick,* and the determinism in Hardy's novels.

Still more demanding of the student as reader and thinker is the *evaluation*. The evaluation requires the student not only to explain and interpret what he finds but also to assess its worth by relevant standards. There are two weaknesses, it seems to me, in our typical handling of this kind of critical paper in the introductory course. The first is that such papers are assigned before the students are ready for them. Literary criticism is a complicated and demanding process that should not be attempted before the student has learned how to read with considerable skill and how to write specifically about what he has read. It would seem, then, that the evaluation should not be assigned until the student has had considerable practice with papers calling for explication and interpretation. The second weakness in much current practice is that the student is not encouraged to be sufficiently explicit about his criteria for judgment. Often students write so-called critical papers without knowing themselves what their criteria are. And even when they do have some idea of their criteria, they may fail to make them clear to the reader. Requiring students to be explicit about their criteria, at least in their early critical papers, results ordinarily not only in more careful reading but also in better organization and clearer argument.

Since competent literary criticism is such a difficult task, it would seem important to give students as much practice in the discipline as possible. Consequently, a series of short papers, each more difficult than the one preceding, is likely to be more helpful to most students than one or two long papers. The series might well start with an assignment requiring measurement by a single, relatively simple criterion, such as clarity of structure, probability of action, or appropriateness of diction. The assignments can then be made more difficult by making the criterion more difficult: for example, internal consistency, harmony of poetic form with content, depth of insight. Still more difficult assignments can be achieved by requiring judgments based on two or more criteria or by requiring comparisons of two or more works based on one or more criteria.

One other kind of paper requiring purposeful reading, especially for style, is the *imitation*. Indeed, nothing that I can think of is so likely to make students aware of the intricacies of the style in, say, *Huckleberry Finn* or "When Lilacs Last in the Dooryard Bloom'd" as an assignment calling for a short prose selection or poem to be written in the style of the original. As exaggerated imitations, parodies are often of value in this respect too. To parody Whitman successfully, the student must first be able to recognize the salient char-

acteristics of his material and his style—hence the need for great
perspicuity in reading. Moreover, a parody now and then can en-
liven a sequence of writing assignments, and sharpen a student's
reading ability considerably. Too, it can quicken his critical acumen
since it is not long before at least the better students realize that the
meretricious is what lends itself best to parody—that Whitman's
sillier catalogues are easy to parody whereas the more moving sections in "When Lilacs Last in the Dooryard Bloom'd" almost defy
such treatment.

Whatever its type—explication, interpretation, evaluation, imitation—the main point is that in the introductory literature course the
paper should be clearly a support for the reading program. The
subject of every paper, its nature, and its degree of difficulty should
all be determined not only by what the students are reading but also
by what they are looking for as they read. In short, the writing
program in the literature course can be designed to encourage purposeful reading. To a large degree, it becomes an inexcusable waste of
everyone's time when it is not so designed.

IV

At the beginning of this essay I proposed three objectives for
the introductory course in literature: (1) to create an interest in
literature, (2) to develop skill in the reading of literary works, and
(3) to develop some understanding of certain acknowledged literary
masterpieces. It seems unnecessary to discuss the third objective since,
happily, it will be achieved if the second is achieved. As the student
develops skill in reading, he, willy-nilly, develops a high measure of
understanding of the works he reads. And we shall assume that in
most of our colleges he is asked to read *Hamlet* and *Tom Jones*, not
Ten Nights in a Bar Room and *Fern Leaves from Fannie's Portfolio*.

In his little book in *The Aims of Education*, Alfred North White-
head describes the cycle of mental growth in three stages: romance,
precision, and generalization. Education, he goes on to say, for both
the teacher and the student should consist of the continual repetition of such a cycle: the romantic excitement of the first apprehension
of a subject, the systematic ordering of the material after the subject
has been carefully studied, and, finally, the synthesis of the two in

a return to romanticism with the added advantage of classified ideas and developed techniques.

As English teachers, we seem unfortunately prone to get stuck at one of the first two stages. Either we remain well-meaning but undisciplined enthusiasts or we become dry-as-dust pedants fretting over little scholarly predicaments of our own making. In days when truly liberalizing education is so sorely needed, we cannot afford to waste any of our precious undergraduate class hours quivering over the lines of a poem or orating at length on obscurities in the life of the poet. Especially, we cannot afford such personal luxuries in the introductory course. If we are to achieve our objectives in this course, we must maintain in some miraculous fashion a blend of that excitement necessary for communicating an interest in literature and that discipline necessary for training students to read it. Maintaining this blend is no easy task; yet in no other course can it have such profound effects or yield such satisfying rewards.

7

LENNOX GREY

Cultivating
Literary Audiences

". . . getting to know, on all the matters which most concern us, the best which has been thought and said in the world. . . ."

PROBABLY these few clipped words from Matthew Arnold's *Culture and Anarchy* (1869) have been our most frequently invoked sanction or slogan for the teaching of literature since English became a school subject in the last quarter of the nineteenth century, and English departments (as distinct from chairs of rhetoric and belles-lettres) took form in our schools and colleges. The easily remembered words were well timed to give a sense of dignity and mission to teaching in a society said to put more value on other things. Along with them echoed certain other familiar polarized fighting words from the same source on values and audiences: notably the "universal" *vs.* the "provincial," and the "cultured" *vs.* the "Philistines" —often in senses considerably different from what Arnold intended.

An echo-with-a-difference is to be heard in the recent bulletin, *The Basic Issues in the Teaching of English,* [1] reporting conclusions from a series of conferences on the subject held throughout 1958 by some thirty members of four associations with a grant-in-aid from the Ford Foundation: [2]

Are we teaching English in such a way that it truly has a civilizing value, or have we watered down the subject so much, in an attempt to

LENNOX GREY   Professor of English; Head, Department of the Teaching of English and Foreign Languages, Teachers College, Columbia University. Formerly Instructor, University of Minnesota. Instructor and Adviser in Humanities, University of Chicago. President of NCTE, 1951-1952. Awarded General Education Board Traveling Fellowship, Fulbright Lecturer, University of Sydney. Cochairman of NCTE Committee on Bibliography of the College Teaching of English. Author of *A. A.:* [Allan Abbott] *Teacher of English Teachers,* 1940; *What Communication Means Today,* 1944; "Literary Audience," in *Contemporary Literary Scholarship,* NCTE, 1958.

[1] *The Basic Issues in the Teaching of English/* Being Definitions And Clarifications/ Presented by Members of the American Studies Association/ College English Association/ Modern Language Association,/ and National Council of Teachers of English/ From a Series of Conferences Held Throughout 1958 (Supplement to *College English,* October, 1959).

[2] *Ibid.,* pp. 5-6.

fit it to the supposed interests of the many whom we teach, that we have deprived them of the opportunity to become acquainted with and to experience the best thought and expression of their own time and the cultural heritage which is rightfully theirs? This is a vexing question, and most English teachers have at one time or another asked it of themselves.

This observation is significant on several scores. It corrects the too frequent assumption that by the "best" we English teachers (or Arnold) meant only, or even chiefly, the ancient and classical. In its reference to "the many whom we teach," it touches our concerns about audience, but it avoids that current equating of "Philistine," "mass," "anti-intellectual" which characterizes our hot debates today about audience in books like *Mass Culture*. In "the many," it recognizes that we are concerned with individuals, not with a unitary mass.

Such an explication might be reading too much into the paragraph if it were not for an earlier paragraph which recognizes modern complexities hardly dreamed of by Arnold: [3]

We are in the midst of what some people call a "communications revolution." This means more than saying, whether justifiably or not, that Johnny looks at television instead of reading books. It means that mass media of all sorts—picture magazines, radio, television, recordings, films, and the like—have significantly affected the environment in which young people learn to read and write. . . . The power of mass media, frightening to some people, has led to courses which emphasize propaganda analysis, general semantics, and other means of resistance to "pressure communications."

There can be little doubt where the loyalty of the writer, or of most teachers of English, lies. It is with neither the "elite" nor the "mass." It is with "the best which has been thought and said" and with making it available to "the many whom we teach."

But, for many reasons, this third position is not easy to establish and maintain. The literary canon itself shifts with new audiences, both scholarly and popular: Melville, forgotten in 1920, a "world classic" in 1960; Faulkner, omitted from the twenty best American writers in 1949, near the top in 1959. Interpretations shift on the

[3] *Ibid.*, p. 5.

most durable works: Hamlet psychoanalyzed; the *Odyssey* translated as a novel; *Huckleberry Finn* made a symbol of "integration." But these are familiar and documentable. The greatest uncertainty, and perhaps the most important for our purposes, is the nature of the "many"—for whom we lack identifying names beyond the dichotomous epithets and a few crude but perhaps significant mediating terms like "average reader" or the half-playful "middlebrow." Yet we have sensibilities on these matters. Can we begin to examine and articulate our sense of them by taking up the "cultured–Philistine" and "elite–mass" threads and seeing what twists and turns and variations have been given them since Arnold's day: first, outside our English field; then, within it at several presumably significant points in our history as recorded in the *English Journal* and *College English*; and finally in an unpretentious little spot-check of the views of some of our more thoughtful students?

II

Perhaps it was inescapable that Arnold's hope for a new active middle-class "culture" in England (to succeed what little was left of the culture of the "once splendid," but now "barbarian," aristocracy; to transform the narrowly educated, sectarian, mechanically minded "Philistine" middle classes with this "best which has been thought and said"; and to be extended ultimately to the currently brutalized lower classes or "populace," whose elementary schools Arnold served as Her Majesty's inspector) should be converted in middle-class America into a simple conflict between the "cultured" (with aristocratic overtones) and the "Philistines." Inevitable or not, American reactions quickly took this either-or form. When Arnold visited the United States in 1883-84, popular newspapers caricatured Arnold, his monocle and speech as symbols of British aristocracy. Part of the phenomenon may have been anti-intellectual as well as Philistine. But more of it would seem to have been simply anti–British (anti-aristocratic)—as a neat way of defining our Americanism. Thus the dichotomy was born in a confusion of issues, and the slogans have remained confused ever since.

We may, of course, dismiss such dichotomizing as a modern shadowboxing Battle of the Books (now "real books" *vs.* "mass media"), as something whipped up by "the intellectuals" but of little significance to most people. There is a good deal of credible testimony, certainly, that it has been whipped up by "intellectuals." Russell Lynes and others have made *Harper's Magazine* a good-humored reviewing stand of the phenomenon. In *A Surfeit of Honey* [4] Russell Lynes summed it up:

As David Riesman pointed out some time ago (and as *Time* magazine recently reiterated) the position of the intellectual has never been stronger in America than it is today. It is popular among intellectuals to bemoan the fact that nobody pays any attention to them, that they have never before encountered such a wave of anti-intellectualism, and that they are voices crying in a wilderness. But an intellectual without a wilderness is a missionary without a cannibal.

It would be a mistake, however, to assume that this is an academic tempest, without general significance. It is general enough to have been considered recently at the two poles of the New York press on a single day—Tuesday, January 26, 1960.

A review of Leon Howard's *Literature and the American Tradition* by Charles Poore in *The New York Times* [5] gives a highly suggestive perspective, refusing to take either side in the "elite" *vs.* "mass" debate, yet implying his leaning:

. . . the strongest impression of all, I found, is that American writing, from the earliest times to the present, always seems to contain a sort of continuous Boston Tea Party. The movers and shakers among our writers, in other words, are constantly rebelling against something or other . . . the austerities of the Puritans . . . the proprieties of the Victorian Age . . . the machine-tooled short story . . . the ineffable historical novel . . . that recurring impulse to accent nationalism under the guise of internationalism that populates European cafes with . . . bearded expatriates. Right now highbrow and middlebrow are happily, if unusually, allied in the fight against conformity—a blight that perplexingly creates its own conformities among those who combat it.

In the *New York Daily News* on the same day, two columnists react also to the narrow choice—worth quoting at greater length as symptoms of what happens when the choice is so narrow.

---

[4] (New York, Harper & Brothers, 1957), p. 18.
[5] *New York Times*, January 26, 1960, p. 31.

John Chapman in "Mainly About Theatre: Gold in Them Thar Lowbrows," shows the typical first polarized response:

This newspaper had a sensible editorial the other day—as it almost always does—expressing the hope that the reformers and intellectuals won't mess around too drastically with television.

It pointed out that many more millions enjoy Westerns and crime detection than the comparative handful who go for the deep stuff, and suggested that these deserving millions be not forgotten.

I'd like to make the same kind of case for the theatre. . . . It is no crime to be a lowbrow; it's fun—but hardly anybody is catering to the lowbrow any more, even though a fortune lies waiting.

Yet Chapman has a hopeful vision of "an open-minded lowbrow, if we can develop one," and even concedes value in an "intellectual" level, provided there is a "meat and potatoes" level also:

The ideal theatregoer might be an open-minded lowbrow, if we can develop one. When it is suggested that he see *The Miracle Worker* he won't say, "Aw, I don't want to see a play about a deaf mute who can't see." He will take the suggestion—and find one of the most robust and entertaining dramas on the boards. . . .

Today's theatre—the over-all Boardway playbill—seems to be obliged, through economic necessity, to cater to the critics instead of to the public direct—because if you don't get a good notice you're dead. And, as I wrote in a column long before I was annointed as a critic, the way to get a good notice is to make a critic think he is thinking. . . .

Our playwrights and managers are admirably devoted to being intelligent and introspective, and the intellectual level of the theatre has risen greatly in two decades . . . "mood" plays . . . fine dramas of the human soul. But hardly anybody is serving us meat and potatoes.

Nancy Randolph's *Chic Chat* also shows the typical defensive first response, reviving the old dichotomies of cultured-and-not, rich-and-not, but it, too, plays with notions of multiple tastes and audiences:

CULTURE IS MAGNET FOR PALM BEACHERS
Like postmen, Palm Beach plutocrats cannot be kept from their appointed rounds by weather. Nor by culture, whose cool winds blew briskly here this week on theatregoers. Rich resort society has survived both an in-

terpretation of Carl Sandburg's poetic world and a presentation of Anton Chekhov's socially significant drama, *The Cherry Orchard.*

THAT OLD WORLD IS NEW AGAIN

Class, which had a vogue some years ago, then died from overwork, has come to life again. *Horizon,* a magazine that looks like a book, carries a current article, "The Cultural Class War," by Eric Larrabee [one of the *Harpers'* observers of the "elite" *vs.* "mass" dialectic].

The author lists four groups and some of their choices in movies, books, buildings, gadgets—"by which you may judge them."

In "strictly for the masses," the author says *Peyton Place* is the masses' choice in novels and Palisades Park their pet resort.

In "pretensions to class," the pretenders' resort is Greenbrier (White Sulphur Springs, Virginia) [*sic*] in "Up From the Masses," the resort is Disneyland, California, and in the last group, "genuine class," Larrabee says classy folk prefer the Tanglewood Music Festival as a resort.

"Listen, Mr. Larrabee, what about Palm Beach for real class?"

Here, obviously, is a highly exploitable theme, inviting irony at one level and sarcasm at another, which we have not heard the last of—one which, as teachers, we must understand and interpret.

The perceptiveness and judiciousness of the *Basic Issues* paragraph is the more evident in the light of such dialectic, and it appears all the more judicious the farther one traces the tangled threads in the current debates on audience. In that convenient anthology of the "elite" *vs.* "mass," *Mass Culture: The Popular Arts in America* (1957), Bernard Rosenberg's [6] pessimistic sociological introduction (opposed to his fellow editor David Manning White's semioptimistic introduction) appears to accept the semantic equation, Mass Media ———→ Mass Audience ———→ Mass Culture ———→ Mass Mind ———→ Mass Man, when he says in all seriousness, "mass culture threatens not merely to cretinize our taste, but to brutalize our senses while paving the way to totalitarianism."

We can take comfort, perhaps, from the ironies of two other reputable sociologists, Paul F. Lazarsfeld and Elihu Katz, [7] in *Personal Influence:*

[6] Bernard Rosenberg and David Manning White, *Mass Culture: The Popular Arts in America* (Glencoe, Ill., The Free Press, 1957), p. 9.

[7] Elihu Katz and Paul F. Lazarsfeld, *Personal Influence: The Part Played by People in the Flow of Mass Communications* (Glencoe, Ill., The Free Press, 1955), pp. 15-32.

When people first began to speculate about the effects of the mass media . . . [their] image, first of all, was of an atomistic mass of millions of readers, listeners and movie-goers prepared to receive the Message; and secondly, they pictured every Message as a direct and powerful stimulus to action which would elicit immediate response . . . [But then we discovered] intervening variables: exposure, medium, content, and predispositions . . . Thus, the image . . . that the media play a direct influencing role, has had to be more and more qualified . . . [And] now . . . the newly accented variable of interpersonal relations . . the discovery of "People" . . . opinion leaders . . . not at all identical with those who are thought of traditionally as the wielders of influence . . . distributed in all occupational groups, and on every social and economic level.

Yet from this hopeful discovery of diffused "influentials," we are brought back sharply: [8]

Who or what influences the influentials? Here . . . the mass media reentered the picture. For the leaders reported much more than the non-opinion leaders that, for them, the mass media were influential.

Are we thrown back, then, to a very serious consideration of L. L. Schücking's contention in *The Sociology of Literary Taste* (1944) [9] that "taste" is no more than a manifestation of a "taste-upholding type," and that the new taste-upholding types now "possess the practical means of success and command the technical media for establishing their view—publishing firm, theater, review, and so forth . . ."?

What has been the view of us as a "taste-upholding type," and of our function in our new "mass medium," the college? If we turn back to the first volume of the *English Journal,* (1912), of the "College Edition" (1928), and of *College English* (1939)—all presumably at times when we might expect considerable articulate self-consciousness—what threads do we find?

III

"Going Forth to the Philistines" (September, 1912) by Thacher H. Guild of the University of Illinois, would seem almost too pat, along

[8] *Ibid.,* p. 32.
[9] *Die Soziologie der Literarischen Geschmacksbildung* (1931).

with other articles liberally invoking "the best." But the obvious is
what we should start with. In this article and many of the others
the emphasis understandably is not on literature alone but on the
problem of getting it and the new "laboratory" practice of composition (replacing the older theoretical rhetoric) to work in congenial
harness. Guild's article conveniently rings most of the changes of
the day, from Professor Lounsbury's then current indictment of
"Compulsory Composition in Colleges" in *Harper's Magazine* (quoted
at some length in Sherwin Cody's "Scientific Principles in the Teaching of Composition" (March, 1912) and referred to in "A Hint
from the Newspaper Office" by Fred N. Scott of the University of
Michigan in the same issue, and by others elsewhere) to a basic
questioning of the whole tradition of the "sedulous ape", condemned
by Frank Aydelotte of Indiana University in "Robert Louis Stevenson's Darkening Counsel" (June, 1912) and mocked by Martha
Hall Shackford of Wellesley College (April, 1912). Here is Guild's
opening, concerned with "people," and also with dichotomies, cul-
tured-and-Philistine, East-and-West, and others:

In current slang, when you strike down to the vital interests of a man
you "get him where he lives" . . . he is at home with you. But even
in a college course in composition, student and instructor may dwell so
far apart that they rarely get into each other's neighborhood. The latter,
for instance, may have an apartment next door to the Literary-Snobs,
while his protégé resides in that far district where the word literature is
understood to mean advertising circulars. Manifestly, the raw air out
yonder is not for sensitive nostrils, and the teacher accordingly summons
the boy to his own apartment. . . . But the student, if indeed he ever
finds the place, is altogether likely to sniff out the odor of moth balls.
The next moment he is gone!

"And thank God you are rid of a knave," says Professor Lounsbury.

But neither the Yale reactionist nor his prophets, Milton and Bacon,
ever had to shoulder the precise responsibility offered by a thousand
students enrolled in a single rhetoric course in a state university. . . . In
the good old days when composition courses were unnecessary, going to
college meant one thing: today it means another—a dozen others. The
type of student now chiefly represented in our thousand theme-writers
was then sticking to his farm or shop or office. . . . He is a Philistine, but
he is canny and open-minded. . . . Perhaps—and this suggestion is the

only excuse for my paper—perhaps we can succeed further if, recognizing not only his resistant practicality, but also his coming-on disposition, we lay aside the tradition which doth so easily beset us, and fare forth with patience to meet him.

The good old days of 1912? Everywhere, then as now, from college and high school teachers alike, the conflict of the artistic and the utilitarian: "Shall Laboratory Work in Composition Be Given Up"; "How to Make English Literature Teaching Utilitarian as Well as Cultural"; "Observations Upon the Teaching of Composition in French Lycées" (Karl Young); "Culture and Efficiency Through Composition," "Composition as a Means of Cultivating Literary Appreciation."

"An Open Letter to Teachers of English" from the New York State Association of English Teachers (first issued at a meeting in New York in December, 1909) was a central subject of consideration at the first annual meeting of the National Council of Teachers of English, Chicago, in December, 1911, and endorsed in principle but not on specifics:

While . . . a great deal has been accomplished by the modern movement toward uniformity in English in . . . twenty years . . . it has developed such limitations that a step forward is imperatively needed.

We feel that the type of entrance requirement and the type of entrance examination which are based upon a closed list of books, however comprehensive, are harmful in many ways . . . a few books . . . treated in such a way as to defeat the ends of literary culture . . . read in an unnatural manner . . . [engendering] an actual distaste for literary masterpieces and a too narrow conception of the bearing of literature upon life, particularly through the exclusion of contemporary literature which interprets to students the life of their own time.

The "Open Letter" recommends three aims, "linguistic, cultural, and ethical," with this revealing observation on the cultural:

The second class of motives should be those of literary culture, a culture which should include, beside the study of classic forms, the attempt to standardize [sic—meaning establish standards for?] the taste of the pupils in regard to the theater [including "moving picture"], fiction, song, and periodic literature, the prevailing contemporary forms of culture and amusement.

Two months before the publishing of "An Open Letter," (which appeared in *News and Notes,* March, 1912) *The Round Table* Department had published a less startling recommendation from the Illinois Association of Teachers of English, signed by W. W. Hatfield of Farragut High School, Chicago, saying that it had "instructed its delegates to the National Council to bring to attention the matter of current literature suitable for high-school use:"

To include in its [the NCTE's] list for class reading, study, or whatever you choose to call it, some books of the last ten years. Our present custom of using only old books in the classroom leaves the pupil with no acquaintance with the literature of the present day, from which he is sure to choose his reading after graduation.

Among high school and college teachers alike there was a generally strong feeling for bringing literature to the many, to those affectionately regarded as Philistines, in no narrow way.

With such bearings from 1912, we can note much more sharply the turnings of 1928 and 1939 as they relate to the old dichotomies and to newer sensibilities about literate persons and literary audiences.

In 1928, the first year of the "College Edition" of the *English Journal,* college entrance examinations have faded from the picture; college composition has largely been separated from the study of literature (though the literary merits of the essay collections "to give students something to write about" are vigorously debated); invocations of "the best" are infrequent; "culture" has invisible or visible quotes about it.

In the boom year 1928, the most striking difference from 1912 is the evidence of various "audiences" within the professional literary fellowship, and their struggle to gain or maintain place—philologists, critics, historians. Kemp Malone, of Johns Hopkins, in "Philology and Literature" (April, 1928), states the case for his audience:

The philologist is the lover of literature. But his love is scientific, and, no doubt, it is far from obvious to the general public. With naïveté the so-called literary critics wonder at and damn the work of the philologist. It never occurs to these good men that the scientific study of the human animal demands an examination of literature from the point of view alien to the I-like-this-but-I-don't-like-that of the aesthetic amateur. Fortunately our universities are now committed to philology, and have turned their backs for good on literary dilettantism. The mob howls without, but the philologist works on undisturbed, in his ivory tower. And what better luck could we wish him?

On the next page, in "What The English Teacher Should Know," Allan Abbott of Teachers College, Columbia University reports for the NCTE Committee on Teacher Preparation certain findings from inquiries addressed to various leading teachers and also to boys and girls:

[*From the leaders*]: [Baker] a general college education. . . . Only after these . . . special literary knowledge . . . a scholar's sense of relative values, catholicity of taste. . . . [Holmes] world literature. . . . [Thomas] experience of art, music, dramatics. . . . [Leonard] much genuine experience of excellent literature . . . essential influences in certain literary periods . . . valid criteria of excellence. . . . [Hanford] an amateur enthusiasm for reading beyond the narrowly mapped academic highway . . . art galleries, theater, music, travel; above all, social contacts.
[*From boys and girls*]: . . . talking interestingly on all sorts of literature. . . . [bringing] to my attention the fact that the hustle and bustle of life and the craving for money has tended to drive off the better things of life. . . . Art, Literature and Music . . . ability to forget the classroom and become that character in literature which the class is studying.

O. J. Campbell of the University of Michigan ("Introductory Course in Literature," November, 1928) becomes explicit about the way in which academic audiences get established, as he questions the survey:

Every man wishes to reproduce his own educated kind. With the teacher of any art, this desire appears in an aggravated form. . . . [He] wishes to have his students feel what he feels and has felt. . . . [In] the aesthetic experience, the manner in which the knowledge of a piece of literature came to the teacher has become insensibly . . . a part of his enjoyment of it. . . . The teacher studied his subjects according to the historical method when he was in college. . . . Consequently, he believes that in an emotional matter like literature, he should obey his feelings and encourage the survey.

Probably these observations are more revealing about our sensibility or insensibility toward literary audiences than the one article of the year directly concerned with audience: Montgomery Belgion's "British and American Taste" (March, 1928), prophetic though it was of C. P. Snow's current view that British writers know their audiences, while Americans do not:

In England, a novelist's public is habitually confined to one set of readers, and although he may be indeed famous with that particular set, his name may be almost unknown to the remainder of the reading public [illustrated in England by the Gibbs-Hutchinson-Deeping "public," the Foster-Woolf-Huxley "public," and the Huxley-Wyndham Lewis-T. S. Eliot "cult"]; in America, on the contrary, all novel-readers so mix their reading that in that sense, if in no other, American novel-readers all belong to the same class.

The reasons are matters of both tradition and money [with some implications for us that Arnold's efforts for middle-class culture had some effect, even if not the one he intended.]

In America an extremely large number of people find themselves during middle life suddenly lifted . . . into a position of comfort, and even of plenty . . . [they] want to enjoy the fruit of their wealth . . . [in] . . . the possession of "culture". . . . So they try to acquire this "culture" by reading any and every book they hear well spoken of.
But in England any real change of social position is comparatively rare. . . . Either the secrets of this "culture" have been revealed to them in youth or they go to the grave blissfully unaware of its very existence. . . . Education or "culture" has little to do with brains; it is, after all, no more than having a feeling for the arts, for behavior, for human relations.

Belgion, variously an editor of the Paris *New York Herald*, literary adviser to Jonathan Cape, London, and to Harcourt, Brace, New York, wrote with too much tact to say "American Philistine," but we can be fairly sure that American teachers read it in, and that the good things in his article consequently had little effect on our thinking about varieties of audience.

College English, Volume I (1939-1940), provides in its topical index a useful sequel to the evidence of a varied professional audience in the "College Edition" of 1928: "Aims and Curriculum" (10 items), "The English Language" (6); "Graduate Courses" (4); "Literary Criticism" (4); "American Literature" (10; 7 contemporary); "English and European Literature" (7); "Teacher Education" (3); . . . "Teaching Composition (19), "Teaching Literature" (20) —with overlapping of references where articles touch more than one subject.

Pearl Hogrefe of Iowa State College ("Our Opportunities in a Democracy Today," April, 1940) notes these separations of interest, and sounds another note—the War:

Wherever we turn in the world today we confront chaos or near chaos . . .

This macrocosm of world-chaos is repeated by a microcosm of chaos in the teaching of college English. . . .

We have all seen lopsided teachers: those with the aesthetes' slant, the philologists' slant, the methods-of-education slant (in its extreme form a shadow without substance), the concern with ideas only, the research slant.

After a familiar nod to such phrases as "appeal to the Philistine" in "Freshman Composition: Its Great Middle Class" (December, 1939) and "carrying culture to the masses" in "The Freshman Intellect" (May, 1940), we may briefly consider three pieces which show the web into which not only our "cultured-Philistine" and "intellectual-mass" threads but the "universal-provincial" have been interwoven in a striking way: "American Books and French Readers" (March, 1940) by Justin O'Brien of Columbia University, "Provinciality" (March, 1940) by Joseph E. Baker of the State University of Iowa, and "The Responsibility of the English Teacher" (April, 1940) by Theodore Spencer of Cambridge University and Harvard —the first and third pivoting on the subject of war, the second on the issue of American "regionalism" and "provincialism" which stirred the Thirties and saw a number of our previously avowed American regionalists move to the universality of the New Criticism. The volume has six articles on regionalism.

O'Brien shows American literature, including regional literature, becoming "universal". He has just observed in Paris:

. . . how difficult it was becoming to discuss contemporary French literature with enlightened Frenchmen, since all the young and enthusiastic intellectuals would much prefer to talk of American literature . . . Stein-

beck or Faulkner . . . one comes to wonder if the French public reads
chiefly in English . . . at least for an intelligent minority. . . . [Magazines
and] reviews . . . contain articles on such subjects as "Social Evolution
in the Southern States According to the Novels of T. S. Stribling". . . .

In "Provinciality," Baker defines his subject as "the neutral
state produced by living in a 'region dependent on a distant authority.'" Starting from the question "Should we look upon America
as a mere province of Europe, culturally, and on the South and
West as mere provinces of our North Atlantic States?" he answers
"in the negative" and proceeds to a rebuttal of the widespread identification of "regionalism" with "provincialism" (echoing Arnold's
"best" in the process) and strikes out at "superficial cosmopolitanism."

. . . America should share as much as anyone in European culture. . . .
The culture of Frederick the Great and his court was provincial; it was
dependent on Paris. Nazi culture is chauvinistic; it refuses to enjoy the
best that has been thought and said in Paris. But the culture of Weimar
. . . was neither dependent nor chauvinistic.

Regionalism aims to discover matters of universal interest in the
actual life of one's own region.

Sinclair Lewis . . . probably . . . has the most powerful provincial
mind of the twentieth century . . . his is the kind of provinciality produced by a superficial cosmopolitanism . . . the result of the kind of
culture maintained by our universities, our critical periodicals, our
scholarly and literary circles. We have ourselves to blame if his vision
of our life is sometimes blurred.

In turning from this complex of Midwest regionalism and Ar-
noldian "universality" to Spencer's "The Responsibility of the English
Teacher," one is tempted to consider instead either "Our Social Contract" (March, 1940), in which Merritt Y. Hughes of Wisconsin is
concerned with the "undeclared four-sided war" among (1) "literary
history," (2) ". . . the linguistic advance guard—the light artillery
of human semantics", (3) "the advance guard of Marxism" and (4)
"the discouraged humanists"—but hopeful that I. A. Richards's
efforts toward "widening the sphere of human sensibility" will bear
fruit; or to "Understanding Modern Poetry" (April, 1940) by Allen
Tate, recently of North Carolina and Princeton, which, after starting
most relevantly with "the confident analogy between the audience
of the modern poet and the audience that the English Romantics

had to win in the early nineteenth century . . . [in which people hope] T. S. Eliot will be as easy for high school teachers as 'The Solitary Reaper,' " forsees no comparable audience for Eliot because " 'progressive education' is rapidly making us a nation of illiterates", and to understand Eliot "perhaps we had better begin, young, to read the classical languages."

But Spencer provides a still more useful complex of "individuality" *vs.* "mass", "universality", Great Books, an observation on "the conduct of life," and a thrust at "progressive education" for cultivating the wrong kind of individuality:

Last August an event occurred which is apparently remote from anything connected with the teaching of English but which has, nevertheless, an intimate bearing on it . . . the German-Russian pact . . . a kind of deathblow to the belief . . . that what matters if one is to be a human being, is the nature of the ideology in which one believes. . . . It has . . . shocked us out of the kind of complacency where the problem of being a human being is solved by immersion in an idealistic mass movement. . . .

The decade of the 1930's was a decade in which the main human problem was how to merge the individual experience in the mass experience. The decade upon which we are about to enter will probably be a decade concerned with a reawareness of the individual experience now that the pre-eminence of the mass has led to chaos. . . .

What sort of individual experience must we look for and try to cultivate?

Primarily it should be based on two things: on a sense of values that is not purely local and on an imaginative comprehension . . . [Both] are fighting a set of obstacles difficult to overcome . . . The first . . . has been well summed up by Aldous Huxley ". . . there exists no single set of authoritative books." . . . The vicarious experience gained from literature is not a substitute for direct personal experience, but . . . without it, direct experience is meager and thin. Nor is literature necessarily a guide to the conduct of life . . . ; it gives a basis for comparison and judgment by implying the universal through a particular representation.

IV

In 1958 and 1959 opportunities offered to make a simple comparative check of the views of Australian and American college students of comparable liberal arts background who were preparing to be teachers, and who would presumably be cultivating the literary audiences of the future.

They were given a single-page check-sheet listing our familiar dichotomies, trichotomies ("highbrow, middlebrow, lowbrow"; "upper class, middle class, lower class"), and several descriptions of more various audiences, from "Great Books" readers to "mystery fans." They were asked to delete any that were not common usage and weight the ones that did apply.

The forty-six American students and twenty-five Australian students gave these returns on the items most applicable here, drawn from a detailed report to be published elsewhere:

95 per cent of the Australians deleted "Philistine," no American did so.

All Australians accepted "cultured" as current usage; 32 per cent of the Americans said they use the dichotomy themselves.

64 per cent of the Australians deleted "anti-intellectuals"; 15 per cent of the Americans did so.

95 per cent of the Australians thought "intellectuals" alone widely used; 58 per cent of the Americans thought both were used.

52 per cent of the Australians deleted "middlebrows;" only one American did so; and 43 per cent of the Americans said they used the trichotomy themselves.

73 per cent of the Australians either deleted "upper . . . middle . . . lower" or indicated that it did not apply to literary audience in Australia; only one American thought it did not apply in America.

From these returns it is fairly clear that, if the groups were representative, the "cultured–Philistine" and "intellectual–anti-intellectual" dichotomies, and the class differentiating trichotomies, are characteristic of Amreican thinking and usage, but not of Australian. Australians said they left Arnold some time ago.

48 per cent of the Australians volunteered "educated" and "uneducated" as the ends of a continuum applying to literary audiences; 4 per cent of the Americans did so—possibly reflecting the relative prestige of education in Australia and the United States?

But with both the Americans and Australians, preferences supported the following ways of characterizing literary audience, for themselves and for their fellow Americans or fellow Australians, as they understood their attitudes:

95 per cent of the Australians thought "overlapping audiences with somewhat distinguishable tastes" for various kinds of literature ("Great Books," "mysteries," and so on) would most accurately describe current thinking; 82 per cent of the Americans thought so; both groups gave it their heaviest relative weighting.

Our conclusions?—or our cumulative sensibility?—as we have followed the labyrinthine course of our uses and abuses of Arnold's sanctions and slogans, and as we now try to conceive "the many whom we teach" and their "supposed interests"? Not, I hope, a conclusion that Arnold was wrong. He was remarkably right and effective for his time and his England, encouraging a new secondary education and a broadened culture by what F. R. Leavis has called his "higher pamphleteering." And despite our distortions he did important service in America as (to quote John Crowe Ransom in "The Concrete Universal") "the most engaging schoolmaster who ever teased and scolded his bad pupils into bothering about 'the best that has been thought and uttered in the world.'"

But our persistent nineteenth century American, narrow-choice, "taste-upholding" usage of "Philistines," "intellectual," "mass," (all of which Arnold used), and so on, must be critically examined in much the same way, apparently, as we have been examining other aspects of "academic usage" *vs.* other "educated usage," as in the study of vestigial eighteenth century grammar, most conspicuously.

As one clue to *real audiences* and *real usage,* slender though it may be from our spot-checking along Ariadne's thread, should we take seriously the disposition of our young Americans and Australians to think of audiences as many, and encourage these many audiences as substitutes (or antidotes) for "the mass" (antidotes, if there really should be danger of a mass), with no offhand, cliché, a priori, invidious distinctions between "Great Books readers" and "mystery" or "sports" fans. For, if we violate or ignore such current usage about real identifiable audiences, we may not only alienate large parts of the audience we would like to cultivate, but will violate our very scholarship—a scholarship which is seeing more and more that Faulkner's compelling power comes in part from his use of mystery story techniques in his symbolizing of the tragic 'mystery of the South' (see Frances O'Brien's forthcoming study of Faulkner's indebtedness to Willard Huntington Wright, alias "S. S. Van Dine") most obvious in *Intruder in the Dust,* while Hemingway's power owes no small debt to Ring Lardner, in his raising of the "defeat-victory" theme in the sports story to increasingly high potential between *In Our Time* and *The Old Man and the Sea* (note the counterpoint of the Di Maggio "myth" there).

For literary audiences, as for literature itself, shouldn't we take "variousness and possibility" (to quote, finally, our foremost American interpreter of Arnold, Lionel Trilling) as a more viable sanction or slogan (noting a word used often at a recent MLA meeting concerned with audiences)—*viable* meaning "with capacity or power to live"?

8

HAROLD A. ANDERSON

Teaching the
Art of Listening

CENTURIES before man learned to communicate by means of written symbols he communicated with his fellowmen by word of mouth. Indeed, for ages listening was the primary means possessed by man for gaining an education and for enlarging his experiences vicariously. The literature of the race, too, was kept alive by oral tradition. Then, listening was an indispensable art; the ear held precedence over the eye. Bonaro W. Overstreet[1] phrased this well when she said: "The individual who, in the long preliterate stages of history, had no keen ability as a listener, must have remained a prisoner within his own small cell of experience."

Then, with the invention of the printing press five centuries ago, listening slowly gave way to reading the printed page. Through the centuries, the Western World became increasingly print-minded, and the major burden in obtaining an education or in enlarging experiences generally was placed on the eye. The art of reading became the dominant facility for gaining an education, particularly in the schools, and it was said with conviction that reading makes the man. The very concept of literacy, even, came to be limited to the arts of reading and writing.

Now, in a little more than a quarter of a century, the mass media of oral communication have returned to the ear its former preeminence. The radio, the sound motion picture, and television have made the spoken word the most powerful medium of communication the world has ever known.

Of course, we have always spoken a thousand times more words than we write and listened to a thousand times more words than we read—even though, as a nation, we consume countless tons of print

HAROLD A. ANDERSON   Associate Professor of Education, University of Chicago. Formerly Head of Department of English, University of Chicago High School; Executive Secretary, University of Chicago Committee on the Preparation of Teachers. President of NCTE, 1944-1945. President, National Conference on Research in English, 1949. Member NCTE Commission on the Curriculum. Chairman, Committee on Public Relations, NCTE, 1941-1949. Author and coauthor of textbooks and articles in the teaching of English.

[1] Bonaro W. Overstreet, "After This Manner, Therefore, Listen. . . .", *Wilson Library Bulletin*, XX (April, 1946), 598.

daily. Studies by Paul T. Rankin, made twenty-five years ago, showed that children and young people spent a great deal of time in listening. More recent studies by I. Keith Tyler, Edgar Dale, Paul A. Witty, and others show that the radio, sound motion pictures, and television have greatly increased the amount of time spent in listening. The American people, indeed, have found in these media their habitual pastimes. They probably devote more time to these pastimes than to any other activities save work and sleep.

It is not, of course, the amount of listening which should concern us most. It is the impact of the spoken word that matters. Through the instrumentality of the mass media of communication the spoken word has a potential power for good beyond the dreams of man. But, because the human ear is a willing subject, it is also easy prey for those who would use the spoken word for evil purposes. Whether the tremendous increase in the volume of the spoken word will serve us well depends in large measure on our listening habits. Wendell Johnson [2] made this clear when he said:

. . . As the world grows more ominously voluble by the hour, the words we hurl at each other are no more confusing and maddening, or clarifying and calming, than our habits of listening permit them to be. Until they reach our ears they are mere sound waves, gentle breezes, harmless as a baby's breath. It is through the alchemy of listening that they become transformed into the paralyzing and convulsant toxins of distrust and hate—or the beneficent potions of good will and intelligence.

Much has been written in recent years about the impact of the mass media of oral communication on children, young people, and adults. It is clear that people at all age levels rely more and more on the spoken word for information about their local, national, and world communities. Their economic concepts, political ideals, and ethical standards are influenced, if not largely determined, by their listening. Attitudes toward marriage and family relationships, principles of nutrition and habits of food selection, understanding of human motives, and notions of personal habits are left increasingly to the tutelage of the mass media.

[2] Wendell Johnson, "Do You Know How to Listen?" *Etc.: A Review of General Semantics,* XII (Autumn, 1949), 9.

NEGLECT OF LISTENING IN THE SCHOOLS

The shift from the eye back to the ear is, in itself, no tragedy. The tragedy lies in the fact that only our eyes are trained. Except for isolated instances, virtually the only instruction in listening that children and young people receive in the schools is the quite useless admonition to "pay attention" and "listen carefully." Listening, at all educational levels, has been the neglected language art for generations.

Evidence of this neglect is not difficult to document. In 1945, the National Council of Teachers of English appointed a national Commission on the English Curriculum. The Commission was charged with the responsibility of producing a series of volumes on the English curriculum from kindergarten through the university. At the outset, the Commission agreed that listening should be accorded its rightful emphasis as one of the four language arts—reading, writing, speaking, and listening.

In an effort to ascertain the extent to which listening was then taught in the schools and in the hope of obtaining illustrative materials for the curriculum series, an appeal was directed to several thousand teachers of English throughout the nation. This appeal asked teachers to supply brief descriptions of units of instruction or language activities in which training in the art of listening received focal or, at least, special attention. The response was disappointing. Other efforts have been equally fruitless.

The neglect of listening until recent years is further shown by the paucity of professional literature and research studies in the field. In 1950, the writer prepared an exhaustive bibliography of articles, monographs, and theses on listening. Only one hundred and seventy-five titles were found of which perhaps fifty could be called research studies. In contrast, William S. Gray reported in the 1950 edition of the *Encyclopedia of Educational Research* that 2700 studies in reading had been published between 1881 and 1945. In the five-year period from 1940-1945 alone, four hundred and sixty-two studies in reading appeared.

A number of reasons may be advanced for the neglect of listening in the schools. One is the fact that children begin to acquire the art of listening at a very early age. Before children enter school at five or six, they already have learned how to listen and how to speak remarkably well. They appear to have acquired, without any systematic instruction, an amazing control of oral language. It is understandable that teachers and school administrators would assume that instruction in listening (and too often in speaking, too) is unnecessary. But in the case of reading and writing, children usually enter school with little, if any, facility. These become school subjects. Not so with listening.

Many teachers and school administrators, furthermore, obtained their training and acquired their thought patterns in a day when the spoken word was of relatively less importance. Mass oral communication played only a minor role in their lives. For them, the eye still holds precedence over the ear. Neglect of listening is also due to the fairly common belief that listening is probably determined by hearing acuity and intelligence, and hence, not subject to improvement through instruction.

Our neglect of listening may be attributed in part, perhaps, to the facts that deficiences in listening are less easily detected and that the act of listening has few outward signs of activity. At least we seem to be less sensitive to shortcomings in listening than in reading, for example. For many years teachers and school administrators have shown by tests that large numbers of pupils are seriously retarded in reading. It is common practice to measure periodically the reading ability of all pupils in an effort to discover their shortcomings and to provide instruction in reading. Not so in listening. There has been very little complaint about listening retardation. True, no tests of listening ability have been available until recently, but this dearth of tests probably indicates that school people have been insensitive to the problem. Usually, instruments become available when the needs for them are recognized. Don Brown, in an unpublished paper, put it this way:

The art of "auding" bears its orphan status for several reasons. One is that we engage in frantic practice of the art while lying supinely in apparent lassitude or while bucking cotton bales or rush-hour traffic. These need no outward sign of inward activity. The process has the deceptive aspect of passivity even when most energetic because, unlike our eyes when we read, our ears don't wiggle when we "aud."

Recent Accent on Listening

Formation of the NCTE Commission on the English Curriculum in 1945 marked the turning point in concern about the role of listening in modern life and about the inclusion of listening in the program of instruction at all educational levels.

In 1951, the Committee on Listening Comprehension of the NSSC sent a letter to speech chairmen and deans in over five hundred colleges and universities informing them of its projects in listening and inviting them to participate.

The introduction of courses in communications skills at the college level in place of courses in freshman English and speech also did a great deal to further instruction in listening.

First of all, the Commission recognized listening as one of the four basic language arts and accorded it equal status with reading, writing, and speaking in the formation of its Commission organization and curriculum production committees. Throughout its deliberations and in the production of its series of volumes on the English curriculum, the Commission accorded listening the status it had come to hold in the thinking of the Commission. This, in itself, drew nation-wide attention to listening as an area of instruction in the language arts at all educational levels.

The Commission's Committee on Listening also took steps to promote instruction in listening and to stimulate research. Through correspondence with several hundred English teachers the Committee on Listening sought to facilitate the exchange of experiences on teaching listening, to disseminate units of instruction, and to promote inquiry and experimentation. Steps were also taken to encourage local, state, and regional organizations of teachers of English to include listening in their programs.

A third fruitful step was the stimulation of research in the area of of listening. Letters were sent to most of the major colleges and universities urging the appropriate departments to encourage graduate students to undertake theses and dissertations in the field. A list of suggested research areas was enclosed with the letter.

The growth of interest in listening as a language art and the productivity of writing in the field in the last decade have been remarkable. Listening now finds a place on virtually every program whether local, state, regional, or national. Courses of study in language arts and English reveal the new emphasis. Textbooks writers today give listening more than a passing comment.

As indicated earlier in this essay, by 1950 an exhaustive bibliography on listening yielded only one hundred and seventy-five items. A recent bibliography contains five hundred and eighty items. Of these, one hundred and eleven are theses and dissertations. Only eleven of these research studies appeared prior to 1945.

LISTENING AS A MODE OF LEARNING IN SCHOOL

Most of the literature on listening prior to 1945, and much of it today, relates to the listening habits of people in their response to the mass media. No one will gainsay the importance which these media have given to listening today. But the importance of listening is not to be measured alone by the phenomenal growth of these media. Listening is an important medium in the normal learning processes in the schools. In spite of the heavy reliance on the printed page in most schools, a high proportion of instruction at all educational levels is addressed to the ear. Miriam Wilt's [3] study in 1949 revealed the large role listening plays in school learning. Miss Wilt secured data from 1405 teachers in forty-seven states concerning the number of minutes each school day that pupils were taught by each of the four language arts. These teachers reported that learning was dependent on listening seventy-five minutes of an average school day.

Listening also plays an important role in everyday life quite apart from the mass media and the schools. Table talk and conversation in the family circle; informal and more formal group discussion in thousands of small groups (Sunday school classes, young people's societies, Scout groups, fraternal groups, to mention only a few); sermons and public addresses—these are only a few of the language situations in modern life which call for skill in listening. Unless children and young people develop good habits of listening in these

[3] Miriam E. Wilt, "A Study of Teacher Awareness of Listening as a Factor in Elementary Education" (Unpublished doctor's dissertation, Pennsylvania State College, 1949).

areas, their educational development and the quality of their family and community living will suffer.

AUDING—A NEW TERM FOR LISTENING

Some writers, notably Don Brown and John G. Caffrey, have argued the need for a new term to represent the complex act of listening to oral language. They contend that the term *listening* is not precise enough, insisting that the term is no more acceptable as representative of the full act of listening than *looking* or *seeing* would be for reading. It is true that listening embraces more than comprehending spoken language. We listen to music, to a clap of thunder, and to a multitude of other nonlanguage sounds. In the familiar "Stop! Look! Listen!" we are not admonished to attend to spoken words. Likewise, listening embraces more than hearing. Listening to oral language involves also recognition of sound symbols and comprehension of the meanings of the sounds. But, in a sense, so does the hearing of musical notes or the whistle of an engine.

In an effort to provide a more precise term and one more descriptive of the total act of listening, Brown and Caffrey have proposed *auding*, a term not found, of course, in a standard dictionary. They have also introduced the related words *auder, auded, audable*. In support of the proposal "the verb, *'to aud'*, would embrace the hearing act, the listening act, and the comprehending act as one total experience". [4] Stated slightly differently, Caffrey defines *auding* as "the process of hearing, listening to, recognizing and interpreting or comprehending spoken language". [5]

It is too early to predict whether the term *auding* will become widely accepted as a substitute term for listening as applied to listening to spoken language. At present, its use is limited virtually to the writings of Brown and Caffrey. In all probability the term *listening* itself will come to be used by writers in the field in a manner more in keeping with the broader concept.

[4] John Caffrey, " 'Auding' as a Research Problem," *California Journal of Educational Research*, IV (September, 1953), 155.

[5] John G. Caffrey, "Auding," *Review of Educational Research*, XXV (April, 1955), 121.

RESEARCH IN LISTENING

No attempt will be made here to review the research studies on listening. This has already been done by Artley and Caffrey. [6] While no one would gainsay the fact that research in listening has thrown some light on a wide range of questions, an examination of the fairly substantial body of research literature reveals at once our fragmentary state of knowledge about listening and many unanswered questions.

A number of generalizations about listening may be drawn from the studies reported in the literature. First of all, listening is a language activity in which children, young people, and adults alike spend a great deal of time. Even before the advent of radio, this was true; but with the coming of mass media of oral communication the amount of time devoted to listening has greatly increased. People at all age levels devote more time to listening than to any other language activity. Even in school, where the printed page has played such an important role, listening is an important medium of learning.

Such fragmentary research as is available indicates that people at all age levels in this country are influenced by what they hear. The almost ceaseless bombardment of words develops opinions, forms attitudes, imparts information, and, in a wide variety of ways, shapes the thinking and feelings of the populace. The extent to which this tidal wave of words is for the common good is not clearly known.

Unfortunately, there is a lack of careful research on individual differences in listening ability. Instruments for measuring listening ability comparable to those available in reading have not been constructed. A good beginning has been made. With the use of these new instruments some evidence has been collected to show that pupils do differ quite widely in their ability to comprehend the spoken word, but the precise nature and full range of these differences have yet to be discovered.

Reading and listening have much in common. Training in one seems to support the other, but competence in one does not necessarily mean competence in the other. Some good readers are poor

[6] A. S. Artley, "Research Concerning Interrelationships among the Language Arts," *Elementary English*, XXVII (December, 1950), 527-37; John Caffrey, "Auding," *Review of Educational Research*, XXV (April, 1955), 121-38.

listeners and some good listeners are poor readers. Where objective studies in listening have been undertaken, the evidence is clear that listening habits and skills can be improved at all age levels through systematic instruction. In a number of instances notable improvement in listening has been achieved.

NEEDED RESEARCH IN LISTENING

As indicated earlier, there has been a marked increase in the number of research studies on listening in recent years. However, many questions remain unanswered or only partially answered.

How important is listening? Quantitatively speaking, listening is without doubt the most important of the four language arts. There are, however, other criteria for assessing the importance of an activity. One is its role or influence in the lives of men. The literature on listening is replete with warnings of the potential dangers of mass oral communication unless people are trained to listen critically. There is fear that these unlicensed teachers—the radio, the motion picture, and television—will capture the hearts and minds of audiences and employ the spoken word for questionable purposes.

At present, we have very little factual information about the way in which people are affected by the listening they do. We need answers to questions like these: What information do people now obtain largely through listening? To what extent are their notions about food, nutrition, marriage and family relationships, political ideals, personal health, and moral virtues obtained through radio listening and to the impact of the spoken word in television and in the motion picture? To what extent may misconceptions or perverted notions about many aspects of human living be traced to the influence of these mass media of oral communication? To what extent do they increase public enlightenment of the important social, economic, and political issues of the times? In what degree does mass listening make for unity and social solidarity, and in what degree does it produce hysteria, confusion, and discontent?

It must not be inferred from the foregoing questions that all listening is confined to the mass media. Children and young people listen to their teachers in school and to one another; they listen to sermons and to their Sunday school teachers; they listen to one another on the playground and on the street. Wherever they are, they are listening a great part of every waking hour. What do they learn? What is the effect of this listening upon their value systems, their ideals, their morals, their understanding of the physical and biological universe? Certainly, it would be naive to assume that their education comes solely, or even largely, from the printed page.

We need information, too, about the kinds of activities in modern life which demand a high degree of skill in listening. In what situations is the major burden placed on the ear? Obviously, the radio is a supreme instance. We also need to know how to listen to the oral element of television and motion pictures. We need to know how to listen to conversation, to group discussion, to talks, and to drama. Teachers take the importance of these listening situations for granted. But how much study has been given to the importance of listening skills for the salesperson on the job, for the foreman in the factory, for the teacher or preacher, for the secretary taking dictation, to mention only a few? Studies are needed to ascertain the ways in which listening skills are needed in all walks of life.

What is the nature of listening as a language art? Research in reading has afforded considerably knowledge about, and insight into, the physiology, psychology, and sociology of reading. To date, the body of literature concerning the nature of listening is meager. The mental processes involved in listening are complex and not very well understood. Until research provides more guidance, instruction in listening will be based on hunches.

The kinds of studies needed in this area are suggested by such questions as these: What higher mental processes are involved in listening? What actually goes on physiologically and psychologically during listening? Are the processes similar or different from those in reading? If different, in what ways? Can the good listener be identified and described as we now identify and describe the good reader? How important are auditory acuity, vocabulary, knowledge of grammar, general linguistic competence? Is selective listening, that is, the ability to listen only to that which one wishes to hear, a desirable listening faculty? If so, can it be taught? What is the essential difference, psychologically, between mere hearing and actual listening?

The literature in the field differentiates among several kinds of listening, but little is known about the skills needed in each. Are the skills needed for listening to expository speech the same as those needed for narrative, argument, or persuasion? How does effective listening to lyric poetry differ, if at all, from listening to directions on how to make a box kite? How validly may listening be differentiated into such categories as comprehensional, discriminative, appreciational, critical? What different skills might be needed in listening to political or partisan speeches, radio advertising, group discussion, drama, propaganda? What factors in face-to-face listening differ from those of radio, sound films, and television?

What factors influence the quality of listening in and out of school? Research in reading reveals that certain factors influence the quality of a person's reading. Even such seemingly minor matters as length of type line, spacing between lines, margins, size of type, quality of paper, color of binding, paragraphing, and side and center headings affect reading. Vocabulary load, sentence patterns, and organization of ideas play a much larger role. The notable progress which has been made in recent years in the preparation and production of reading materials for all age levels stems in no small measure from studies of these and other factors affecting reading rate and comprehension.

Comparable factors, presumably, affect listening, but few objective data are available as to what these factors might be or how important they are. Common sense would suggest that one's listening comprehension is affected by the speaker's voice quality, his personality, his speaking manners, his organization of ideas, the absence of noises and other distractions, and the temperature and condition of the air in the room, to mention some of the more obvious factors.

The research needed in this area is suggested by these questions: To what extent do unfavorable factors in the listening situation, such as noise and other distractions, lack of motivation, and poor speaking, result in inattention, daydreaming, passive or marginal listening, and even an immunity to listening? What effect do the listener's interests, motivation, and purpose have on his listening? What effect does the listener's emotional state have on his listening performance? Are there marked individual differences in the listening attention span? How influential upon the quality of listening is the speaker's reputation, authority, affiliation, sponsor?

If more were known about the factors influencing listening performance, it might be possible to develop a score card comparable to a readability formula against which to measure the adequacy of the listening situations to which pupils are subjected. In the study of reading, we are able to say with some assurance what qualities makes a book readable. To date, we have little basis on which to appraise a listening situation. Until we do, teachers are not likely to improve the listening climates in their classrooms.

How well do pupils listen? The periodic measurement of the reading ability of pupils at virtually all educational levels through the administration of standardized tests is now almost universal in this country. Teachers and school administrators know a great deal about the reading abilities and disabilities of their pupils. But they know virtually nothing about the listening abilities and disabilities of their pupils. Why? One reason may be that we have been insensitive to the importance of listening as a language art and hence have not thought it necessary to be concerned about the level of listening competence. The more immediate reason is that until recently no tests for measuring listening ability have been available. Even now the tests fall far short of meeting the full range of needs.

Again, the research needed in this area may best be suggested by raising questions. Are there wide individual differences in listening ability? Do pupils improve in listening competence progressively from grade to grade, or do their listening habits deteriorate? Anyone who has read stories aloud to very young children knows that they are able to listen remarkably well. Indeed, their ability to remember the details of a story is amazing. This keen ability to listen attentively is probably what Coleridge had in mind when, in "The Ancient Mariner," he refers to the good listener as one who "listened like a three years' child." As children grow older, they appear to lose their sharpness in listening. At any rate, there seems to be very little evidence that their powers of listening improve with increasing maturity in other respects. Why? Might it be that the listening situations to which they are subjected both in an out of school are such as to develop slovenly habits?

What is, or should be, normal performance at each grade level? Can listening norms be established? What weaknesses or disabilities do poor listeners manifest? What is the correlation between listening ability and intelligence? Between listening and school achievement? How can poor listening habits be identified and detected? What characteristics differentiate the good listener from the poor listener? What is the relation between listening performance and such personality factors as emotional stability, social adjustment, and mental health? How widely do pupils vary in their ability to learn through listening? What proportion of pupils are so retarded in listening skills as to require remedial instruction?

There is need, also, for research to ascertain the relation between listening competence and intelligence and between listening and school achievement. We need to know whether intelligence is a factor in language competence quite independent of the mode of presentation. Do slow pupils learn more readily, as is sometimes alleged and for which there appears to be some evidence, through listening than through reading? Do bright children know how to listen better than slow ones? Do pupils who achieve well in school possess better listening habits and skills?

TEACHING LISTENING SKILLS

The growing body of literature on listening contains a number of descriptive reports on successful practices in the teaching of listening. Space limitations preclude a full description of these practices. Only brief guidelines can be given here.

1. It is generally agreed that the first step in organizing a school program for the teaching of listening is the *establishment of a favorable listening climate*. Anyone familiar with school practices will readily admit that the listening situations to which most pupils are subjected leave much to be desired. If we are candid, we must acknowledge that much which goes on in the schools actually breeds poor listening attitudes and habits. Too many pupils are compelled to listen to things which fail to command challenging intellectual participation. The question-answer recitation, the rehashing of textbook assignments by both students and teacher, the delivery of book reports designed primarily to satisfy the teacher that the book has been read, and the repetitious announcements and lesson assignments are not conducive to the building of good listening habits.

Someone has said that, if students are to learn to write and speak effectively, they must have something to say, a reason for saying it, someone to whom to say it, and facility for saying it. That is no less true of listening. The fundamental attack which teachers should make on the problem of improving listening habits and abilities is the provision of abundant opportunities for meaningful listening. Students should have something worthwhile to which to listen, a reason for listening, someone to whom they care to listen, and facility for listening. Unless all listening situations in school are made conducive to the practice of good listening habits, instruction in listening per se is likely to be fruitless.

The teaching of listening is not the task of the language arts teacher alone. All teachers share this responsibility. Indeed, no teacher is likely to be effective in any subject, be it mathematics or physical education, unless he provides a favorable listening climate. The school assembly, student rallies, meetings of the Student Council, and a wide range of nonclassroom situations also can provide excellent opportunities, if properly conducted, for developing good listening habits.

2. A second important step in organizing a school program for improvement in listening is to *make clear to pupils—at all grade levels—why good listening habits are important and what skills must be achieved to be a good listener.* This includes an awareness of the role of listening in modern life, of the relationship between good listening and school achievement, and of the need for competence in listening in virtually all vocations and professions.

Far too often teachers embark upon instructional programs without making clear to their pupils the nature of the learning products they are seeking to achieve. If a program in listening is to succeed, pupils must be informed about the skills, abilities, attitudes, and appreciations which constitute good listening. Making clear to pupils the ends and means of instruction has the salutary effect of clarifying in the mind of the teacher as well the goals of instruction.

3. A third element in a program of listening, closely related to the foregoing to be sure, is *an awareness on the part of both student and teacher of the similarities and differences in the receiving language arts—reading and listening.*

There are some ways in which they are clearly different. The ear is the receiving organ in one and the eye in the other. Obviously, there are important individual differences in the effectiveness of these organs as receptive agents of communication. In the areas of visual and auditory acuity alone the differences are marked. For some, hearing may be seriously impaired while visual acuity may be superior or vice versa. Others may suffer degrees of impairment in both.

In listening, the speaker sets the pace of communication; in reading, the reader sets it for himself. The reader may pause to reread a sentence or a longer passage. He may stop to think about what he has just read, letting his mind follow a number of voluntary excursions of interpretation, association, and implication. Not so in listening. The listener must weigh some bit of evidence or proposal against his own information or opinion while listening as the speaker goes on to make his point. The listener cannot pause to reflect on a metaphor or to organize his own ideas in silent debate. Most of our listening does not permit the reflective processes so valuable in reading. The speaker's pace or the relentless sound track in motion pictures hurries the listener along sometimes faster than he can absorb what he hears; for some people it moves so slowly it produces boredom.

There are other differences of which both teachers and students should be aware. Listening is usually a socialized activity while reading is, for the most part, a personalized one. Furthermore, in oral communication the listener has the advantage of both the style of the speech itself and the personality of the speaker. On the other hand, sometimes, because of the speaker's manner or appearance, the listener may reject an idea or fact he would be quite ready to accept in print.

An understanding of these and other differences and similarities will do much to motivate the student to improve his listening habits and skills.

4. A fourth, and clearly the most important ingredient, in a program of listening is *provision for systematic instruction in the art of listening*. No attempt will be made here to outline such a program. Only a few suggestions can be given.

The program should provide both an analysis of the skills needed in effective listening and abundant purposeful practice in these skills. Pupils need to know something of the skills required for listening to various types of oral discourse: narration, exposition, persuasion; lyric poetry and dramatic productions; informal conversation and more formal group discussion; structured and unstructured speech. They need not only to know about these differences but also to analyze their own listening habits.

Systematic instruction should also be provided concerning the purposes for which people listen and the relation between the purpose for listening and the skills involved. Some of the reasons we listen are: to be informed; to be entertained; to get the main idea of a discourse or to note supporting details; to attend appreciatively to oral delivery or beauty of language; to follow the thread of a story. An awareness of these and other purposes and the acquisition of appropriate habits and skills constitute an important aspect of instruction in listening.

Pupils need also to understand the effect on the listener of such factors as the speaker's reputation, affiliation, voice quality, mannerisms, facial expression, and gestures, and use of colored or loaded words.

Another important aspect of effective listening is an awareness of word cues which signal the sequence of events or ideas, such as *moreover, on the other hand, still another thing, finally*. An awareness of the use of these words and phrases to indicate sequence and practice in attending to them will do much to improve listening.

The foregoing practices are only illustrative of the elements of a sound program of instruction in listening. The interested teacher will find in the literature fruitful suggestions for developing units of instruction in the many facets of the art of listening.

THE CHALLENGE

It is patently clear to the thoughtful observer of the communications scene that the spoken word in recent years has come to play an increasingly vital role in the personal and corporate lives of men. There is every indication, too, that we are only at the threshold of the communications revolution. It is incumbent upon the schools at all educational levels to accept the challenge to teach this generation and the next the indispensable are of listening.

9

HARLEN M. ADAMS

Speak the Speech!

THE STUDY of oral communication and the oral study of literature constitute two basic essentials of education. The young
speaker should learn to listen to himself and to others; in this
he can be aided by the use of guides to the evaluation of his speech.
Likewise the reader can gain a better understanding and appreciation of literature, especially poetry, through instruction in oral
interpretation. Classroom procedures in these two areas are here
suggested.

I

ORAL COMMUNICATION

One of the best ways to encourage students to grow is to let them
see how much they are growing. The student who is learning how
to improve his public speaking can be motivated by some simple
diagnostic and checking techniques.

First, the student needs to know specifically what he should work
on. He can discover this, with the aid of his teacher and classmates,
by a diagnosis of his needs.

Second, he should have frequent evidence of his progress. This,
too, can be obtained through the help of his fellow students. They
are his listeners, and their reactions are the real evidence of his
effectiveness.

The chart shown below is a simple form for making the initial
diagnosis of his needs. If a recording is made of his speech while
he presents it, the student himself can participate in the analysis.
Even if the speech is not recorded, the audience of classmates and
teacher should use the diagnostic chart as a guide for listening and
for discussion afterwards. On the basis of the discussion the speaker
can check his own chart in order to record the relative degree of his
need in each area.

HARLEN M. ADAMS   Executive Dean, Chico State College, Chico, California.
Formerly Assistant Professor of Speech, Drama, and Education, Stanford
University. Professor of Language Arts Education, Chico State College. Pres-
ident of NCTE, 1953-1954. Currently member of the Commission on the
English Curriculum, NCTE. Author of *Speak Up!*, 1956; *Speech Guide*, 1940.
Coauthor of *Language Arts and Skills*, 1955.

DIAGNOSIS OF MY SPEAKING

AREAS OF NEED FOR IMPROVEMENT	DEGREES OF NEED		
	Least	*Moderate*	*Greatest*
I. *Material*			
A. Choosing what I have to say (Content)			
B. Arranging what I have to say (Organization)			
II. *Techniques*			
A. Expressing what I say (Language)			
B. Controlling my voice (Voice)			
C. Articulating my words (Speech)			
D. Using my body (Physical Behavior)			
III. *General Communication*			
A. Holding interest (Projection)			
B. Gaining response (Audience Reaction)			

This chart is brief, but the topics listed require careful analysis. A discussion of what each topic covers provides an excellent means of presenting the essentials of public speaking. Such a discussion should precede the diagnosis of the needs of individual students.

The following questions outline the scope of the various topics and are designed to stimulate attentive listening. They are addressed to the listener rather than to the speaker. The test of a speaker is not merely his preparation (as in choosing a title) but rather the response he receives (as in the reaction of the listener to the title).

LISTENER'S GUIDE QUESTIONS

I. MATERIAL

   A. *Content*

      1. Topic

      a. Has the speaker chosen an effective title for his speech?

      b. Is his topic well chosen with regard to the audience and the occasion?

      c. Is his material timely and interesting?

      d. Does he show familiarity with and control of his material?

2. Unified theme and purpose

      a. Does he have a clear-cut aim? For example: to inform, entertain, convince, impress, arouse to action?

      b. Do you detect a single theme, well stated and easily followed?

      c. Is his point of view well thought through?

      d. Are you certain as to what response you should make?

3. Selection of detail

      a. Do you feel that the general ideas are adequately interpreted?

      b. Has he chosen supporting material carefully?

      c. Is his detail concrete and exact?

B. *Organization*

1. Beginning

      a. Does he make an easy transition from the previous speaker, or from what immediately preceded, to his talk?

      b. Is your curiosity aroused or your interest awakened by his opening remarks?

      c. Do you note any appeal to some common interest or experience of the audience?

      d. Have you learned why you ought to know something about the subject?

      e. Have you discovered the main divisions or topics around which the talk will be organized?

2. Body

      a. Does he gain your consideration of his material and ideas by a careful organization of his talk?

      b. Does his line of thought develop logically, cumulatively, clearly, and climactically?

      c. Is he easy to follow? Does he clarify or repeat when necessary?

      d. Are the vital points stressed?

      e. Is there evidence of good subordination of ideas and proper proportion of material?

      f. Are the transitions clear?

      g. Is the material sufficient, insufficient, or excessive?

3. Ending
   a. Has the speech been adequately rounded out or summed up so that it seems final and complete?
   b. Is the conclusion appropriate, too long, anticlimactic?
   c. Does he gain a response from you suitable to the apparent purpose?
   d. Has he planned for the time limit?

II. TECHNIQUES

A. *Language*
   1. Vocabulary
      a. Do you feel that his vocabulary is adequate or that a few words have been overworked?
      b. Are his words dull or vivid, ordinary or well chosen without being either "slangy" or "pedantic"?
      c. Does his language flow easily and fluently?
   2. Usage and Style
      a. Is his sentence construction clear, effective, and in conformity with a good level of usage?
      b. Is his rhetorical style striking and original without being ornate?
      c. Do you note distinctive turns of phrase, avoidance of repetition, and facility of expression?

B. *Voice*
   1. Control
      a. Does he show ease, relaxation, and poise?
      b. Is his breathing adequate and well controlled?
   2. Phonation
      a. Is his vocal quality clear, pure, pleasant, free from disturbing characteristics?
      b. Is his pitch level pleasing? Does he have adequate range or variety of pitch?
      c. Does he have adequate resonance and power? Can you hear him easily at all times?
      d. Does he have vocal flexibility, variety, and expressiveness?

C. *Speech*
   1. Articulation
      a. Are his vowels and consonants clear-cut and distinct?
      b. Do you detect any slurring or clipping of sounds?
      c. Can you understand what he says?

    2. Pronunciation
       a. Is his pronunciation accurate?
    3. Tempo
       a. Is his tempo varied?
       b. Does the flow of speech seem to be rhythmical and regular?
    4. Phrasing and emphasizing
       a. Does he think ahead and speak smoothly?
       b. Are groups of words which express a unit idea spoken together as a unit?
       c. Is due emphasis given to the major ideas and important words?
       d. Does he make adequate and effective use of pause, stress, and inflection?

  D. *Physical Behavior*
    1. Poise and manner
       a. Is he at ease and self-assured?
       b. Is his stance easy, enthusiastic, and dignified?
       c. Does he approach and leave the platform effectively?
    2. Gestures and movements
       a. Does he make effective use of his body?
       b. Are his movements effective, easy, and meaningful?
       c. Does he mark transitions with physical movement? Does he move his head, arms, legs meaningfully?
    3. Facial expression
       a. Does he use his face to help convey meaning?
       b. Are his brow, eyes, lips alive and expressive?

III. GENERAL COMMUNICATION

  A. *Projection*
    1. Does he project his personality? Do you know something about his personality from his voice, appearance, purpose?
    2. Does he give you the impression that he is conversing interestedly with you?
    3. Is he natural, sincere, friendly, enthusiastic?
    4. Does he have a sense of humor and of imagination?
    5. Does he hold your interest?
    6. Would you say that his type of delivery (whether read, memorized, or extemporaneous) is direct and forceful?

  B. *Audience Reaction*
    1. Does he show respect for the audience?
    2. Does he receive a good response from the audience?

The guide questions define the essentials of public speaking in some detail. The diagnosis determines the major needs of the student. Every practice effort thereafter should be an opportunity for improvement.

For each speech a student should receive a chart which has been checked by his classmates, indicating the relative degree of achievement in each essential. The following chart outlines a method for obtaining such an evaluation.

EVALUATION CHART FOR A SPEECH

	Poor	Fair	Average	Good	Excellent
GENERAL IMPRESSION					
CONTENT					
1. Topic					
2. Purpose					
3. Detail					
ORGANIZATION					
4. Beginning					
5. Body					
6. Ending					
LANGUAGE					
7. Vocabulary					
8. Usage					
VOICE					
9. Control					
10. Phonation					
SPEECH					
11. Articulation					
12. Pronunciation					
13. Tempo					
14. Phrasing and Emphasizing					
BODY					
15. Poise					
16. Gesture					
17. Facial expression					
COMMUNICATION					
18. Projection					
19. Audience reaction					

II

ORAL INTERPRETATION

A generation or so ago the attitude of the times was: "Children should be seen, not heard." Modern school programs in the language arts have helped to reverse that idea and are teaching children how to speak so that they can be well heard.

A comparable reversal has not, oddly enough, taken place in the teaching of poetry. Poetry is still too much "seen, not heard." Yet Homer, the Troubadors, Vachel Lindsay, and many others, have long taught us that the spoken word is the very essence of poetry. Truly, poetry should be heard. It should be studied and enjoyed not by the eye but by the ear.

The modern language arts program, in high school as well as in the elementary school, can well give increased attention to the oral approach to the study of poetry. As Longfellow said:

> Then read from the treasured volume
> The poem of thy choice,
> And lend to the rhyme of the poet
> The beauty of thy voice.

By its very nature poetry is usually more difficult reading than is most prose. The thought is very often complex, involved in form, and usually concentrated or condensed. Children of all ages need frequent opportunities to hear it in order to become accustomed to the language of poetry—to thought in rhythmical form. Reading aloud by the teacher and the use of the many excellent recordings which are available provide these opportunities.

The plan for the oral study of poetry on any single day might draw upon either (1) the steps in the preparation for oral reading, or (2) the techniques in effective oral reading. The major objective, however, should never be lost sight of, namely "listening for enjoyment to 'what oft was thought but ne'er so well expressed.'"

Get the meaning. Good listening and good reading go hand in hand. First, get the meaning. The student who wrote "wanation in the visible with liberty and gusted for all" really had no understanding of what he daily recited as a pledge of allegiance to the flag. Let students read aloud and talk about the meanings of words, sentences, stanzas.

In addition, preparation for reading aloud requires a full understanding of the total meaning. The central idea or the purpose must be as clear as the meanings of the parts. In order to help his listeners, the reader of "The Fool's Prayer" must recognize the message of the author which is couched in the episode between the king and the jester.

An excellent preface to an oral reading which aids in understanding is the explanatory introduction. The story behind the writing of "On First Looking into Chapman's Homer," or the fact of Elizabeth Barrett Browning's death before Robert Browning wrote "Prospice," if recounted before reading the poem, prepares the hearers for a better understanding of the thought.

Respond to the feeling. Full appreciation of a poem requires also a recognition of and response to its emotional content. Oral reading reveals the extent to which the reader understands the feelings of a poet or a poem and the ability to enter into the mood of the selection. A reader does not recite words but rather reproduces ideas and emotions. Only by feeling "like some watcher of the skies" can one "breathe the pure serene" of poetry.

Most poetry expresses not only an idea but a mood. The mood may be one of joy, grief, pensiveness, awe. A knowledge of the background for the writing of "Old Ironsides" helps to explain the attitude of Oliver Wendell Holmes when he wrote. A recognition of his strong feelings makes the poem more meaningful. Students should have an opportunity to hear such a poem in order to understand it fully. Their own reading aloud with attention to the feeling of the author is a profitable vicarious experience.

Recognize the form. Of course the form of poetry first catches the eye—and the ear. Singsong reading results from the form. But overcoming singsong reading results from a fuller understanding and appreciation of the form. Hearing the gallop of the ride from Ghent to Aix or the flow of "even the weariest river [that] winds somewhere safe to sea" requires ear training and adds to the pleasure from poetry. Help students to catch the rhythm, hear the sounds, and enjoy the imagery—which are the essence of poetry.

Phrase appropriately. Developing an understanding of poetry through the oral approach requires mastery of certain techniques of interpretation. The listener will comprehend the thought only if the reader phrases it properly. Suitable grouping of words helps to convey the idea. In the sentence, "What do you think I'll give away free a bottle of ink," there are three different meanings. The first, "What/do you think I'll give away free a bottle of ink"—requires, for the eye, a question mark at the end. For the ear it calls for the pause indicated. "What do you think/I'll give away free a bottle of ink"—when written would need exclamation points. "What do you think I'll give away free/a bottle of ink"—provides both a question and an answer and when written requires a question mark and a period. The student should get the meaning and phrase the words properly in order to make the meaning clear to others.

Emphasize meaningfully. Greater clarity will result also from careful emphasis. "That pen is mine" can change its meaning as the emphasis is placed on each word:

> *That* pen is mine. (not this one)
> That *pen* is mine. (not the pencil)
> That pen *is* mine. (don't dispute it)
> That pen is *mine.* (not yours)

Speak clearly. Meaningful emphasis requires good vocal variety. Change of pitch, change of tempo, change of quality are essential to good oral reading; therefore, to the pleasurable hearing of poetry as well. Help students to improve their voices, to sharpen their articulation, to read aloud, to enjoy poetry.

Practice in groups. Some students do not read aloud easily and well alone. They can, however, benefit from an opportunity to read with a group. Choral speaking, reading aloud together, affords an excellent experience in getting the thought and feeling of poetry. The purpose of choral speaking is not display. It is an avenue to the appreciation of poetry. It should be used as a classroom method of helping all students get a complete understanding of the meaning and make a full response to the emotion of the selection. Good group reading requires a consensus for interpretation. A poem must be understood in the same way by all. Agreement must be reached on the best phrasing and emphasizing.

All English classes should include the study of poetry, which means that all English classes should provide an opportunity for poetry to be heard.

10

PORTER G. PERRIN

Freshman Composition
and the
Tradition of Rhetoric

As we enter the 1960's, there is a fairly widespread desire to raise the required work in freshman composition to a level appropriate to a college course. The first moves seem to be primarily in economy and method (closed television instruction, lecture and quiz sections) and in organization (tossing the remedial work to an extension course or some precollege unit, and sectioning according to ability). The need, it seems to me, is not so much for a change in method or format as in the content and emphasis of the course, the sort of curriculum change that springs from the best thinking of teachers rather than from administrators. As a contribution to this thinking, this paper considers *composition* (actual writing in courses) against the background of *rhetoric* (theory, principles of discourse). The recommendation is not for startling novelty but for a courageous shift of emphasis.

I

The present emphasis follows the historical pattern of college instruction in composition from its beginnings in America. When, after the Revolution, college work that had previously been carried on in Latin began to be expressed in English, the faculty found the students' native language as unsatisfactory as their Latin had often been and, naturally, turned their energies to "purifying" it as before they had "purified" the language of learning. The first professional theme reader at Harvard, Eliphalet Pearson (1752-1826), Professor of Hebrew, was given the job because trade in his own subject was slow. He was a conscientious corrector and pruner of papers, as student diaries record. He was also more grammarian than rhetorician, as suggested by John Quincy Adams' [1] verses of 1787:

PORTER G. PERRIN   Professor of English, University of Washington. Formerly Professor of English, Colgate University. President of NCTE, 1946-1947. Member of Curriculum Commission, NCTE, and Associate Director to 1957. Author, *Writer's Guide and Index to English*, 1942; third edition, 1959. Contributor to *College English, American Speech*.

[1] Henry Adams, "Harvard College, 1786-1787," *Historical Essays* (New York, 1891), p. 120.

> But Pearson, with an awful frown,
> Full of his article and noun,
> Spoke thus: "By all the parts of speech,
> Which with such elegance I teach . . ."

Later, the emphasis was, as now, conditioned in part by available textbooks, especially in the nineteenth century by importations from Scotland, where a social concern for language was strong as it was in the newer country. George Campbell's *Philosophy of Rhetoric* (1776), along with proper rhetorical matter, enunciated the principles of present, reputable, and national usage. After 1866 and at a lower level, Alexander Bain's texts (*Composition and Grammar, Grammar as Bearing upon Composition*) were probably the immediate ancestors of our handbooks.

There was considerable activity at the end of the century in the name of rhetoric, and though, for instance, Genung treated invention and style quite fully, the general emphasis was on a static doctrine. The frame was the four forms of discourse, that typical nineteenth century abstraction, and much emphasis was on qualities, so that the main heads, in addition to description—narration—exposition—argumentation—were: unity—coherence—emphasis—and, in style, clearness—force—elegance. [2] The "communication" movement of the 1930's and 1940's was, in some respects, a revival of rhetoric, though too often the actual courses simply fused elementary exercises from former composition and speech courses. [3] For the last seventy-five years a large part of the instructor's time and effort has been spent in purifying the students' English.

In the tradition of rhetoric this is a weak and static doctrine, on a par with the medieval limitation to the topics of style and delivery. The emphasis has been reinforced by the general neglect of *rhetoric* in the study of literature in which the term is conventionally construed to comprise structure and style or style alone. The theoretical concerns of departments of English lie in literary criticism, which, from the point of view of an ancient (and if anything too stable)

---

[2] John F. Genung, *The Practical Elements of Rhetoric* (1886-), *Working Principles of Rhetoric*, (1901-); Barrett Wendell, *English Composition* (1891-); A. R. Kitzhaber, "Rhetoric in American Colleges, 1850-1900," (Unpublished dissertation, University of Washington, 1953).

[3] Earl J. McGrath, ed., *Communication in General Education* (Dubuque, Iowa, 1949).

tradition, seems a fickle and even faddist activity, changing its pre-occupations from decade to decade: the twenties, moral concerns; the thirties, social issues; the forties, metaphor and minute analysis; the fifties, symbol and myth; the sixties,——? The field of speech has profited from its rediscovery of classical rhetoric, even though the ancient categories are perhaps still insufficiently modified to fit modern conditions. But, so far, the doctrine of the rhetoric of written discourse remains insufficient and somewhat flabby.

More specifically, the focus of the freshman course has been kept on *grammar* (as an inclusive term for some sort of elementary atten-tion to the language) for the main reason, alas, that composition instructors wish to eliminate so much bad spelling, so many frag-mentary and run-on sentences, and such truck; by their fear of colleagues in their own and other departments—that they are not performing their police duty with sufficient enthusiasm; by the text-books, the handbooks on one side and on the other reading volumes of items to titillate the intelligence and conceit of instructors rather than to serve as material for rhetorical study, and the relative lack of immediacy in the books with *rhetoric* or *composition,* or even *com-munication* in their titles; and, finally, by the fact that correcting "mechanics" is quicker and easier for us (easiest of all in workbooks) than the more complex consideration of qualities of whole papers. These various influences have all been intensified by the progressive increase in enrollments of the last several decades, not only adding sheer bulk of work but, since the social base from which students come has been somewhat broadened, giving plausibility to the pre-occupation with "grammar."

II

This view of the course is not quite fair to ourselves; and it is not intended to be, since in the round of curriculum scrutiny now coming up we should not take the most successful courses and the best teachers as the norm. Nor should we allow pressures of enrollment or the itch for economy to dictate. The motivations are, negatively, the pervasive dissatisfactions of the staff and, positively, the pro-fessional and human desire to do a more satisfactory job. [4] The

[4] John C. Sherwood, "How to Escape Teaching Composition," *Bulletin of the American Association of University Professors,* XL (1954), 282-290.

means is a changed emphasis, a new balancing of our regular stock
in trade, specifically subordinating *grammar* to *rhetoric,* taken as the
traditional name for the study of the making, the qualities, and the
effects of verbal discourse. Since rhetoric, of all the academic disciplines, is perhaps the closest to common sense, hardly more than the
systematizing of what competent people do in using words, it will be
difficult to say anything new or surprising about it. (But the tradition
is strong enough to assimilate bits from general semantics, psycho-
analysis, information theory, or what have you, if one's tastes require
—and fit them into a comprehensive scheme.)

The basic premise of rhetoric is that discourse is an act (something
done) studied as an art in the old sense. It is the result of a process
that can be seen in stages for each of which pertinent advice can
be given. The "five parts" of classical rhetoric were topics arranged
in roughly a chronological series of concerns: *inventio,* the gathering
and scrutiny of material; *dispositio,* its arrangement to meet the given
situation; *elocutio,* style broadly considered; *memoria,* amplification
of points at the time of delivery [or writing]; and *pronuntiatio,* the
delivery of a speech. [5] These heads, and others, can be translated
into modern terms and elaborated by borrowing from fields not
available to Aristotle and Quintilian. Actually, we have made considerable progress away from the static rhetoric of form and quality
but need to go somewhat further with the five parts of classical
rhetoric.

1. Many textbooks and more teachers now give suggestions on
the stages in turning out a paper, from focusing on a subject to re-
vising and making the fair copy. Students need not now immediately
try to visualize the finished paper and realize that their failures come
usually from neglecting the earlier stages, those that come before
they sit down to face blank paper. Cultivating businesslike habits of
work, resembling those of competent writers, takes most of the
mystery and much of the pain out of writing.

2. A second premise of rhetoric is that discourse occurs in a situation that defines to a considerable extent the mental "set" of the
writer as well as the content, arrangement, and tone of what is
written. The situation includes a sense of one or more readers: "To

[5] See Charles Sears Baldwin, *Ancient Rhetoric and Poetic* (New York,
1924).

write is to raise a claim for the attention of readers." [6] Writing lacks the possibility of immediate "audience contact" of even classroom speeches. It is a lonely business and requires imagination, sometimes to remember even the recipient of a letter. Most mature or professional writing is for books or periodicals; the readers are selected groups of the general population, represented more or less accurately by editors. We are not training professional writers at this level; yet we are pointing humbly in their direction. Most themes should be of publishable patterns and an instructor needs to develop as part of his professional equipment some editorial sensitiveness, to see who might read the piece with possible interest or profit.

Obviously, the instructor is the immediate and unavoidable reader, and if he reads both as an individual and as a professional, he can create at least an illusion of audience. [7] There is also the class—a freshman class can be an alert and intelligent audience, and, with training, can improve their receptiveness. The class is the actual audience for themes read aloud and those so read and, especially, those published in some form should be chosen for subject matter and rhetorical excellence: some of the dullest prose in print is in course publications selected primarily on the basis of surface correctness. Some awareness of readers can move students in the direction of mature writing and away from the deadly theme smell.

3. Perhaps the real key to giving rhetoric the upper hand again is by attending to subject matter, and the tougher tradition of rhetoric since Aristotle has taken for granted some jurisdiction over content. Teachers who write these days on reading themes stress the need to regard content first. [8] The rhetorical approach to subject matter considers accuracy, definiteness, completeness (relative to scale and purpose), consistency, discrimination of fact from opinion, and the treatment of other facts and points of view. Such considerations help put matters of surface finish in proper perspective. (A resort to logic is not the way out, for, though it may contribute a

[6] C. Wright Mills, *The Sociological Imagination* (New York, 1959), p. 218.

[7] Jeffrey Fleece, "Teacher as Audience," *College English*, XIII (1952), 272-275. See also Barriss Mills, "Writing as Process," *College English*, XV (1953), 19-26; James H. Pitman, "How to Read Freshman Themes," *Journal of Engineering Education*, XLI (1951), 402-405.

[8] Delmer Rodabaugh, "Assigning and Commenting on Themes," *College English*, XVI (1954), 33-37.

means of checking certain elementary relationships between state-ments, it cannot test the relation of the statements to actuality or to purpose, and as at present practised seems principally to exhibit the instructor's virtuosity.)

4. Our best developed rhetorical topic is plan, so well developed that organization is too glibly spoken of and students say "My organi-zation is poor" with almost as much assurance and even pride as they speak of being bad spellers. A good deal of the effort spent on outlining is devoted to the form and perhaps teaches more about by-products, such as parallel phrasing, than about the shape of the paper. But outline or no we try to encourage students to see the paper in stages growing out of the material actually available, and to consider beginning, ending, proportion, emphasis. [9]

5. A less developed topic is what has been traditionally called amplification in rhetoric. In simple matters and especially in narrative it consists principally in good judgment of what to put in and what to leave out, selection of detail. In expository papers it is in part interrelation of details and more general statements. Partly from fear of irrelevance or "padding," partly from lack of experience, students tend to write barely. They do not realize that ideas have to be de-veloped to guide and hold a reader's attention. The symptom of successful amplification is tolerable paragraphs, not necessarily the full dress paragraphs of the nineteenth century but still definite blocks of material. We will hardly get adequate development unless we do something to encourage facility and "amplification."

There are other rhetorical topics too: types of papers, in relation to articles that appear in print, offering patterns and items for imi-tation; tone or perspective, from the neutral tone of much academic writing to humor, satire, invective, and even tragedy, each with various freedoms and limitations in development; suggestions for gauging readers' response and possible effects of what is written; the ethics of verbal action, which it is part of our social role to en-courage; and so on.

The privilege of helping young people in their efforts at communi-cation, and even more the right to tamper with what they have written, depends on professional training, made up in large part of such rhetorical topics as these. One is not automatically equipped

[9] Ednah S. Thomas, *Evaluating Student Themes* (Madison, Wis., 1955).

by becoming a member of an English department, or by reading elementary texts alone. With more lore from the main rhetorical tradition there would be less excuse for dodging the central problems of composition; the work would have more inherent interest, could stand more nearly on its own feet, and would be more of college caliber.

III

Within some such frame for the study of discourse rhetoric has always included an account of language as the medium of discourse. The change we need is this, from an apparent emphasis on language as *end* to language as *means*. A composition course has a responsibility to further the students' facility in the usage of the publicly articulate class and even more in the various styles that can increase the effectiveness of their particular papers.

Not to be entirely idealistic, there is no blinking the fact that many of our customers do not have when they come to us the command of language we would like or that they should have. (Students have never satisfied college faculties in language or in various other matters.) There may be momentary satisfaction but little use in castigating their previous teachers of the preceding schools—though steady pressure on school administrations might eventually encourage them to establish working conditions that would allow high school teachers of English to do what they would already like to do. (And back of the schools is our society, specifically parents and their fuzzy expectations and even lack of appreciation of mental as opposed to manual skills.)

To a considerable extent the remedy is in our own hands, or at least that is the part of it for us to be first concerned with, and it lies in the conditions of admission. The revolt against college entrance requirements of the earlier generation was directed primarily at requirements of subject matter, and was well taken; but the colleges did little to meet the situation except grumble. They could have instituted requirements in *skills,* and it is not too late to do this. Even state universities could sell their supporting public on the idea that entering students should have sufficient skill in the Three R's to carry on college work. There may be quite proper conditions for high school graduation that are not pertinent to admission to college. It is the responsibility of the higher institutions to define their needs and to find ways of securing them.

Even if admission customs were improved, there would always be the lowest quarter of an entering class, who would probably need some help in elementary language matters. But even now there are only a few items of this sort: a score or so of verb forms, the use of two or three pronoun forms (where the written usage is more precise than the spoken), verb agreement with concealed or complex subjects, the position and relation of occasional modifiers, and once in a dog's age a predicate adjective (which with a *real* now and then is almost the only actual application in syntax of the parts of speech category so elaborately taught). All together there are not enough to serve as the basis for a college course.

Looking at the situation squarely shows that the argument now flourishing over "traditional grammar" *vs.* "linguistics" is a secondary issue. The basic question is How much direct attention to the language should be given in a course in writing? The answer is, As much as is necessary to encourage habits of effective expression. We need to present a few items of current usage and of written convention, general practices and exceptions to them. The description should be accurate, its first responsibility to represent the choices of verbotropic people in what they say or write, with reasons where possible. These reasons are for the most part social and not linguistic, since the problems wouldn't arise if there wasn't divergence within the "structure" of English. There should be good undergraduate courses in a head-on approach to language, especially to the English language, and a good case could be made for requiring such a course, as a contribution to general education and understanding. But it is not the function of a course intended to improve immediately habits of expression.

Within a rhetorical framework the focus of attention is style, choices among words, word groups, sentence patterns offered by our rangey language, variations that lie within Standard English. The process of maturing in language is in growth in the flexibility and precision in the use of these variables in actual writing. This can be elaborated at a theoretical level from gestalt psychology, as opposed to the limited behaviorism to which we seem to subscribe, especially in exercises and workbooks: by setting the whole above the part, by a determined effort at relating means to ends. To a considerable degree development in language is a by-product of extensive and more or less purposeful practice in writing. The growth is furthered unconsciously by lengthened contact with the educated community, by reading, by all college courses. (This is one reason why for maximum efficiency and for bringing the course to an actual college level the required work in composition or at least a part of it might well be postponed to a later time, say to the junior year.)

A course can speed up this process of growth somewhat by emphasizing items to be observed, by showing students how to isolate the small features of language of which they are ordinarily unaware. We have to remember that we are above the average verbotropic; they are not, often not even average, but the early curiosity they had about language can perhaps be reawakened.

The concrete suggestion is that the course should be conspicuously organized on rhetorical principles, and matters of language not stressed for a time. A little later matters of usage and style can be introduced and fall into place as means rather than ends. It takes considerable control—not to say faith—for the old hands to overlook "mechanics," but if they would, or at least no more than check items on papers, [10] they would find that when they did take them up after a month or so many would have disappeared, just from the students' attending to saying something. And we could concentrate on style—at an elementary level to be sure—on the effectiveness of language in the particular paper, and use "grammar" in the service of "rhetoric."

IV

It is not, thank heaven, the function of this paper to present a model plan for the course, but a few specific comments may amplify the theory that has been presented. It is obvious that the time to establish the emphasis, to stress subject matter and rhetorical topics, is at the beginning and end of a course and of the terms or semesters within it. In this way often a shift can be made from earlier work in English.

[10] Nelius O. Halvorson, "Two Methods of Indicating Errors in Themes," *College English*, II (1940), 277-279.

Although doctrine is important, even more important is application of it in assignment and handling of written work. We want everything at once, naturally, but we need to parcel out our demands and see them in a progressive course of action, and to discriminate consciously the functions of assignments and to make the functions clear to students. There is usually some need for exercises, and the only objection to them is that teachers often come to rely on them too much. Checking right or wrong, filling in blanks is primarily a device for driving in definitions. We know that there is not much carryover to their actual writing.

Practice pieces are in a sense exercises for which the student produces the copy. These have to do typically with rhetorical matters: amplification, continuity of development, variety in style and effect, reader direction. The old daily theme, now impossible, encouraged observation, facility, apt development, and was a practice piece. People, for example, do not ordinarily write from topic sentences, but developing a topic sentence may be a useful way of practising amplification. The reference paper may and at its best does rise to the level of actual communication, but the emphasis on method and form makes it basically a practice piece. Practice pieces are of special importance and might well be numerous early in a course—and, throughout a remedial course, far more useful than exercises, because the strugglers have a fear of paper and usually a long record of unsuccessful writing. [11]

But the core of the work in composition is the paper that develops information or ideas for reading by others: the theme. Our view of the course is principally conveyed to students by our handling of themes, more clearly than by our doctrine. Reading themes is an elementary form of criticism, with subject matter and development first, usage and style second. Fortunately actual theme criticisms are rarely published, but the classic pattern is seen in the comment by William Vaughn Moody on a theme by Gertrude Stein, 29 December 1894:

The analysis of character is, as far as the limits of your space have allowed, convincing and suggestive. The point of view wavers strangely.

[11] Ray C. Maize, "A Writing Laboratory for Retarded Students," *College English*, XVI (1954), 44-48; Porter G. Perrin, "The Remedial Racket," *The English Journal*, College Edition, XXII (1933), 382-388.

We have an instinctive feeling, from the tone in which the young lady is treated, that the point of view is really hers, and that the analysis which deals with her character is self-analysis, but ostensibly the point of view is that of the author or omniscient spectator. The result is a trifle confusing—the opening is oddly awkward and formal. I wish that you might overcome your disdain for the more necessary marks of punctuation.

Rewrite the first page and revise the rest. [12]

Students expect us to manhandle their papers, feel cheated if we don't. [13] In their appearances at conventions they are likely to seem more hardboiled than the teachers, though they may be compensating for ruffled feelings, just as some of our public sentimentality may be compensating for past rudeness. But they are sensitive to injustice and extreme or arbitrary emphases, and do not accept readily, for example, a failing mark on a four page paper of good content because of one comma fault. Things that may bulk large in practice pieces have to be seen in perspective in more serious papers.

In the long run, attitude is more important than even the content of the criticisms. Studies in "method" in our field often show that one particular approach or device has some identifiable advantages over another, but these are usually extremely slight. The same studies show that the essential condition for improvement is a sense of progress, of accomplishment. For that we have to guard against what is perhaps an occupational disease, negativism. "It is obviously easier to find flaws in an essay than to recognize virtues," says the CEEB, [14] and "Teachers enjoy passively but find fault actively," says another study. [15] The writer-critic relationship should develop some inter-action of positive and negative, with an accent on the positive. It is just good pedagogy. No matter the low condition of the present

[12] Rosalin S. Miller, *Gertrude Stein: Form and Intelligibility* (New York, 1949), p. 126.

[13] Katherine Keene, "Students Like Corrections," *The English Journal*, XLV (1956), 212-215.

[14] *Report on the First Six Tests in English Composition* (New York, 1945), p. 27.

[15] William J. Dusel, "Some Semantic Implications of Theme Correcting," *The English Journal*, XLIV (1955), 390-397; compare William G. Perry, Jr., "The 600-Word Theme and Human Dignity," *College English*, XIV (1953), 454-460. These two articles are recommended as a starting point for future reflection.

paper, the view is toward the future and the fruit of our criticism is in later papers:

Will your comments lead him to write again, or to fear writing? Will they stimulate a desire to write better, or merely a fear of making errors? Will you be opening an exchange of understanding, or will you and the student communicate less and less from now on? What happens when the paper is returned, carrying your addition to the ideas expressed? [16]

The perspective of rhetoric is often pedestrian, but its long pre-occupation with *rhetorica docens* stresses leading to virtue by presenting the successful and by pointing forward. We hold the whip hand and in the long run will get the sort of papers we praise—and so the sort that we deserve. This pointing to the future rather than a tense preoccupation with the present takes imagination and forti-tude. But such a courageous re-emphasis in the too usual practices of our profession would go far to recondition the freshman course and help restore it to its rightful place in the tradition of rhetoric and in the college program today.

[16] Lou La Brant, *We Teach English* (New York, 1951), p. 171.

11

CHARLES C. FRIES

Linguistic Science
and the
Teaching of English

SCIENCE, as science, aims at pushing out the boundaries of human knowledge and understanding—the boundaries of man's intellectual freedom. Science, as science, does not concern itself with building better machines for transportation or for mass communication, nor with improving the food supply, nor with the curing of diseases. Linguistic science, like other sciences, aims solely at knowledge and understanding. Linguistic science concerns itself with our knowledge and understanding of the nature and functioning of human language. As science, linguistics is not concerned with the teaching of English or of foreign language or of reading.

The knowledge and understanding won by science in its various fields, has, however, been of great use to man in his struggle to control his living. Scientists have helped to interpret the significance of the knowledge they have won and have often filled the roles of engineers as well. But it is the function of our professions—the doctor, the teacher, the engineer—to take the knowledge and understanding that has been achieved by science and to explore its usefulness for man. We must not assume or expect that the scientists themselves can or should be able to lead the way in practical applications of the knowledge of their science, or even to take the responsibility for explaining its practical significance. The applications of scientific knowledge to the practical problems of invention, of construction, of disease, of learning and teaching, demand their own types of research and must be done by those who know and understand both the practical problems and the results of science.

To insist thus upon the separation of science (the search for knowledge and understanding) from the applications of science (the struggle to make full use of all that is known) is not to belittle the

CHARLES C. FRIES Professor Emeritus of English, University of Michigan. President of NCTE, 1927-1928. President, Linguistic Society of America, 1939. Honorary Litt. D., Bucknell University, 1946. Editor-in-chief *Early Modern English Dictionary* since 1928. Represented the United States in the Fifth International Congress of Linguistics, 1939; Seventh, 1952; Eighth, 1957. Author of *The Teaching of the English Language*, 1927; *American English Grammar*, 1940; *Teaching and Learning English as a Foreign Language*, 1945; *The Structure of English*, 1952. Coauthor of *The Teaching of Literature*, 1925. Contributor to numerous journals and encyclopedias.

importance of either. In our modern society, however, technology (the applications of science, the *doing*) receives much greater consideration than *mere knowing*. We tend to measure the worth of what we know only in terms of doing, not in terms of understanding or intellectual freedom. And modern linguistic science is no exception.

The efforts to take the knowledge achieved by modern linguistic science and to use it in solving the problems of teaching English in our schools have not thus far been wholly successful. Perhaps an examination of some of the obstacles to this application of linguistics might help to remove them.

I

IGNORANCE OF THE FACT THAT THERE IS A LINGUISTIC SCIENCE

Efforts to change the patterns of our dealing with matters concerning the English language have been resisted because the public (even the "educated" public), the school administrators, and the teachers have not been aware (and could not believe) that a linguistic science actually existed.

In 1921, Professor Henry Cecil Wyld delivered his inaugural lecture as Professor of English Philology at the University of Oxford, England. In that lecture he made the following statement:

The subject matter of English philology [*linguistics* in United States usage] possesses a strange fascination for the man in the street, but almost everything he thinks and says about it is incredibly and hopelessly wrong. In no subject, probably, is the knowledge of the educated public at a lower ebb. The general ignorance concerning it is so profound that it is very difficult to persuade people that there really is a considerable mass of well-ascertained fact and a definite body of scientific doctrine on linguistic questions.

Professor Wyld was, of course, speaking especially of the situation in England. In 1924, at the foundation meeting of the Linguistic Society of America, Professor Leonard Bloomfield in his paper *Why a Linguistic Society?* made an equally severe statement about the situation in the United States.

To speak, finally, of the public interest, it is evident that a great and important, indeed the fundamental phase of our social life consists of linguistic activities, and that, in particular, elementary education is largely linguistic, . . . Yet . . . our schools are conducted by persons who, from professors of education down to teachers in the classroom, know nothing of the results of linguistic science, nor even the relation of writing to speech, or of standard language to dialect. In short, they do not know what language is, and yet must teach it, and in consequence waste years of every child's life and reach a poor result.

Professor Wyld's statement was made in 1921, the very year in which Edward Sapir's great book *Language* appeared. It was three years before the founding of the Linguistic Society of America, and seven years before the organization of the first International Congress of Linguists. [1]

Before 1921, however, linguistic science, or more precisely, *the "modern" linguistic science of Europe and America*, had had a fruitful development lasting through a complete century.

Linguistics may be said to have begun its scientific career with the comparative study and reconstruction of the Indo–European languages. In the course of their detailed researches Indo–European linguists have gradually developed a technique which is probably more nearly perfect than that of any other science dealing with man's institutions. Many of the formulations of comparative Indo–European linguistics have a neatness and a regularity which recall the formulae, or the so-called laws, of natural science. . . .

The methods developed by the Indo-Europeanists have been applied with marked success to other groups of languages. It is abundantly clear that they apply as rigorously to the unwritten primitive languages of Africa and America as to the better known forms of speech of the more sophisticated peoples. . . . The more we devote ourselves to the comparative study of the languages of a primitive linguistic stock, the more clearly we realize that phonetic law and analogical leveling are the only satisfactory key to the unravelling of the development of dialects and

---

[1] The word *linguist* as here used does not mean one who speaks a number of different languages. A practical speaking, reading, and writing control of several languages, no matter how many, does not necessarily give one any understanding of what is here called *linguistic science*. A *linguist* is one whose special field of scholarship is linguistic science. See Section II below for a definition of "linguistic science."

languages from a common base. Professor Leonard Bloomfield's experiences with Central Algonkian and my own with Athabaskan leave nothing to be desired in this respect and are a complete answer to those who find it difficult to accept the large scale regularity of the operation of all those unconscious linguistic forces which, in their totality, give us regular phonetic change and morphological readjustment on the basis of such a change. It is not merely theoretically possible to predict the correctness of specific forms among unlettered peoples on the basis of such phonetic laws as have been worked out for them—such predictions are already on record in considerable number. [2]

But, as late as 1946, Leonard Bloomfield, after pointing out that . . . "the administrations of a few universities have come to understand the place of linguistics in the domain of science," went on to write as follows:

Nevertheless, the community at large does not yet recognize even that a body of linguistic knowledge exists. . . . Even academic groups and learned periodicals in other fields of science are sometimes unaware that there exists any cumulative body of information about language and go for linguistic counsel to persons who, quite evidently, have made no use of it. [3]

Today, among the educated professional groups, there is still practically no general recognition of the existence of a large body of cumulative scientific linguistic knowledge. Even our best popular magazines publish article after article presenting extremely naïve views of language—arguments and opinions based on prescientific assumptions which linguistic science has long ago discarded as untenable. Many of these articles concern English—its "illogical character", [4] its "increasing deterioration and corruption," or its lack of any "lawful pattern of pronunciation." Concerning the "ideas" that come from whole sentences, it is asserted that: "The final idea is the result of the fusion of the meanings of the separate words into a

[2] Edward Sapir, "The Status of Linguistics as a Science" in *Language* 5 (1929) 207, 208.

[3] In "Twenty One Years of the Linguistic Society," *Language*, 22 (1946), 3.

[4] See, for example, the article entitled "English is a Queer Language," by Alice Hamilton, M. D. in *Atlantic Monthly*, June, 1959. The significance here lies not only in the fact that such an article should have been written by one who is highly educated in another professional field but that *The Atlantic Monthly* should have published it.

coherent whole." [5] Some, stimulated by arguments in the United Nations, have written concerning the need for "honest speech—a language in which no word has more than one meaning and everybody knows what that meaning is . . . let each word in every document mean what it says in any language and then proclaim that meaning to all mankind". [6]

Since 1921, the enthusiastic work of a growing body of linguistic scholars has led not only to a refinement and development of the earlier knowledge achieved during the nineteenth century but also to a new view of the very nature of language itself. The Linguistic Society of America, founded in 1924 with two hundred and seventy members, now has a membership of over sixteen hundred. The Eighth International Congress of Linguists, meeting in Oslo, Norway, in 1957, was attended by five hundred and twenty-five invited linguists, from forty-three different countries—from Japan and Australia to Cuba and the Federation of the West Indies, from the Union of South Africa and Ghana to Russia and Scotland, from Argentina and Uruguay to the United States and Canada.

The first task to be accomplished, if we are to use to the full the linguistic knowledge and understanding now available, is to make the educated lay public aware that there is actually a linguistic science with a cumulative body of scientific knowledge and understanding concerning the nature and functioning of language.

II

MISUNDERSTANDING AND MISREPRESENTATION OF THE ATTITUDES AND THE WORK OF THE LINGUIST

Linguistic science, with its very solid achievements of knowledge and understanding during the last hundred and forty years, has not

[5] UNESCO Report, *The Teaching of Reading and Writing*, Monographs on Fundamental Education, X (1956), 68. The view expressed in this quotation from 1956 doesn't seem to differ fundamentally from that of the following quotation from Richard Grant White, *Words and Their Uses* (1870). "In English, words are formed into sentences by the operation of an invisible power, which is like magnetism. Each [word] is charged with a meaning which gives it a tendency towards some of the other words in the sentence and particularly to one, and which repels it from others."

[6] Editorial, *Detroit Free Press*.

only been very generally ignored, it has been much misunderstood and grossly misrepresented. This misunderstanding and misrepresentation has also stimulated resistance to the efforts to apply and use, in teaching, the new linguistic knowledge.

Journalists, in reporting upon lectures and interviews given by linguists, have sought sensational headlines without regard for the truth or the damage that might be done to those who sorely needed the help that linguistic science could give. The following headline from the *Detroit Free Press* of December 29, 1951 is an example:

> "GRAMMAR? IT AIN'T GOTTA BE PERFECT"
> *Prof Defends Us as Says 'It's Me', 'None Are,' 'Lay Down'*

The United Press wire services took this material from the *Detroit Free Press* and sent it throughout the country. Papers from New England to California carried the item with variations *ad lib*. The heading in the Oneida (N. Y.) *Daily Dispatch* was "It Don't Make No Difference." It is, perhaps, unnecessary to add that the headings and the articles themselves were completely wrong in attitude, point of view, and all details of content. Not a single item indicated in the headlines above was even mentioned in this particular effort to explain some of the work of the linguist. Subsequent letters of protest were completely ignored.

Even serious writing from university professors furnishes many examples of misunderstanding and misrepresentation of the work and point of view of linguistic scientists:

It is a question whether philologists [linguists] should ever be allowed to teach English Composition: with them, whatever is, is right. [7]

. . . the linguists who measure language propriety by statistics. [8]

All linguistic facts [For linguistics as science] are per se of equal importance or of equal unimportance. [9]

[7] Professor H.S.P. Woodhouse, Head, Department of English, University College, University of Toronto, Canada, in "The Nature and Function of the Humanities," *Transactions of the Royal Society of Canada*, 46, Ser. 3, Sec. 2, (June, 1952).

[8] Louis B. Salomon, Associate Professor of English, Brooklyn College, "Whose Good English?" in *Bulletin of the American Association of University Professors*, 38 (1952) p. 446.

[9] Morton W. Bloomfield, Professor of English, Ohio State University, in *College English*, 15 (1953) p. 36.

The great cry is for improved communication, and yet under the pretext of being free and easy and above quibbling, those who do the most talking and writing indulge themselves in the very obscurities and ambiguities that cause the outcry.

They are abetted, moreover, by another offspring of the scientific spirit, the professional student of language. In his modern embodiment, the linguist takes the view that whatever occurs in anybody's speech is a fact of language and must not be tampered with, but only caught in flight and pinned on a card. This is "scientific detachment," and it has gone so far that under its influence in many schools all the categories of grammar, syntax, and rhetoric have been discarded. The modern way to learn English or a foreign language is to absorb a phrase-by-phrase enumeration of all that might conceivably be said in ordinary talk—a directory instead of a grammar. [10]

Every assertion concerning the linguist in the last three sentences of this quotation is fundamentally wrong in fact. More than that, the evidence for the facts concerning the work and attitude of the linguist was not only abundant before 1953 but had been easily accessible for more than twenty years. No one, recognized as a linguistic scientist, doing serious research and publication in linguistics, has ever, to my knowledge, taken the point of view that "whatever occurs in anybody's speech is a fact of language and must not be tampered with, but only caught in flight and pinned on a card." No linguist has ever, so far as I know, even held the view that *in practical use* "one form is as good as another" or that "if a language form is used anywhere, by anyone, it is acceptable to use it everywhere." Linguists have used statistics in a variety of ways but never have they "measured *language propriety*" by raw quantitative preponderance of one form over another. Throughout the history of linguistic science, linguists have sought (1) to collect and record sound samplings of linguistic facts, (2) to determine which facts are significant for each kind of inquiry, (3) to develop techniques and procedures for studying these facts in order to arrive at sound conclusions—conclusions that could be stated in such terms that they could be verified, and used by further research, and thus aid in

[10] Jaques Barzun, Professor of History, Columbia University, "English as She's Not Taught," in *Atlantic Monthly* (December, 1953) p. 53. See also the article "Grammar is Obsolete," by Wilson Follett, *Atlantic Monthly* (February, 1960), and compare C. C. Fries, *The Teaching of the English Language* (New York, 1927), especially Chapter V, "The Scientific and the Artistic Points of View in Language."

building up a cumulative body of sound knowledge. The following books furnish an impressive display of some of the things *the linguists have been doing with the materials they have collected,* other than pinning on cards whatever occurs in anybody's speech that they happen to catch by chance. William Dwight Whitney, *Language and the Study of Language* (1867) and *Life and Growth of Language* (1874); Herman Paul, *Prinzipien der Sprachgeschichte* (1st edition 1880, 5th edition 1920); Edward Sapir, *Language* (1921); Otto Jespersen, *Language: its Nature, Development, and Origin* (1923); H. Pedersen, *Linguistic Science in the Nineteenth Century,* tr. Spargo (1931); Leonard Bloomfield, *Language* (1933); and Kenneth Pike, *Language* (in Relation to a Unified Theory of the Structure of Human Behavior), Part I, 1954; Part II, 1955; Part III, 1960. Perhaps the best example of the gathering of the facts of usage is the *Oxford English Dictionary.* The body of the material upon which the fifty years of editing was based consisted of some six million quotations. The Early English Text Society was founded in order to provide satisfactory texts of early English books to be excerpted for this dictionary. [11]

A *linguist,* then, is one whose special field of scholarship is lin-

[11] Preface to the first edition of Volume I of the *Oxford English Dictionary* (1888), p. v. ". . . It was proposed that materials should be collected for a Dictionary which, by the completeness of its vocabulary, and by the application of the historical method to the life and use of words, might be worthy of the English language and of English scholarship. With this view, it was resolved to begin at the beginning, and extract anew typical quotations for the use of words, from all the great English writers of all ages, and from all the writers on special subjects whose works might illustrate the history of words employed in special senses, from all writers whatever before the 16th century, and from as many as possible of the more important writers of later times. . . . p. vi. ". . . The aim of this Dictionary is to furnish an adequate account of the meaning, origin, and history of English words now in general use, or known to have been in use at any time during the last seven hundred years. It endeavours (1) to show, with regard to each individual word, when, how, in what shape, and with what signification, it became English; what development of form and meaning it has since received; which of its uses have, in the course of time, become obsolete, and which still survive; what new uses have since arisen, by what processes, and when; (2) to illustrate these facts by a series of quotations ranging from the first known occurrence of the word to the latest, or down to the present day; the word being thus made to exhibit its own history and meaning; and (3) to treat the etymology of each word strictly on the basis of historical fact, and in accordance with the methods and results of modern philological science."

guistic science. *Linguistic science* is here understood to be a body of knowledge and understanding concerning the nature and functioning of human language built up out of information about the structure, the operation, and the history of a wide range of very diverse human languages by means of those techniques and procedures that have proved most successful in establishing verifiable generalizations concerning relationships among linguistic phenomena.

In this much loaded and difficult definition there are five essential features that cannot be separated, for each succeeding feature is a qualifier of what has preceded. Perhaps the following arrangement of the parts of this definition may serve to give these important features their relative prominence.

LINGUISTIC SCIENCE IS

1. *a body of knowledge and understanding*

2. (knowledge and understanding) concerning the *nature and functioning of human language*

3. (this knowledge and understanding) built up out of *information* about the *structure,* the *operation,* and the *history* of a *wide range* of *very diverse human languages*

4. (this knowledge and understanding built up) *by* means of those *techniques and procedures* that have proved *most successful* in *establishing verifiable generalizations*

5. (verifiable generalizations) concerning *relationships among linguistic phenomena.*

III

TRADITIONAL VIEWS OF LANGUAGE CONTRADICTED BY THE KNOWLEDGE AND UNDERSTANDING ACHIEVED BY LINGUISTIC SCIENCE

Every science has developed its own special techniques for investigation, analysis, and the testing of generalizations concerning the data it accumulates. Modern linguistic science began early in the nineteenth century with the use of sets of phonological correspondences as a means of exploring and proving genetic relationships between different languages. These techniques became more refined and more rigorously controlled after 1875. Later came the growth of sound techniques for language history, for linguistic geography, for the analysis and description of unwritten languages, for finding and checking the structurally significant contrasts that make the special signals of each different language. The validity of the basic approach to these techniques has been verified again and again, and the techniques themselves have been and are being constantly improved by rigorous experimentation and criticism. But the heart and substance of linguistic science is not simply in the techniques of operation—not in the tools of analysis. The heart and substance of linguistic science is, rather, in the growing understanding of certain features of the nature and functioning of human language itself that have become clear as the *unexpected results* of the use of these tools in the study of a great variety of languages.

Some of these results that constitute our present knowledge are the following:

1. It became clear that all the languages investigated were always, and had always been, in a state of constant change. There has, for example, never been a time in English during the last thousand years, when the recorded materials do not show evidence of change in progress—evidence of divided usage in some features of the language.

2. It became clear that these changes could not have been corruptions arising from the ignorance of the speakers—accidental and lawless. These changes have shown themselves to be astonishingly regular and systematic—large patterns of change that stretched over long periods of time.

It may be urged that change in language is due ultimately to the deviations of individuals from the rigid system. But it appears that even here individual deviations are ineffective; whole groups of speakers must, for some reason unknown to us, coincide in a deviation, if it is to result in a linguistic change. Change in language does not reflect individual variability, but seems to be a massive, uniform, and gradual alteration, at every moment of which the system is just as rigid as at any other time. [12]

[12] Leonard Bloomfield, Review of Jespersen's *Philosophy of Grammar,* in *Journal of English and Germanic Philology,* 26 (1927), 444-446.

The facts of language history destroyed the myth of a golden age of a language in perfection at some time in the past—a perfection from which it has deteriorated.

3. It became clear that the most stable features of a language were its sounds—not its vocabulary; not its grammar. Linguistic science in the first period of its modern development set up "laws" or generalizations of "sound change." These were generalizations concerning correspondences of "sound" features between several languages, or between different periods of a single language. They were correspondences that could be grasped in statements applicable to the whole body of the native words in the languages concerned. It was these correspondences of "sound" features that established a rigorous basis for the treatment of etymology.

4. It became clear that the only basis for "correctness" in a language had to be the usage of the native speakers of that language. Language history provided the evidence to identify new forms and older forms. The studies in linguistic geography showed the language characteristics of different language and dialect areas and the centers of language dispersion. Together, linguistic history and linguistic geography led to a much clearer understanding of the significance of dialect differences in a language and the basis for the special prestige through which one regional dialect out of many becomes the "standard" language.

5. It became clear that "standard" and "literary" languages are not the bases from which "dialects" diverge through mistakes, lawlessness, and incomplete learning. The "dialects" come first and preserve older forms. On the whole, the language forms of colonists tend to keep more of the older patterns than do the forms of the speakers who stay in the homeland. In similar fashion, the differing grammatical forms of the uneducated are usually more conservative or older than those of the educated.

6. It became clear, from the more than seventy-five years of work upon the great historical dictionaries, that multiple meanings for words is normal, not "queer." We must everywhere in language expect to find that the most frequently used words have a variety of meanings—not just one literal meaning and a few so-called figurative meanings. Words cover whole areas of meaning, and, except for

highly technical words, there are no words in two languages that cover precisely the same areas. The number of different meanings for each of the commonly used words in English (as recorded and illustrated by verifiable quotations in the *Oxford English Dictionary*) is almost incredible.

7. It became clear, with the development of the work in phonetics, that all the "mysterious" qualities of the sounds and "accents" of human language are matters that can be analyzed and described in terms of the physical movements by which they are produced and also in terms of the specific kinds of vibrations that make up their acoustic characteristics. [13] The increasing accuracy and completeness of the recording, reproduction, and transmission of vocal sounds grew out of the work of the phonetics laboratories. In other words, linguistic science, through the techniques of phonetics, has now successfully been able to isolate, describe, produce, and control mechanically a great many of the specific features that comprise the total complex of human speech sounds.

8. It has become clear, with the developments in linguistic science during the last forty years, that the habits that constitute the control of one's native language are not habits concerning items of language as separate items—that is, of separate segments of sound as represented by the letters or of individual grammatical forms. Practical language habits are always habits concerning *contrastive shapes of linguistic items, in structural patterns, functioning in a system*. No item has linguistic significance by itself. Its significance can arise only out of its contrast with other items in the structural patterns that function as signals in a particular language system. "Structural" linguistics has attempted to discover and describe:

(*a*). The basic contrastive sound features that function in identifying or separating the various meaning units (morphemes or words) in a linguistic community—*pan* from *pen* and *pin* and *pun*.
(*b*). The basic contrastive features that identify and separate the grammatical units that function in the patterns that signal structural meanings.

[13] See Kenneth L. Pike, *Phonetics: A Critical Analysis of Phonetic Theory and a Technic for the Practical Description of Sounds.* University of Michigan Publications in Language and Literature, XXI (1943).

Martin Joos, *Acoustic Phonetics*, Linguistic Society of America, Language Monograph, No. 23 (1948).

(c). The basic contrastive arrangements and forms of these functioning grammatical units that identify and separate the patterns that signal the structural meanings of a language.

It is assumed that all the significant materials that signal linguistic meanings are matters of contrast within a limited number of patterns.

9. It has become clear that that which is objectively the same uttered sound will be perceived and responded to very differently in accord with the specific patterns of the particular native language of the hearer. Or, in other words, the same phonetic differences may have (usually do have) entirely different structural values from language to language. In general, there are no language sounds that are easy or difficult in themselves. Ease or difficulty of pronunciation or of hearing turns out to be a function of the way the phonetic material patterns in a person's native language. Native speakers of English respond easily to the sound contrasts which distinguish *river* from *liver*, *pray* from *play*, *correction* from *collection*, *variable* from *valuable*, *storing* from *string*. Native speakers of Japanese, in the first stages of learning English, not only find it difficult to produce these significant differences consistently—they cannot hear them. The child, in learning his native language, must develop not only great facility and accuracy in responding to the limited number of contrastive physical features that identify the functioning units of the structural patterns of his particular language, he must learn to ignore all those physical features that are not relevant to those patterns. His great facility and accuracy in recognizing and producing the signalling patterns of his native language is thus bought at a price. He develops blind spots for a whole range of physical differences that form the signalling devices of other languages. Thus, the power or force in the structural arrangements of the first language (the native language) makes the learning of a second language as an adult a very different matter from the learning of the first language.

Altogether a tremendous body of knowledge and understanding has been won by linguistic science during the last hundred and forty years. In this cumulative body of basic knowledge concerning the nature and functioning of language there is much that ought to be of use in helping to deal with those practical teaching problems that have not yet been satisfactorily analyzed. Considerable resistance to its use arises from the fact that it contradicts many of the older views of language which are still vigorously maintained.

IV

RESISTANCE OF A "GRAMMAR" SANCTIFIED BY TWO HUNDRED YEARS OF ENGLISH TEACHING

The minds of most of us who have taught English have been deeply channeled to think of language in terms of the "grammar" we first met in the early years of our school life. We had not been conscious of our language. Language was like the air we breathed—part of the undifferentiated background of our experience. To many of us in these early years, this "grammar" came as a revelation. Some of us (I, for one) liked it immensely. On the whole, it was those who "liked grammar" and really mastered it who have become the teachers of English who have stayed in the profession. And the material of this grammar, with its *definitions* and *"analysis" of sentences for the sake of classification,* was pressed into our thinking habits not only by the teachers who revealed it to us as one of our early intellectual experiences but also later by our own repeated teaching of grammar to class after class. More teachers have taught more "grammar" and usage in the schools than anyone has taught anything else. As a result, English teachers of considerable experience have found it extremely difficult and confusing to read a "new" grammar with a different outlook and a *different purpose.* They *read* new collocations of words but, they *think* the old definitions and the old processes of classification. A "new" grammar to them means simply a different (and more confusing way) of *doing the same thing.*

For the sake of clarity and sharp contrast let me use my own book, the *Structure of English* (1952), as an example of the "new" grammar in this very brief comparison of some basic features of the "old" and the "new." This "new" grammar presents a very different view of what English grammar really is. Its central concern is not with "definitions" or with any special set of names for the "parts of speech." It does not attempt to analyze "dead" sentences or anything else for the sake of "classification."

The basic difference between the "old" grammar and the "new" grammar is, in brief, set forth in the following statements under

(A) for the "old" grammar, and under (B) for the "new" grammar.

A. The "Old" Grammar

1. The "old" grammar starts with the full knowledge of the linguistic meaning communicated by a sentence. This linguistic meaning of a sentence includes:

(a) the dictionary meanings of the separate words, and

(b) another set of meanings, like the facts that the particular utterance makes a statement or asks a question, that certain words in this utterance represent the one that performs the action, the one to or for whom the action is done, the thing which was acted upon.

2. Starting with these two kinds of meanings the "old" grammar demands that the words and the groups of words which represent the meanings of (b) above, be classified under certain technical words, like *declarative sentence, subject, object, indirect object,* and so on.

3. The basic procedure of the "old" grammar consists of examining this second set of meanings, in (b) above, for the sake of "classifying" the words or groups of words that represent them.

B. The "New" Grammar

1. The *Structure of English* does not propose the *adoption* of a new set of terms under which to "classify" the "parts of speech" or anything else in English grammar. In my view, the answer to only one important question should provide the basis for decisions concerning the choice of special names to substitute for long descriptive statements. Through what terms can we achieve the most complete understanding between writer and reader? When the meanings are new there are only two means of approach. Either we can use old terms that have the advantage of familiarity in their shape but the disadvantage of being misunderstood by readers who just cannot keep in mind that the old meanings must be changed. Or else we can use new terms that have the disadvantage of unfamiliarity in their shapes but the advantage of being given the meaning content that fits. I have used numbers (*Class 1, Class 2, Class 3, Class 4*) instead of the old names for the major parts of speech in an attempt to keep close to familiarity in the form of the labels and to avoid the misunderstandings that would inevitably attach to the old names, especially to the names *adjective* and *adverb*. In the *Structure of English,* Chapter VII gives the formal characteristics of these parts of speech, *not* Chapter V. [14] Chapter X treats "modifiers." In spite of my

---

[14] Chapter V of the *Structure of English* has been taken by many reviewers as stating my general criteria for "determining the parts of speech". This

many assertions concerning the fact *that the modifying function is not and cannot be used as any part of the formal markers of Class 3 and Class 4,* many teachers equate my Class 3 with the old term *adjective* and my Class 4 with the old term *adverb.* The force of this old thinking, in which the function of *modification* as the chief identifying characteristic of *adjective* and of *adverb,* is so great that, in spite of my specific statements and marked examples under descriptive headings, these same and similar examples are given quite different markings and offered as evidence that I follow the old pattern. The following are examples from a recent book by one who is really seeking to understand and evaluate the "new" grammar.

From *Teaching English Grammar* (p. 67)	From the *Structure of English* (p. 208 and p. 229)
"The system of grammar presented by Fries . . . Identifying words in classes according to functional use. . . ."	[Heading] "**Class 1** *words* with **Class 2** *words* as 'modifiers.' "
"The *running water* sparkles." **Class 3**	"A *burning fire* is in the fireplace." **Class 2-ng Class 1**
	[Heading] "*Class* **2** *words* with *Class* **2** *words* as modifiers."
"The boys came *running.*" **Class 4**	"Both the boys *came running* when C——— yelled." **Class 2 Class 2-ng**

Chapter V, however, gives only a sketch of the *procedure* by which I procured from my corpus of material a large body of words to be examined in order to *find out* what the characteristic contrastive markers of each class were. See pp. 73-74, and footnotes No. 12 and No. 13. See also pp. 86 and 104-109 for the basic difference between the four "parts of speech" and "function words". In spite of negative warnings in footnote No. 2, page 88, and the descriptive characteristics set forth on pp. 104-109, many still see in my "function words" only the old distinction between words with lexical content and words with no such content—a distinction which I have repeatedly insisted was not only wrongly stated (See ¶ 3, p. 106) but does not represent the chief characteristics of "function words". For the relation between the procedures of Chapter V and the description of the "markers" in Chapter VII see pp. 110-113. It is important also to separate the use of "positions in a test frame" as part of the procedure to find the words to be examined (See pp. 73-75, including footnotes 6, 7, 8) from the use of "position as a marker" (for example, *poorest* preceded by *the*), pp. 140-141.

This "new" grammar is not tied to any special names for the parts of speech. It presents the conclusion that the functioning units which make up the signals of structural meanings are not *words as vocabulary items* but rather *classes of words* for which we have here used the old term "parts of speech." In order to respond to the signals of the structural meanings in our utterances one need not know the lexical meanings of the words but he must have learned to respond to the form classes to which the words belong. A description of the structural signals must have some way of identifying these form classes other than listing them. But the names by which they are identified are not important. The matter of real importance is the distinguishing contrastive markers to which those who use English have learned to respond. Only when the essential form-class markers are responded to does the word receive its form-class meaning which makes it fulfill its functions as a unit of some pattern that signals a structural meaning.

2. The *Structure of English* reports the results of an investigation. It starts with the view that the group of meanings, other than dictionary meanings, by which the old grammar classifies the parts of the sentence that represent them—that these meanings (called structural meanings) must be signalled or communicated in some way. English-speaking children have learned to respond to these signals of structural meanings very early in learning to talk, and foreigners who seek to learn English must learn them early. The investigation of which the *Structure of English* is the report undertook the task of finding out what these signals are in modern English and describing how they operate. This report gives some brief statements of parts of the procedures of the investigation, but the center of attention is on trying to describe what the signals actually are. The purpose of the "new" grammar is, thus, quite different from that of the "old" grammar in that the "new" grammar does *not* seek to "classify" the words and word groups of the sentences, but rather to describe the precise contrasts of patterns of form classes that elicit the range of meanings that we have called structural meanings. It seeks not to *classify* but to *predict* the recognition responses that will regularly follow certain patterns of form class arrangement.

3. The "new" grammarian does not "classify" for the purpose of removing ambiguities from sentences. Faced with the headline "Doctor Stoops Low in Medic Meet" he simply says that this, like a great many printed newspaper headlines, [15] is, as it stands, structurally ambiguous *because it does not have the form-class markers*. Wherever the essential form class markers are entirely absent (and where, as in printed material

[15] See *Structure of English*, pp. 62, 63, 64.

generally, there is no special signal from the intonation pattern) the "new" grammarian predicts that there will be structural ambiguity. He can go further and indicate the precise formal markers that would resolve the ambiguity. For example, any determiner before the word *Doctor* would give one clear structural meaning, for example, "A Doctor Stoops Low. . . ." Or any Class 2 word-form after the word *Stoops* would give another clear structural meaning, for example, "Doctor Stoops is. . . ." The "new" grammarian insists that there is in our utterances a separate layer of meaning, structural meanings, and that these particular meanings are definitely signalled by the arrangements and forms of the four major parts of speech and by function words. He would insist, too, that these signals of structural meanings can be *described in physical terms,* so that, given the formal description of the signals, he can predict what the recognition responses will be in an English-speaking community. He would also insist that, whenever necessary portions of the signals are not present in the utterance or whenever the signals overlap, there will be some type of structural ambiguity. [16]

Perhaps the obstacle most difficult to remove from the path of those who really strive to understand a "new" approach to grammar consists of the hold upon our thinking of the practices and purposes of the traditional *grammatical analysis for the sake of classification.* The weight of two hundred years of teaching has so channeled the responses of the more experienced teachers that a variety of blind spots seem to prevent an understanding of the materials of a "new" grammar aiming at *description* for the sake of *prediction* rather than *analysis* for the sake of *classification.*

V

FOR THE TASK AHEAD

Enough concerning obstacles. There are others, of course, including the overly enthusiastic assertions of those with very little contact

---

[16] Of course, in the actual live use of language for communication the signals of structural meaning are not separated from all the other signals, so that what would be structural ambiguity if there were no other clues, is often clarified because the hearer uses all the kinds of clues together. See concerning signals of immediate constituents, *Structure of English,* pp. 272, 273. For the kind of procedure that will determine whether "The wind blew up the street" and "The powder blew up the ship" are structurally the same, see note 7, p. 75 of the *Structure of English* and the University of Michigan dissertation by Edward J. Anthony.

with linguistics, who, in the manner of science fiction, imaginatively project the claims for linguistic science far beyond anything that that science is at present able to deliver. This "linguistic-science" fiction helps to stimulate an even more extravagant "antilinguistic science" fiction from those of greater ignorance of the facts who have built up a hideous mask to hide the real face of the linguistic scientist. (See *College English* for January, 1960). But there are those real leaders in the teaching profession who have patiently tried to understand the not always simple writing of linguistic scholars and to find in it helpful materials to report and explain to classroom teachers. (See W. W. Hatfield "Will Structural Grammar Help?" in *College English*, December, 1958.) These leaders must form the nucleus of the group we need to undertake the co-operative task of using to the full the solid achievements of more then a century of linguistic research. For this co-operative effort we must have (*a*) some of the producing scholars in the English language who are willing to struggle hard to understand the practical problems of the broad field of English teaching, (*b*) some of the leaders of the teaching profession devoted to the task of understanding both the problems of English teaching and the contributions of linguists, and (*c*) some of the best classroom teachers who will try to understand the significance of the work of both the linguistic scholars and the professional leaders and then assume the chief burden of the task of putting the results of that work into specific materials for the guidance of textbook writers. This will be a long hard task but is one worthy of a top level Commission.

Such a group must have available for their work those who have achieved understanding and control of the tremendous body of material produced by a host of workers in the field of English language— from Old English up to and including the descriptive analysis of present-day English. This material is not all easily available and nicely laid out. Great masses of it are in a form that needs to be reworked and restudied in the terms of our recent developments in structural linguistics.

In the teaching of English, the major problems themselves need to be much more thoroughly analyzed and more definitely identified and described. In this task some of the tools and techniques of modern linguistic science should provide new insights and sharper methods of statement if these tools and techniques are carefully explored. They must not be woodenly and unimaginatively applied without critical evaluation and adaptation.

Teachers cannot be equipped to provide the "applications of linguistic science" to the problems of teaching English by taking "one or two courses in linguistics." It seems to have been assumed that everybody knew what subject-matter content any course of study labelled *linguistics* would include, and that any course with a "linguistic" label would provide the necessary enlightenment. As a matter of fact, however, *linguistics* covers a very wide range of material and one cannot predict what even an introductory course will stress. Very frequently, "training in linguistics" as recommended to language teachers has meant mastering only the tools, techniques, and procedures of linguistic analysis. Many "introductory" courses are set up to offer what are thought to be the necessary first steps for those who aim to become practitioners in the analysis of an unknown language. Some "linguists" seem to believe, or act as if they believed, that tools, techniques, and classificatory definitions alone constituted the substance of the science of linguistics. I do not want to belittle the scientific importance of adequate tools, sound techniques, and sharp classifications. I should like, however, to insist that one can achieve a sufficient mastery of these tools and techniques of linguistic analysis to be a good practitioner of linguistic analysis, without any real understanding of the significance of the achievements of linguistic science. Perhaps this is the reason that some of those teachers of English who have earnestly sought help in linguistic courses have come away disappointed, having found nothing directly applicable to their needs.

The Conference of 1958, in the pamphlet, *The Basic Issues in the Teaching of English* ["Issue" 13, p. 9], raised the question of the part linguistics should have in the teaching of English, in the following manner.

Up to the present, only a few textbooks have attempted *to adapt the approach of the structural linguists to use in the classroom.* Nevertheless, we must ask whether *this new method offers a clue to a better correlation* of the knowledge of language structure with writing ability. How much, if any, of *such linguistic knowledge* is appropriate for each level? How may teachers best be trained *to develop this knowledge in their pupils?* [The italics are mine.]

This paragraph seems to suggest that "the approach of the structural linguist," his methods and techniques, might be adapted "to use in the classroom" as "a new method" for achieving "a better correlation of the knowledge of language structure with writing ability." It then raises the questions of "how much, if any, of such knowledge" of language structure is appropriate for each level, and how best to train teachers to pass on "this knowledge" to their pupils. I shall be greatly disappointed if, at this point, the reader of this paper does not realize quite clearly that the program I have advocated here is something quite different. In my view it is not the tools and the techniques of linguistic science that should be brought into the classroom. In some way, the substance of the knowledge and understanding won by linguistic science must be thoroughly assimilated and used to shed new light upon the problems that arise wherever language is concerned.

12

DORA V. SMITH

Developing a
Love of Good Reading

loving wrote and her brother and sisters remained for hours, "as socially unaware as the treasure at El last formed in Alaska with Aladdin

RECENTLY, in an article in the Saturday Review, Clifton Fadiman divided all subjects of study into two classes: *generative* and *self-terminating*.[1] The *generative* included such disciplines as history, science, literature, and languages; the *self-terminating*, the how-to-do subjects like "how to bake a cake" or "how to drive a car." The idea is intriguing, especially if one's favorite subject falls in the class of *generatives*, because it goes straight to the heart of every English teacher's ambition to generate a love of good reading which will enrich the lives of students.

But, on second thought, one wonders if the generalization is a bit too facile. One suddenly remembers the boy for whom physics proved so generative that he became a great scientist, but for whose sister the same course was completely self-terminating. One recalls also with a tinge of discouragement certain courses in the history of English literature which, for many pupils in the class, have eventuated in the determination "never to crack a book again" as long as they live. It is doubtful if a course in "how to drive a car" ever resulted in a comparable wholehearted repudiation of automobiles.

It takes two poles to generate a spark. The book alone cannot do it. The reception end must be in working order. And in the field of reading guidance, the reception end varies constantly. No two readers are alike in native ability, in power to read, in family background and traditions, or in personal interests and drives.

Mary Ellen Chase, before she had reached school age, sat aloft in her kitchen Parnassus on top of the huge secretary in her Maine

DORA V. SMITH Emeritus Professor of Education, University of Minnesota. President of NCTE, 1935-36. Chairman, NCTE Committee on Selection of Textbooks in Composition; Committee on Research; Director, Curriculum Commission since 1945. Awarded honorary Ed.D. by Rhode Island College of Education, 1957. W. Wilbur Hatfield Award, NCTE, 1957. Named Minnesota "Teacher of the Year," 1958. Author of *Communication, the Miracle of Shared Living* (Kappa Delta Pi lecture series), 1955; *Instruction in English*, Monograph No. 20 of the National Survey of Secondary English, 1932; *Evaluating Instruction in Elementary School English, Evaluating Instruction in Secondary School English*, 1937. Editor-in-chief of NCTE curriculum volumes.

[1] Clifton Fadiman, "Roots of the School Dilemma," *Saturday Review* 42 (September 12, 1959), 13-15 and 55-56.

home, where she and her brother and sisters remained for hours "not actually upon the secretary at all, but instead in Arabia with Aladdin or in the dark forest with Hansel and Gretel, with the four ingenious Robinsons on their mysterious island or with Oliver Twist in the workhouse, with David Copperfield in the Peggottys' houseboat, loving the alluring smell of crabs and lobsters and the blue mug holding a nosegay of seaweed, or with Jim Hawkins, crouching in the apple barrel of the *Hispaniola*." [2] For this magic childhood she "pays tribute to two young parents, who knew well that in opening the wide doors of reading to their children, they were building for them houses, not made with hands, but dwelling places of the mind, which would always furnish them with food, shelter, and delight." [3]

Early in the same decade Irvin Cobb was struggling with Mc-Guffey's readers, which, according to William McAndrew of Chicago, were "books that quietly stole into you, and made you different." [4] But for some reason they did not steal into Irvin Cobb, who insisted in his plea for Deadwood Dick and other favorites from the "nickul library" that all the "impossible idiots of literature" found their way into the McGuffey readers of his generation; for instance, the boy who stood on the burning deck "when everyone else had had sense enough to beat it." [5]

Then there was Mr. Adhem whose name led all the rest. "Why shouldn't it have led all the rest?" he remonstrated: "A man whose front name begins with *Ab,*, whose middle initial is *B.,* and whose last name begins with *Ad,* will be found leading all the rest in any city directory or telephone list anywhere." [6] Or take, for example, "Sir Walter Scott's poetic contribution touching on Young Lochinvar, who came out of the West. ... The West appears to have been a favorite place for upsetting things

[2] Mary Ellen Chase, *Recipe for a Magic Childhood* (New York, The Macmillan Co., 1952), p. 8.

[3] *Ibid.*, p. 11.

[4] William McAndrew, "School Book Famine," in Phyllis Fenner, *Something Shared: Children and Books* (New York, The John Day Co., 1959), p. 143.

[5] Irvin S. Cobb, *Irvin Cobb at His Best* (Garden City, New York, The Sun Dial Press, 1940), p. 174.

[6] *Ibid.*, p. 157.

to come from; so I can't take issue with Sir Walter there. But I do take issue with him where he says:

> So light to the croupe the fair lady he swung,
> So light to the saddle *before her* he sprung.

for I was born and brought up in a horseback-riding country.

"Here we have Young Lochinvar swinging the lady to the croupe, and then he springs to the saddle *in front of her*. Now to do this, he must either take a long running start, and leapfrog clear over the lady's head as she sits there, and land accurately in the saddle, which is scarcely a proper thing to do to any lady, aside from the difficulty of springing ten to fifteen feet into the air, and coming down, crotched out, on a given spot, or else he must contribute a feat in contortion the like of which has never been duplicated since. . . . I deny that he could have done that croupe trick. There isn't a croupier at Monte Carlo who could have done it. Buffalo Bill couldn't have done it. Ned Buntline wouldn't have had Buffalo Bill trying to do it. Doug Fairbanks couldn't do it. I couldn't do it myself." [7]

Apparently, the kitchen Parnassas on a Maine homestead and the "horseback-riding country" produced two very different problems for the English teacher who wanted to make his subject generate interest in good reading.

Clifton Fadiman, two or three decades later, found himself in a New York City high school in an underprivileged district where all followed the same course "in pursuit of excellence." They came out, he reports, with a regard for Shakespeare far above their regard for the Frank Sinatras of their day and with a comforting sense of security in their cultural heritage both in time and in space. [8]

He, himself, learned Latin outside of school because it was not offered in his secondary school program, and he wanted to have access to the literary treasures of Rome. Evidently, he credits the general atmosphere of the school and the superiority of his teachers for the unusual success of the program.

Earlier in the same decade, George Boas, philosopher, who was also in secondary school and college on the Atlantic seaboard, had a very different experience. He says:

[7] *Ibid.*, pp. 180-181.
[8] Clifton Fadiman, *op. cit.*, pp. 55-56.

But, alas, I was soon told that Greek did not exist so that you might read Plato and Sophocles and perhaps even Aristophanes; it existed to teach you how and when acute accents changed to grave, how circumflexes would never dream of alighting on a short vowel, how to distinguish between *paeon primus* and the *paeon quartus*—which I have forgotten how to do but I still recall their musical names—and, of course, how to conjugate mi-verbs.

Latin was a little better, for as I remember we had a professor of Latin who was not a Great Scholar, and so he treated Horace, Catullus, and Propertius as if they were poets and not collections of strange verbal and metric forms. [9]

Recalling his own instruction in elementary and high school English as "just as boring to the child as it was to the teacher," he remarks:

I am not blaming the teachers for trying to make the process as pleasant as possible. I think that it is a wonderful and kindly idea, for, personally, I found life in the primary and secondary schools, when I went to them in the Dark Ages before Dewey, an uninterrupted torture. If reading Burke's conciliation speech and *Silas Marner* and *Viri Romae* and Caesar can be made pleasant, I am all for it, assuming that the student has got to read them. This may be one of the lower forms of hedonism, but I fail to see why anyone should suffer agony until he has to, Admiral Rickover to the contrary. [10]

In this case, the choice of selections and the way in which they were presented both had bearing upon whether the study of literature was generative. These literary individuals were undoubtedly classed among "the gifted" when they were in school. Love of good reading appears to be an individual affair, and nothing is more dangerous for a teacher than generalizing on the basis of his personal recollection of his own likes and dislikes in reading during childhood or adolescence.

Perhaps we should add a contrasting picture—the truck driver interrogated in the Denver library survey some fifteen years ago as to when he last used the public library:

"Well, you see," he replied, "it's fifteen years since I left high school, and I ain't had much use for the library since."

Although individual differences in taste and in reading ability are

[9] George Boas, "Superstitions in Education," *The Johns Hopkins Magazine* 10 (April, 1959), 7.
[10] *Ibid.*, p. 28.

well-known, too many schools persist in an effort to make lovers of reading by forcing every pupil in the classroom to read the same book.

As one reading specialist has pointed out, "One cannot comprehend something which is written in a strange vocabulary, in sentences too long for one's mind to encompass, a context that assumes experiences one has not had, and in a complexity of organization that requires a mentality beyond one's own." [11]

It is particularly important to emphasize this fact today because there are those among us who would fix the literature program grade by grade—and not only that, but fix it in a sequence from the graduate school *down*. "*This*," they say, "is required for a Ph. D. in English: therefore, *these things* must be taught during the four years of college; *these* must be covered during the high school years; and *these* in the elementary school." Wasn't it Jonathan Swift who satirized the impractical philosophers of Laputa for building their houses from the roof down? Moreover, it is interesting to note that in June, 1959, of some fifteen thousand students who were given bachelor's degrees at twelve major universities in the United States, only 5½ per cent were English majors. Would anyone propose that the elementary and high school literature programs of this country should stem from needs of the small fraction of that 5½ per cent who ultimately go on to the doctorate in English?

But suppose we begin at the other end and let boys and girls grow into reading through every experience of childhood. Reading preferences reveal themselves early, and there is nothing in the annals of psychology to suggest that they grow from the top down. One Christmas a child of two, seeing his father unwrap a book, ran across the room to examine it. It was Norman Cousins's *Modern Man Is Obsolete*. Holding it in one hand, he frantically turned the pages with the chubby palm of the other. Then he dropped the book to the floor in disgust, announcing, "Too bad! No twains!" Already he had learned to look for trains in books because they were a dominant interest in his two-year-old world.

Like Mary Ellen Chase, other fortunate children have learned to love books long before they have come to school. With their mothers

[11] Constance McCullough, "What Does Research Reveal about Practices in Teaching Reading?", *The English Journal*, Vol. 46 (November, 1957), pp. 478-79

they have gleefully recited the galloping measures of Mother Goose or pointed triumphantly to familiar animals and toys in colorful object books. They have listened to stories like *Angus and the Ducks* and *Make Way for Ducklings* read from well-illustrated picture books. Again, they have matched their own experience with such real-life stories as *Hi, Mister Robin!* or *The Giant Story,* or with delightful verses from books like John Brewton's *Under the Tent of the Sky* which open their eyes to the things about them. Still others have phonographs they, themselves, can operate on which to play recordings by gifted storytellers.

The schools have a part to play in helping young mothers to recognize their responsibility for developing early a love of books and a desire to learn to read. Some schools have a picture-book library from which they lend books to mothers of preschool children. Others, during National Children's Book Week in November, distribute lists of stories, poems, and recordings which preschool and other children enjoy, and use the P.T.A. meeting that month to urge parents of pupils of all ages to give their children a wealth of experience with books. Local libraries often co-operate by furnishing displays of books available at the neighborhood branch. Such programs have been proved to produce results clearly compensating for the work involved. Since Book Week falls in November, parents are often eager for suggestions of books to buy for their children for Christmas.

It is important that the kindergarten continue this program, making up to those who have not had the privilege of such contact with books during preschool years and extending it for those who have. Since it is possible in the kindergarten to enjoy stories and simple poems of the children's own experience *every day,* the teacher has a unique opportunity to lay the foundation for a love of reading and to build a wealth of vocabulary and interests preparatory to the beginning reading program. Parents should be helped to understand that associating books with a good time and with all the experiences of the child's day is infinitely more important for later success in reading than teaching him to find the *the's* and *and's* in the newspaper.

Storytelling and reading aloud to the children in the kindergarten and primary grades should be a part of each day's program. If the kindergarten children on a walk around the block stand in awe before a huge steam shovel opening its jaws on a neighboring bank,

Mike Mulligan and His Steam Shovel should be awaiting them on their return to the classroom. After the teacher has read the story, it should remain on the browsing table in the library corner along with giant picture books of diggers, builders, and other large machines which delight the hearts of the boys.

The next step is to read aloud to the children Julia Sauer's *Mike's House,* the story of Robert, who named the library *Mike's House* because every Tuesday, when he went to the preschool story hour, he took home *Mike Mulligan and His Steam Shovel* for his mother to read to him. The girls like Mike Mulligan as well as the boys, but they may have their own story in *Rosa Too-Little,* the child who learned to write her own name so that she could have a library card.

There is no experience of childhood which cannot be matched in story or poetry. Do the children make a snowman at recess? There is "The Best Time of All" by Nancy Byrd Turner with a snowman just like theirs. Do the birds build their nests in the spring? There is George Cooper's "What Robin Told." Does an aeroplane pass overhead? So does one "zoom" through Mary Greene's "Aeroplane." Little children memorize poetry so readily that they should have a whole stock of poems made their own before they leave the kindergarten and first grade. Many of these, too, will come from *The Real Mother Goose, Tenggren's Mother Goose,* or other favorite editions.

Sometimes, it is the individual child whose experience dictates the story to be read on a particular day. One has a birthday; then a birthday story accompanies the birthday cake into the classroom. One has a father just returned by plane from Washington. He has a chance to show the children the pictures of airplanes in a book in the library corner. Another has announced during morning news that he has a new baby brother. Then out comes Marjorie Flack's *The New Pet.* Still another child may be excited about the arrival of a grandmother from overseas, and that is the time for Marjorie Clark's *Poppy Seed Cakes.* The possibilities in Christmas and other special days are infinite, and most teachers and parents take full advantage of them. John Brewton's *Christmas Bells Are Ringing* is invaluable for both sacred and secular poetry.

But some of the choicest classics of childhood are not about things seen or heard. They come from the realm of the imagination. Children never tire of hearing and playing afterward such folk-tale favorites as *The Three Bears, The Three Pigs, The Three Billy Goats Gruff,* and *The Travelling Musicians.* All of them are now available in slender little volumes with excellent illustrations, the first two by Leslie Brooke, the third by Marcia Brown, and the last by Hans Fischer. Such colorful picture books on the kindergarten browsing table make children long to be able to read them for themselves. They can be matched also in poetry in such selections as Rose Fyleman's *Fairies and Chimneys,* Clement Moore's *A Visit from St. Nicholas,* and Edward Lear's *The Jumblies.* A careful balance among fun, fact, and fancy is important in the development of a program which will stimulate a lifelong interest in reading. Particularly to be deplored is a steady diet of dull, moralistic, made-to-order stories intended to influence the behavior of children—"poor stories," says Paul Hazard, "full of a good bit of authoritative ethics to be applied externally without any internal consent." [12]

The transition from this story-book world to first-grade reading is a particularly precarious one so far as the love of reading is concerned, for it means a shift from being read to to the job of reading for oneself. Continued storytelling and reading aloud need to be kept up by both teacher and parent so that the child may retain his enthusiasm for what he may be able to read for himself once the skills of reading are mastered. The kinds of material and the challenging vocabulary and ideas of the picture books are often beyond the skill of the first-grade reader; yet he needs the stimulation of more literary materials while he is learning to read the simpler stories of everyday life which are controlled in vocabulary to meet the needs of the beginner.

On the other hand, he should have opportunity to read with pride to his parents and other children the new stories for beginners which are appearing annually for first-grade children. Books like Else Minarik's *Little Bear* and *Little Bear's Father Comes Home,* Syd Hoff's *Danny and the Dinosaur,* Elizabeth Guilfoile's *Nobody Listens to Andrew,* and Dr. Seuss's *Cat in the Hat* have all proved the tremendous interest they have for first-grade children. And what pride the beginners take in reading them to others!

First-grade rooms should display constantly both books which be-

[12] Paul Hazard, *Books, Children, and Men* (Boston, The Horn Book, 1944), p.4.

ginners can read for themselves and books which should continue to be read to them until they are capable of reading on a higher level.

Again, books of fun, fact, and fancy should play an equal part in the child's reading experience: *Tim and the Brave Sea Captain,* for example, for fun and adventure; *White Snow, Bright Snow* and *Little Toot* for both fact and everyday experience; and *Millions of Cats, Hansel and Gretel,* and *Snow White and the Seven Dwarfs* for fun and fantasy.

By the end of the first grade the range of reading ability within each class begins to show itself. Some children have made more than two years' progress in reading during their first year in school. Some have progressed only three months. These differences are due to a wide variety of causes such as ability to learn, the richness of experience provided by the home, or the attitudes and interests of the child himself. If, in every year of the pupils' school experience, all of them are stimulated to achieve up to the level of their potentialities, these differences should increase in even greater proportion from grade to grade. Bond and Tinker, for example, have published a table revealing a range from first to nearly fourth grade reading ability in the second grade, from first to sixth in the fourth grade, and from second to ninth in the sixth grade. [13]

Hence, it is necessary, if skill and interest are to be maintained, that books paralleling each level of reading represented by pupils in the classroom be provided to care for the needs and interests of all of them. If the circus is being studied in the first grade, books available should range from a large picture book of circus animals through the Haders' *Circus Baby* and Marjorie Flack's *Wait for William* to William Du Bois's *Great Geppy.* If the seasons are the subject of discussion in the second grade, the books will range from Lois Lenski's seasonal picture books, such as *I Like Spring,* through titles like Tresselt's *Autumn Harvest* or *Rain Drop Splash,* the Haders' *Big Snow* or Charlotte Zolotow's *The Storm Book* to the high level of Schneider's *Let's Find Out.* If, on the other hand, the third grade is at work on *Pets and How to Care for Them,* a range of books available may go from C. W. Anderson's *Billy and Blaze* or Clare New-

[13] Guy L. Bond and Miles A. Tinker, *Reading Difficulties: Their Diagnosis and Correction* (New York, Appleton-Century-Crofts, Inc., 1957), p. 37.

berry's *Mittens* through Illa Podendorf's *True Book of Pets* or Beverly Cleary's *Henry and Ribsy* up to A. P. Morgan's *Pet Book for Boys and Girls*.

Stories of humor and adventure top the list of favorites among children of all ages. [14] There is no area which better illustrates the development of interests in relation to the growth of children than their choices in books of humor. Appreciation of subtle humor comes late in most children's experience. That is why one must avoid using *Winnie the Pooh* or *Rabbit Hill* with children too young to recognize their subtleties. Humor is based on incongruity, and much experience with the normal relationships of things must precede recognition of the incongruous. Kindergarten children laugh hilariously at a teddy bear which has slid off a window seat and is found standing on his head. They know that he belongs on his feet. Obstreperous humor catches their attention immediately—Dr. Seuss's *Cat in the Hat*, for example, or *Curious George* or *Cecily G. and the Nine Monkeys*. They love Will and Nicolas's *Circus Ruckus* because a boy and his pet dog are literally catapulted into a circus act and land squarely on the back of the donkey to be unexpectedly a part of the performance. Children readily sense the humor in *The Happy Lion* who, when the zoo gate is left open, attempts to return in friendly fashion the calls of the people who have come to see him at the zoo. From these books they may be led to *Petunia*, the goose who expects to grow wise by carrying a book under her arm, or to *The Loudest Noise in the World*, which didn't make such a good birthday present after all. Again, in order to enjoy *If I Ran the Zoo*, a child must know what the animals of an ordinary zoo are like.

Middle-grade children rejoice in Atwater's *Mr. Popper's Penguins*, in Virginia Kahl's *Away Went Wolfgang!*, and in Natalie Carlson's *Alphonse, That Bearded One*, finally reaching such heights as *Mary Poppins*, *The Just-So Stories*, *Mr. Revere and I*, and *Tom Sawyer*. Any program to develop children's love of reading finds an invaluable ally in humor. Children's reading textbooks in the past have been almost devoid of it.

Studies of children's interests in reading reveal a special interest

[14] George W. Norvell, *What Boys and Girls Like to Read* (Morristown, N. J., Silver Burdett Co., 1958), pp. 182-185.

in animal stories during these early years. [15] Perhaps little children see a reflection of themselves in the troubles of Angus brought on by his curiosity and his difficulties with the cat, or in *Flip*, the pony who lacks confidence in himself. Gradually they work up into stories of more adventuresome animals like *Burlap*, who finds the circus bear, or *The Biggest Bear* by Lynd Ward.

Intermediate-grade boys, especially, crave adventure thrillers with animals as heroes. Many of these also serve to satisfy their desire for mystery stories. Stephen Meader's *Red Horse Hill*, O'Brien's *Silver Chief, Dog of the North*, and Machetanz's *Panuck, Eskimo Sled Dog* combine mystery, adventure, and an animal hero. Jim Kjelgaard's *Big Red* does the same for the more mature readers. Dr. Carlsen suggests that in these stories boys find a kind of "assurance of human greatness" in the heroic deeds of courageous animals. [16] A taste for this kind of reading gives teachers a chance to lead gifted pupils to more mature and better rounded stories such as Marguerite Henry's *Misty of Chincoteague, King of the Winds,* and *Brighty of the Grand Canyon,* which, like Eric Knight's *Lassie Come Home,* combine action with characterization, and a richness of setting and of language with a good story. Randolph Caldecott's picture book of Cowper's *John Gilpin's Ride,* displayed on the chalk tray along with these horse stories, could not fail to attract readers looking for "thin" books. For less mature pupils, Kipling's *Jungle Book* and *Just-So Stories* go especially well after the teacher has read aloud enticing samples.

The nature of the children's interest in adventure changes through the years. At one time it is the Wild West; at another, it is war. At still another, it is adventure in space. Ruthven Todd's *Space Cat* and Ellen MacGregor's *Miss Pickerell Goes to Mars* intrigue the younger intermediate-grade readers while Robert Heinlein, writing for more mature readers in *Rocket Ship Galileo* and *Have a Space Suit—Will Travel,* does with space stories what Tunis does with sports—relates them to some social problem. In between, one of the most popular of all is Eleanor Cameron's *The Wonderful Flight to the Mushroom*

---

[15] *Ibid.,* pp. 182-185.
[16] George Robert Carlsen, "Behind Reading Interests," *The English Journal* 43 (January, 1954), 7-12.

Planet. Fortunately in this area of mystery and adventure girls often read the same books as boys.

Children in these years, one psychologist pointed out, never walk when they can run and never run when they can leap. Enthusiasm and excitement are high, and the reader's need for action has to be met in books. Series like *The Landmark Books* give better readers action aplenty with valuable historical settings. *Daniel Boone* by John Mason Brown and *Paul Revere and the Minute Men* by Dorothy Canfield Fisher are titles boys particularly like. Clyde Bulla's *Riding the Pony Express,* Howard Pease's the *Jinx Ship,* and Stevenson's *Treasure Island* are universal favorites. Armstrong Sperry's *Call It Courage* has a boy hero and a literary flavor which challenges the best readers.

Girls in Grades Four to Six seek many stories of everyday experiences of children like themselves. Boys accept such books only if they are related to sports or some other absorbing interest or if they are told in an altogether humorous fashion. They never tire, for example, of *Homer Price, Henry and his Paper Route, Henry Read, Inc.,* and *Tom Sawyer,* all well-told stories giving them the humor they enjoy.

Girls, on the other hand, add to the daily doings of Carolyn Heywood's *Betsy* books of earlier years such stories as Eleanor Estes's *The Moffats* or *The Hundred Dresses,* Elizabeth Enright's *The Saturdays,* Carol Brink's *Family Grandstand,* and Doris Gates's *Blue Willow.* It is easy to lead from these to regional stories like Virginia Sorensen's *Plain Girl* or to stories with historical settings like *Caddie Woodlawn* for the older girls or the popular *Little House* books by Laura Ingalls Wilder, which reveal the warmth of family life among the pioneers moving westward. During these years when pupils are broadening their horizons in time and space, such books may also lead both boys and girls to similar stories of children of other lands like Spyri's *Heidi,* Meindert De Jong's *Wheel on the School,* Singh and Lownsberry's *Gift of the Forest,* Francis Kalnay's *Chucaroo, Wild Pony of the Pampas,* or Natalie Carlson's *The Family under the Bridge.* Less mature readers may take similar interest in David Fletcher's *Confetti for Cortorelli* or MacKellar's *Wee Joseph.*

Jersild and Tasch, studying children's interests and what they mean for education, found pupils in the intermediate grades especially concerned with problems of human relations. [17] In books like those mentioned above, young readers share vicariously the experiences of many families while they broaden their growing concepts of life in various parts of the world. Such stories have improved tremendously in very recent years and have a much better chance of engaging children's interest than they had some time ago when, as Robert Lawson [18] said:

We had a flood of Little Pedro and his donkey in Mexico, Little Koo Koo the Eskimo and his pet narwhal, Little Kong of Hongkong and his pet duck, and so forth, until every children's book list read like morning roll call at Ellis Island.

Comparison of some of the dull stereotyped stories of other lands, in which the characters are merely pegs on which to hang information, with a rich, vibrating story like *The Good Master,* in which the characters are as alive and unpredictable as their readers, will help children to develop standards of selection among books of this kind.

Teachers in Grades Four to Six face a tremendous challenge in the number of children's classics suitable for these years. Mr. Norvell, in his study of the reading interests of children in the schools of New York State, found *Aesop's Fables* especially enjoyed in Grades Three through Five, after which they dropped off notably in interest. [19] Myths, legends, hero stories, and folk tales were more popular in Grades Five through Seven. Joseph Jacobs's *English Fairy Tales* were read by girls in the early middle grades, followed later by all the *French Fairy Tales,* Asbjornsen and Moe's *East o' the Sun and West o' the Moon, The Household Tales* from the Brothers Grimm, *Andersen's Fairy Tales,* and Lang's color series, notably *The Blue Fairy Book.* Mrs. Juanita Geboe describes a fascinating unit on folklore for gifted pupils in an elementary class in Albuquerque, supplemented by records, films, and tape-recordings. [20] Mrs. Mary G. Dodson also carried on a unique seminar in literature for gifted readers

[17] Arthur T. Jersild and Ruth J. Tasch, *Children's Interests and What They Suggest for Education* (New York, Bureau of Publications, Teachers College, Columbia University, 1949), pp. 54-59.

[18] Robert Lawson, "Make Me a Child Again," *The Horn Book Magazine,* 16 (December, 1940), 450.

[19] Norvell, *op. cit.,* p. 146.

[20] Juanita Geboe, "Folklore for Superior Readers in the Third Grade," *Elementary English* 37 (February, 1960), 93-97.

in two special sessions a week in the upper grades in Long Beach, California. [21]

Boys are more partial to Howard Pyle's *Some Merry Adventures of Robin Hood* and Lanier's *Boy's King Arthur*. Padriac Colum's *Children's Homer* and *The Golden Fleece* or *Heroes Who Lived before Achilles* tell the story of the *Iliad* and the *Odyssey* and the old Greek heroes in a form which middle-grade readers can understand. Sally Benson's *Stories of the Gods and Heroes*, Dorothy Hosford's *Thunder of the Gods* and Padriac Colum's *Children of Odin* present the Greek and Norse myths.

These are the years also of the *Arabian Nights*, of *Uncle Remus*, of *The Jungle Books* and *Just-So Stories*, of *Pinocchio*, of *Robinson Crusoe*, of *Peter Pan*, of *Wind in the Willows*, of *Mary Poppins*, and of *Charlotte's Web*. Old Testament hero stories should also be part of every child's heritage. As told by Walter Russell Bowie, they are especially well adapted to children of this age.

Here is an embarrassment of riches. Most of these books challenge good readers in Grades Five and Six. Trying to force every child through such a program would be to destroy his interest in reading for life. As May Hill Arbuthnot [22] and her colleagues have said:

All we ask is that children be exposed to these choice books with the privilege of rejecting those they do not enjoy. Heaven forbid that any child should come to detest a good story—because it was forced upon him. It will, however, be a rare child, indeed, who, through the years, does not develop some favorites among these fine books, provided he meets them at approximately the right time for him.

The teacher who reads aloud well can stimulate interest through the use of single incidents from the longer books. Groups of children may act out their favorite scenes. Boys will be more than glad, for instance, to enact Robin Hood's toppling Little John into the water. Simple retellings of most of these stories are available for weak readers. Films and slides may be had for some of them and hand puppets may be made for others.

Since the interest in folklore and hero stories persists through the

[21] Mary G. Dodson, *Claremont College Reading Conference*, 1957 (Claremont College, Claremont, Calif.), pp. 129-141.

[22] May Hill Arbuthnot and others, *Children's Books Too Good to Miss* (Cleveland, The Press of Western Reserve University, 1959), p. 8.

seventh grade, many schools prefer to use the more mature epics and heroic tales like the *Iliad* and the *Odyssey* with individual readers in the first year of the junior high school. Recordings, tapes, films, and other helps may be used here, also, to great advantage. Gifted children, especially in the seventh grade, enjoy dramatizing a meeting of the gods of Olympus, for example, each offering to a favorite mortal a wedding gift appropriate to his own character.

Another approach to world-renowned stories was made by a seventh-grade class in Detroit. Representatives of the group interviewed consuls of various countries to ask them what books are favorites of the children in their homelands. One child said to the Italian consul who reported the popularity of *Pinocchio* in Italy, "Oh, do you have *Pinocchio* in your country, too?" The class was off on a literary tour to see what stories had been contributed to "the universal republic of childhood" by different nations of the world. They could then discuss what made these stories worthy of such universal esteem.

Some stories, often left to senior high school, are useful for certain gifted readers in the seventh and eighth grades if presented in editions appropriate for younger readers: the Judge Parry edition of *Don Quixote of the Mancha,* Riggs's *Story of Beowulf,* and Mary Godolphin's *Pilgrim's Progress* with illustrations by Robert Lawson.

Poetry also should find a large place in Grades Four to Six, where it is often forgotten in the press of other reading. When fourth-grade pupils turn to poetry, they often go back to favorites of the primary grades, which they now take pride in reading for themselves. Sharing poems in small groups is especially effective because, while three or four girls may revel in Rose Fyleman and others in Robert Louis Stevenson, most boys will look for animal poems in John Brewton's *Under the Tent of the Sky,* for humorous selections in William Cole's *Humorous Poems for Children* or his simpler *I Went to the Animal Fair.* Attractive collections are more useful for individual reading than large anthologies, though teachers find such volumes as May Hill Arbuthnot's *Time for Poetry* or Helen Ferris's *Favorite Poems Old and New* invaluable sources of poems on many themes. Patriotic and humorous poems, together with simple narratives, delight most children in these years. Much reading aloud by the teacher as he helps his pupils to see and to hear what the poet is presenting is necessary if appropriate responses to poetry are to become habitual.

Choral speaking is also popular in these grades, especially if the poems used with the class as a whole are suitable for both boys and girls.

During the intermediate grades, interest in television is at its height. Evidence has been accumulating that children spend fewer hours before the screen than they did before its novelty wore off. At least half the children seem to be reading more than they did a few years ago. Many teachers find television an asset in stimulating such reading. Hundreds of copies of *Peter Pan* were needed to supply the children's demand after Mary Martin's performance of it on the screen. At Christmas, *Amahl and the Night Visitors*, *The Nutcracker*, and *Alice-in-Wonderland* jumped in circulation because of television showings. Teachers can specifically prepare children for such programs by urging them to read the story in advance.

Recently, the *Saturday Review* carried a cartoon of an eight-year-old boy with his nose against a television screen. To raise himself to the proper level, he sat astride a pile of eight encyclopedias! Showing him the relationship between those encyclopedias or other books of information and what is available on television is an important aspect of guiding reading. Educational television is helping immensely. In the fall, a program on the leaves and seed pods of autumn depleted the library shelves of books on the subject. Science programs on space and on elementary problems in energy have been especially valuable. Celebrations of Hawaiian statehood and President Eisenhower's trips to the Orient and South America have led to a run on geographical material.

Boys who read little will get their start in reading through informative materials related to their personal interests. Schneider's *More Power to You*, Hogben's *The Wonderful World of Mathematics*, Bertha Parker's *Golden Book of Science*, Zim's *Dinosaurs*, and Walt Disney's *Vanishing Prairie* are special favorites. Dr. Shores's study of children's reading in relation to the questions they ask shows a special interest among boys in such subjects as astronomy, geology, science, rockets, and the like, but little knowledge on their part of the many sources of information available to them in books. [23] This

[23] James Harlan Shores, "Reading Interests and Informational Needs of Children in Grades IV to VIII," *Elementary English* 31 (December, 1954), 493-500.

is an important aspect of reading guidance at both the elementary and junior high school levels.

The move from the elementary school to junior high is, perhaps, the most significant in the child's school life. It is a big step toward growing up, accompanied often by significant plans for the future, in the direction of which the young adolescent himself will play a large part. It is a time of anxious self-examination because the desire to "do big things" is strong—self-examination for physical prowess, for courage to meet obstacles, for acceptance by other young people, for the discovery of what one can do best. For girls, at least, there are the beginnings of interest in romance.

These and other elements in the development of young adolescents condition to a large degree the reading interests of the junior high school years. [24] Research indicates clearly that no problem of reading guidance is more important than relating books to the normal interests of growing up. [25]

Finding the right book for the right pupil is particularly important in the junior high school because the range of reading ability within each class widens rapidly. In the eighth grade in New York City, the spread in 1951 was from the top 7 per cent reading at the twelfth grade level to the lowest eight per cent below the norm for the fifth grade. [26] Another complicating factor is that often the younger, less mature pupils are at the top intellectually and many of the older pupils are at the bottom. Hence, the teacher who would guide reading during these years must find simple reading materials suitable in interest for older pupils and more difficult material suited to the social and intellectual maturity of the able young readers. The first of these needs has been recognized for some time and has been met, in some measure, by lists like George Spache's *Good Books for Poor*

[24] John J. De Boer, "What Does Research Reveal about Reading and the High School Student?" *English Journal* 47 (May, 1958), 271-279.

Arno Jewett and others, *Improving Reading in the Junior High School*, Bulletin 1957, No. 10, U. S. Department of Health, Education, and Welfare, Office of Education (Washington D. C., Government Printing Office).

[25] George Robert Carlsen, "Literature and the Gifted Child: Fact and Fantasy," *The Iowa English Yearbook*, Fall, 1959 (Iowa City, Iowa, Iowa State Council of Teachers of English), pp. 14-17; 32.

[26] May Lazar, ed., *The Retarded Reader in the Junior High School* (New York, Board of Education, City of New York, Bureau of Educational Research, 1952).

Readers and Ruth Strang's *Gateways to Readable Books*.[27] The problem of the immature pupil of high intelligence has not been so clearly recognized. Some reading programs for talented twelve-year-olds are pushing them into books which they can read with their eyes but which they cannot encompass in their understanding.[28] One such course gives, among other choices, *Moby Dick, Pride and Prejudice, Green Mansions, Frankenstein, Les Miserables,* and *The Moonstone,* before the pupils are ready for them either emotionally or intellectually. Results are unfortunate for several reasons. Some of the pupils develop a lifelong distaste for reading. All of them miss good books about characters of their own age because they are striving to read beyond their years, and they are deprived of the insights such books can open up to them on problems they face at the moment. Furthermore, they think they have "read" these mature books and will resent the suggestion that they read them again in later years.

For example, a gifted twelve-year-old girl, advanced to the ninth grade in a Middle-Western city, was asked to "report" on Edna Ferber's *So Big.* "Were you satisfied with the ending?" the teacher asked. "Oh, yes, it turned out all right for the boy," she replied. "What about the mother?" said the teacher. "The mother?" asked the child, obviously mystified by the question. "Oh, she was all right in the end, too."

Although many of the interests of Grades Four through Six persist into the junior high school, they appear with new emphases characteristic of early adolescence. Love of adventure is still strong in junior high school boys and girls, but, as they explore their world for challenges they, themselves, hope to meet, the adventure tends to be real or if it is imagined, relates to fields of interest in the adolescent's world. White's *Up Periscope!* and Norton's *Beast Master,* the one real and the other science fiction, are typical of books which are never on the shelves. The Carriers' *Dive!* gives boys the facts they want. Superior readers in the ninth grade will undertake Cousteau's *The Silent World* or, possibly, *Adventuring with Beebe.* Related to

[27] George Spache, *Good Books for Poor Readers* (Champaign, Ill., Garrard Press, 1958).

Ruth M. Strang, *Gateways to Readable Books* (New York, H. W. Wilson Co., 1958).

[28] Carlsen, *op. cit.,* p. 15.

these are the books for better readers revealing man against nature like Herzog's *Annapurna* and Heyerdahl's *Kon-Tiki* or *Aku-Aku*, the story of a scientific adventure to find the origin of giant statues on Easter Island. Ullman's *Banner in the Sky* serves the same purpose for average readers.

Animal adventure is still important in boys' choices. Kjelgaard's *Big Red* remains at the top of the list, and Will James's *Smoky* and similar titles are favorites of those who have not read them earlier. There are many leads a teacher may follow from such books. For example, Lawson's *Mr. Revere and I* finds its horse and rider in Revolutionary days. Leighton's *Comanche of the Seventh* displays his heroism in *Custer's Last Charge*. On the other hand, Jesse Stuart's *Hie to the Hunters!* satisfies a similar interest in the setting of the Southern Highlands, and Haig-Brown's *Starbuck Valley Winter* involves trapping for fur in British Columbia.

Younger adolescents seek adventures in which boys and girls their own age do surpassing things. If the teacher does not satisfy this craving with better books, they will find the cheap juvenile series for themselves. Tom Swift, the inventor, has now gone through twelve volumes of a second generation—*Tom Swift Junior Adventures* by Victor Appleton II—after having appeared in some fifty-four volumes of an earlier series. The junior inventor now specializes in diving seacopters, caves of nuclear fire, outposts in space, and atomic earth blasters. The Hardy Boys, now entering their fortieth volume, have a father who is so universally recognized as a famous detective that he has to call upon his gifted sons to pursue the criminals for him. They still succeed in bringing the villains to justice after adults have given up the chase. *Nancy Drew: The Mystery Girl*, a feminine counterpart of *The Hardy Boys*, is now in her thirty-sixth volume. Judy Bolton furnishes girls some thirty mystery stories like *The Phantom Friend* and the *Haunted Fountain*, and the *Dana Girls* reached Volume Twenty some time ago in such adventures as *The Winking Ruby Mystery*. No wonder boys and girls read these stories by the score as they, like Charles J. Finger, "look out upon a world getting along very well without them."

Teachers who would guide the reading of younger adolescents should know these books and understand the nature of their appeal. They should help boys and girls discover that, incident for incident, the plots are stereotyped and the characters untouched by human experience. They are easy to read. The young adventurers are described by three adjectives in Chapter 1, and the same three characterize them at the end of every volume. There is no growth, no reality of scene or of experience.

In a college class recently, prospective teachers who were asked to write *The Autobiography of My Life of Reading during Junior and Senior High School Years* spoke particularly of the difficulty of knowing what to read next when they had finished the last book in a series. [29] This is the strategic moment for the teacher—to be there and to help the pupil make this transition. Stephen Meader's *Who Rides in the Dark?* and Howard Pease's *Secret Cargo* are good starters on the road up to Stevenson's *Kidnapped*, Masefield's *Jim Davis*, Pyle's *Men of Iron*, Conan-Doyle's *Adventures of Sherlock Holmes*, and Dumas's *Three Musketeers*.

In contrast to these, there are several excellent stories of boys who grow up with animal pets that help them attain maturity. James Street's *Good-bye, My Lady* and Fred Gipson's *Old Yeller* attract average readers; O'Hara's *Green Grass of Wyoming* pursues the same theme for superior readers in the ninth grade. Atwater's *Swiftwater*, combining, as it does, the story of outdoor life and animals with a growing understanding between father and son, is read by both average and better readers. All these stories have a richness of setting which adds to their value for young readers.

Girls in the eighth and ninth grades seek romantic stories of boy and girl relationships. Prime favorites for the older girls, and fortunately among the best, are Maurine Daly's *Seventeenth Summer* and *The Diary of Anne Frank*. Mary Stolz is also much read by ninth- and tenth-grade pupils. For the younger girls, Cavanna's *Going on Sixteen* is popular. It contrasts notably with Nancy Drew, who also lost her mother as a young girl. The dog in *Going on Sixteen* and the problems of country children going to school in town add reality and interest to the story. Cavanna's recent *Scarlet Sail* bids fair to become her most popular story. Dunlop's *Caroline House* is another favorite.

It is important that the teacher guide pupils in evaluating these

---

[29] George Robert Carlsen, "The Magic of Bringing Young Adults to Books," *Wilson Library Bulletin*, 33 (October, 1958), 134-137f.

books. In doing so, he will find extremely useful recent treatments of the subject by Margaret Alexander Edwards, Richard Alm, and Dwight Burton. [30]

In this area of interest the alert teacher can also lead in many directions out from the love theme. For example, older girls are finding Speare's *Witch of Blackbird Pond* a fascinating love story, a top-notch mystery, and an illuminating historical novel set in Puritan days. With unusual richness of setting, with characters that mature in the changing circumstances of their lives, and with a plot growing naturally out of time, place, and character, this recent winner of the Newbery Award is one of the best transition books to adult literature which good readers in the junior high school can find.

Again, one of the major concerns of younger adolescents is what they may do with their lives. At one stage, vocational fiction helps to make vivid for them what people in various vocations do. Mary Stolz's *Organdy Cupcakes* reveals the nurse in the course of her training and Adele De Leeuw's *With a High Heart* introduces a young girl to library work. Part of the appeal of these stories lies in their romantic presentation of young people who, with the highest social motives and with engaging personalities, "make good" on their own as they step out into the world of work. Boys find the same interests chiefly in the more strenuous masculine pursuits like those described in Kjelgaard's *Forest Patrol* and Rush's *Rocky Mountain Ranger*. These are paralleled in such biographies as Alden Hatch's *General Ike*, William Bridgeman's *Lonely Sky*, or Stoutenburg's and Baker's *Snowshoe Thompson*, who carried the mail on skis through the high Sierras.

But the usual question adolescents ask is: "What am I going to be?" They are concerned about themselves, what they look like, how their personalities react upon others, and what service they may render to the world. This interest, under careful guidance, may lead to the reading of biography. Biography for younger adolescents often emphasizes action and adventure. It also makes a great deal of the

[30] Margaret Alexander Edwards, "Let the Lower Lights Be Burning," *English Journal*, 46 (November, 1957), 461-469f.

Richard S. Alm, "The Glitter and the Gold," *English Journal*, 44 (September, 1955), 315-322f.

Dwight L. Burton, *Literature Study in the High Schools* (New York, Holt, Rinehart, and Winston, Inc., 1959).

childhood and youth of famous men and women, revealing what they were like when they were the age of the reader. For the would-be scientists there are Francis Benz's *Pasteur, Knight of the Laboratory,* Sterling North's *Young Thomas Edison,* and Shirley Graham's *Dr. George Washington Carver.* Better readers may try Laura Wood's *Raymond Ditmars* or Clara Ingram Judson's *Soldier Doctor, the Story of William Gorgas.* Biographies of musicians range from the Wheeler and Deucher simple stories of *Joseph Haydn, the Merry Little Peasant* or *Edward MacDowell and His Cabin in the Pines* up to Elliott Arnold's *Finlandia, the Story of Sibelius.* Older girls and boys interested in the theatre will enjoy Jean Latham's *On Stage, Mr. Jefferson,* and the aspiring artist among the less mature pupils, *Benjamin West and His Cat, Grimalkin.* Biographies of moral and social leaders range from Thomas Galt's *Peter Zenger, Fighter for Freedom* to Jeanette Eaton's *Gandhi, Fighter without a Sword.* For the girls, Helen Keller's autobiography is still a favorite along with Elizabeth Yates's *Prudence Crandall, Woman of Courage* and Rachel Baker's *First Woman Doctor.* Biographies of writers serve many purposes. Jean Gould's *That Dunbar Boy; the Story of America's Famous Negro Poet* and Cornelia Meigs's *The Invincible Louisa* are favorites. For the weaker readers, Catherine Peare's *Mark Twain, His Life* fills a need met for mature pupils by Jeanette Eaton's *America's Own Mark Twain.* Josephine Blackstock's *Songs for Sixpence; A Story about John Newbery* reveals the origin of the name of the Newbery Medal awarded for the best children's book of each year. Better readers among the girls can be led to Helen Waite's life of Elizabeth Barrett Browning, *How Do I Love Thee?* or to May Lamberton Becker's *Introducing Charles Dickens.* Miriam Mason's *Yours with Love, Kate* presents to less able readers the ever popular teacher-author, Kate Douglas Wiggin.

Sometimes it is simpler to use with less mature readers single chapters from compiled biographies like McNeer's and Ward's *Armed with Courage,* which presents such people as Florence Nightingale, Wilfred Grenfell, Mahatma Gandhi, or Albert Schweitzer. Eleanor Sickels's accounts of Mary Crockett and Narcissa Whitman in *In Calico and Crinoline* are especially suitable for girls. Some personal reminiscences of women open up new areas of the world to better adolescent readers in such books as Cynthia Bowles's *At Home in India,* Nayantara Sahgal's *Prison and Chocolate Cake,* and Elizabeth Vining's *Windows for the Crown Prince.* Ann Petry's *Harriet Tubman; Conductor on the Underground Railway* takes adolescents back in time to the days of the Civil War.

This last adventure opens up the whole area of Americana of special interest to junior high school boys and girls. Biographies of Daniel Boone range from the very simple one by Esther Averill through John Mason Brown's or James Dougherty's to Stewart Edward White's *Daniel Boone, Wilderness Scout.* Doris Garst's *Jim Bridger, Greatest of the Mountain Men* and her *Buffalo Bill* carry the story further West. Older pupils may pick it up again in Quentin Reynold's *Custer's Last Stand.* Fortunately, good biographies of Lincoln are available at all levels of reading from Genevieve Foster's *Abraham Lincoln* through Clara Ingram Judson's and Sterling North's up to James Daugherty's *A. Lincoln* and Carl Sandburg's *Abe Lincoln Grows Up.* Jeanette Eaton's *That Lively Man, Ben Franklin* and Clara Ingram Judson's *George Washington* and her *Thomas Jefferson* carry America's story back to the days of the Revolution. Howard Fast's *Haym Salomon* and Dorothy Canfield Fisher's *Paul Revere and the Minute Men* help to round out the picture. Carl Carmer has revealed the part played by teen-aged young people in our country's past in his recent *Cavalcade of Young Americans.*

Especially good fiction dealing with America's past is available for average and better readers in the junior high school. Rebecca Caudill's *Tree of Freedom* and Esther Forbes's *Johnny Tremain* are near classics in this area. Older girls revel in Irving Stone's *Immortal Wife,* set during the opening up of California by General Fremont, and in his *Love Is Eternal,* the account of the courtship of Mary Todd and Abraham Lincoln.

In addition to the areas of interest already discussed, many schools find it profitable to develop literary units in the junior high school around such themes as Myths, Hero Stories, Legends, Tall Tales, the Short Story, Plays, and Poetry. [31] Since much of the available

[31] Arno Jewett, *English Language Arts in American High Schools,* Bulletin, No. 13, U. S. Department of Health, Education, and Welfare, Office of Education (Washington D. C.: U. S. Government Printing Office, 1959). National Council of Teachers of English and the National Education As-

material in myths, hero stories, legends, and tall tales is difficult reading for many pupils in the fifth and sixth grades, it is increasingly common to deal with this type of literature in the seventh or eighth grades. Mr. Norvell, in his study of pupil interests, found many individual titles popular in the junior high school. [32] For developing a love of reading, use of individual stories with individual readers seems particularly important. Sharing within the class will then acquaint all of the pupils with all of the stories so often referred to in later literature.

New York State has produced an interesting resource unit for the junior high school called *Tall Tales and Tunes*. [33] It presents many legendary heroes such as Paul Bunyan, Old Stormalong, and Pecos Bill together with popular cowboy ballads from John Lomax and from Carl Carmer's *America Sings*. It includes poems about Johnny Appleseed, John Henry, and Daniel Boone, and eventuates in such literary legends as Irving's *Rip Van Winkle* and the *Legend of Sleepy Hollow*. An ascent from Paul Bunyan and other obstreperously humorous stories to Ichabod Crane is an illuminating one for able pupils.

The Benéts' *Book of Americans,* John Lomax's ballads, and Carl Carmer's collection of songs form a natural bridge from such a unit to the reading of ballads and the introduction of poetry. Mr. Norvell and others have found vigorous narrative and humorous and patriotic verse particularly adaptable to the junior high school years. Lomax's "Bill Peters" and "The Cowboy's Dream," Kipling's *Ballad of East and West,* Noyes's "The Highwayman," and Thayer's "Casey at the Bat" are typical of the poems best liked by this age group. Patriotic selections like "Paul Revere's Ride," "Captain, My Captain," and Guiterman's "Oregon Trail" are popular, and sea poems like "The Pirate Don Durke of Dowdee," the "Ballad of John Silver," and "The Nautical Extravagance" are all much enjoyed. Collections of story poems like Max Hohn's *Stories in Verse* and Elinor Parker's

sociation, Arno Jewett, Editor, *English for the Academically Talented Student in the Secondary School* (Washington D. C., The National Education Association and the Council, Champaign, Ill., 1960).

[32] George W. Norvell, *The Reading Interests of Young People* (Boston, D. C. Heath and Co., 1950).

[33] Bureau of Secondary Curriculum Development, New York State Education Department, *Tall Tales and Tunes* (Albany, N.Y., New York State Education Department, 1959).

100 Story Poems should be explored for poems suitable for the junior high school. *The Courtship of Miles Standish* may be read by gifted pupils, but many others will learn the story from simple prose accounts and a few significant passages read aloud from the poem. Nature and philosophical, or reflective, verse apparently has little appeal unless it involves animals as in Robert Frost's "The Runaway" or "Stopping by the Woods on a Snowy Evening." On the other hand, individual readers may have a special liking for such poems and should be directed to them. All pupils should browse through poetry collections for poems they may share with others who have the same preferences or with the class as a whole. Short stories and plays may often be introduced in the same way in the junior high school.

One of the chief values in the approach through literary types lies in the emphasis the teacher can put upon techniques of reading different kinds of literature. The skills involved in reading poetry and drama differ significantly from those used in other kinds of writing. Imaginative concepts, comparisons, and the use of symbolism present a peculiar problem in poetry. Plays, which necessitate the following of the plot, the development of character, and the creation of setting through dialogue, present a different reading problem. Such skills are carefully analyzed in New York City's recent bulletin on *Reading* for Grades Seven, Eight and Nine. [34]

The first prerequisite, then, for developing in children and younger adolescents a permanent habit of turning to good books for pleasure and satisfaction is to *understand the relationship of reading to the stages of growth* through which boys and girls normally pass at each level of their development. *Timing* so as to capture the inherent interests of young readers is all-important. In addition, the teacher needs to know each child as an individual—his personal interests as well as his reading preferences—so that he may lead him to books that foster both—books which, at the same time, may furnish leads to better and more challenging materials capable of contributing to his growth in maturity, in range of interests, and in literary appreciation.

Informal rather than lock-step procedures in the classroom are

[34] Board of Education, New York City, *Reading—Grades 7, 8, 9: A Teacher's Guide to Curriculum Planning* (Brooklyn, Board of Education of the City of New York, 1957-58, Publication Sales Office, Brooklyn, N. Y.).

necessary to such personal contact with individual pupils. Florence Cleary in her *Blueprints for Better Reading* lists many interest questionnaires available in print. [35] Other informal methods include asking boys and girls to write a paragraph on what they would most like to do with the afternoon if school closed unexpectedly or, the subject for older pupils might be "Sometimes I Worry About————" Such materials as autobiographies, including students' hopes for the future are helpful. One teacher found it valuable to have pupils keep a Reading Plan Book related to their current interests and future educational plans. All reading guidance is also contingent upon the teacher's knowledge of the pupil's ability to read.

Once the teacher knows the needs and interests of his students, he must *develop a broad knowledge of the entire field of children's books* and of the sources by which he may keep up with new ones coming constantly from the press. [36] Furnishing leads from topic to topic and from the child to the book demands firsthand knowledge of what each book contains. For example, single incidents may be the means of making contact with an individual reader, like the heroine's struggle to ride a bicycle in Adam's *Wonderful Year*, the incident of the adopted child in Heywood's *Here's a Penny*, or the efforts of John Haskell to pay his dead father's debts in Walter D. Edmonds's *Two Logs Crossing*.

In the third place, the teacher and librarian working together must *make books available and advertise them constantly*. Colorful editions should be on open shelves in classroom and library. A series of attractive posters advertising the wide variety of interests books can serve may then be used as a device for helping pupils check the breadth of their individual reading programs. In the elementary school, books are often displayed on chalk trays and window sills, on a browsing table in the library corner, or on a shelf of personal projects of individual pupils. They can be related in this way to all the activities of the school day. In junior high school, an English classroom should be recognizable by the number of attractive books always on exhibition. The Olympics, the launching of a satellite, the Kentucky Derby, a Rose Bowl game, or a television

[35] Florence D. Cleary, *Blueprints for Better Reading* (New York, The H. W. Wilson Co., 1957), pp. 24-49.

[36] *Ibid.*, pp. 55-58.

performance all suggest posters with clippings and four or five good books displayed beneath them. The pupils themselves at the junior high school level can work in teams to prepare such exhibits.

If units such as the one on *Great Hero Stories* or *Tall Tales and Legends* are in progress, displays on each subject presenting books of varying difficulty would also be indispensable along with colorful maps of legendary figures.

Attention to the improvement of skill in reading accompanies such a program of reading guidance. Grouping of pupils is necessary at all levels of instruction. If young readers are to grow in ability to read *literature,* considerable emphasis should be upon skills related to foreshadowing and following the plot, to recognition and growth of characters, and to interpreting imagery, visualizing persons and scenes, following inverted word order and rhythm in poetry, and recognizing the emotional connotation of words. All of these problems exist in varying degree from Wanda Gag's *Millions of Cats* through Poe's *The Gold Bug* to a play by Shakespeare.

A program of reading guidance takes time. Certainly, as much time should be allotted to it as is given to reading *together* in the classroom. There should be time for personal selection and some silent reading in the classroom or library. There should be ample provision for sharing day by day and week by week. First, the teacher and librarian should share with the pupils what is available on subjects of interest to them, often reading aloud tempting bits or whole books in the elementary school and sometimes using tapes, slides, and films in the junior high school. It is important that what is read aloud should have literary merit superior to that of books the pupils can read to themselves.

Librarians frequently refer to books which "are never on the shelves" and books which "need pushing." By *pushing* they mean taking the book into the classroom on a truck and telling children what it is about. Then the question, "Who would like to borrow it?" brings a show of three or four or a dozen hands. Librarians complain that junior high school pupils often come into the library asking, "Do you have a biography? I have to read one." They don't know what a biography is nor what it may have to offer them. Time spent preparing the pupils to choose books wisely pays ample dividends.

Plenty of time should also be given for the pupils to share their reading with each other—sometimes individually, sometimes in groups with the same interest. Experience suggests that "book reports" are best when no two are alike and when all are short. Sometimes, pupils "tell about a book;" sometimes, they act out or read a portion of it; sometimes, they use posters, a flannel board, puppets, or a peep show. Often the students share information acquired from the book, as two boys did who demonstrated how sound travels by telephone. Frequently they compare one book with another on the same subject. Always, they give their frank reaction to it.

Finally, the teacher is concerned constantly with *growth*. [37] As Dr. John De Boer has said, "Happily, interests can be kindled, sustained, enriched, redirected, and heightened through skillful guidance." [38] Are the pupils broadening the areas in which they find pleasure in reading? Are they moving from shallowness to depth in their choice of books dealing with the experiences of young people? Are they able to read increasingly mature and difficult material? Are they beginning to detect literary values on which they may build as time goes on? Much of the discussion of these aspects of growth comes after reports are given in class with pupils contributing examples from different books to illustrate the same point. The teacher then has a chance to guide thinking, to draw pupils out concerning elements of strength and weakness in books. *After such discussion,* pupils may be in the best position to *write* their evaluation of the book they have presented.

Literary appreciation has been defined as *personal acceptance of worth*. This genuine relationship between a child and what he reads is the aim of all guidance in reading. No matter how slowly it develops, it is worth waiting for. As George Woodberry has pointed out: "Growth in appreciation is neither rapid nor final; it moves with no swifter step than life itself, and it opens, like life, always on larger horizons." [39]

[37] Bertha Handlan, "How *Free* Should Reading Be?" in C. W. Hunicutt and William J. Iverson, *Research in the Three R's* (New York, Harper & Brothers, 1958), pp. 162-167.

[38] *Op. cit.,* p. 277.

[39] George E. Woodberry, *The Appreciation of Literature* (New York, Harcourt Brace and Co., 1921), p. 5.

13

PAUL FARMER

On Reading Literature

But words, if words are wise, go on and on
To make a longer note of unison
With man and man than living persons make
With one another for whatever sake. *

WITTER BYNNER, "Correspondent"

For SOME TIME now I have been increasingly aware that the teaching of literature is basically the teaching of reading. In planning assignments, directing class discussions, selecting points of emphases, and choosing items for testing, I am conscious as never before of the various ways that reading skills are involved in both the study and teaching of literature. Of course, I had known long before I had ever taught that literature was communicated most commonly through written words and symbols and that the process of getting meaning from them was called *reading*. I had known, too, that reading aloud with "expression" or silently with imagined "expression" could add liveliness and enjoyment to literature. But understanding fully the meaning in the flow of those words—the connotation as well as the denotation, the implied, the inferred, the mood, tone, style, metaphor—all this, I am ashamed to say was missing from my learning.

Worse still was my unawareness of the significance of this meaning —significance of design and structure, of the relation of the parts to the whole, of unity in diversity, and of individuality in universality. As I now look back to those early years of teaching, I trust that perhaps there were times when, by sheer accident, my students got glimpses of the deeper meaning and significance of the literature we had read. As far as I can recall, I made no conscious effort to point up these extended relationships between reading and literature.

Obviously, in this failure to consider the greater significance of

PAUL FARMER Director of Studies, The Lovett School, Atlanta, Georgia. Formerly Co-ordinator of Language Arts, Atlanta Public Schools. President of NCTE, 1950-1951. Honorary Life Member, NCTE. Past President, Georgia Council of Teachers of English. Managing Editor, *Georgia English Counselor*. Coauthor of *The Teaching of English in Georgia*. Coauthor of texts in literature and contributor to journals.

* From "Correspondent," by Witter Bynner in *Guest Book* (New York, Alfred A. Knopf, Inc., 1937), with permission from the author and publisher.

the literature, I had no idea of the relationship between evaluating what we had read and the development of literary taste and appreciation. And providing opportunities for assimilating what we had read—for relating it to personal experience, beliefs, and attitudes—was undreamed of. In short, my earlier concept of reading literature was that of getting meaning from words and whatever pleasure that meaning could give.

During those earlier years of teaching literature, we spent much time in learning facts about writers and their writing as well as historical facts about the times and places in which the writers lived. The textbooks gave almost as much space to the presentation of these facts as to the literature itself. So I taught many facts about literature and saw that my students were well drilled in the factual matter contained in the literary selections.

Now, whatever sin this kind of teaching may have been, it was surely one of omission, not commission. Facts about writers and their times are often important in understanding what the writers say. And the reader must know such things as the conflict underlying the plot and the steps in developing the plot. He must identify the protagonist and the antagonist. A concept of reading limited to matters such as these, however, leaves to chance the greater values of reading literature—the deeper understanding and more lasting satisfactions from responding to it.

And, of course, this extended and broader concept of reading does not imply that the primary step of getting meaning from words is less important than it has always been. Not infrequently college students need review if not elementary training in the structural and phonetic analysis of words, in getting meaning from context, and in using the dictionary. Certainly, not all elementary and high school English teachers are to be condemned for this phenomenon. Many college students manage these basic skills extremely well. Many are having new and more mature demands upon their reading. Think of those who are meeting for the first time the multitude of proper names in a course in world literature, beginning with the Greeks and working through some of the nineteenth century continental novels—perhaps *The Brothers Karamazov*. Facing such a group recently in a technological institute, I decided to spend two class periods in analyzing and practicing the pronunciation of Greek proper names. With considerable surprise, I failed to find in the four textbooks which we were using (three of which had glossaries) or in library sources any generalizations about these pronunciations that were of practical use to the student in deriving pronunciations. Nor could my colleagues refer to such information.

The students and I then correlated as best we could the pronunciation keys in the four textbooks and in the dictionary. Next, we looked for patterns in pronunciation. Finally, but cautiously, we formed generalizations from these patterns. The time was well spent. Relieved from the frequent, annoying interruptions of having to turn to the glossary and from personal embarrassment, we were able to proceed with class discussion much more freely. In noting contrasts with the vowel sounds of English syllabication as well as similarities, students reinforced their understanding of phonetic principles in English pronunciation and its consequent value in getting meaning from unfamiliar words.

But the point of this essay is to extend the concept of the relationship between reading and literature and to justify as best I can that extension. I apologize for taking so long in getting to the point and, particularly, for describing at length a personal experience which I am sure is not unlike many of your own whether you teach in college or elementary school.

No matter how glibly a student pronounces words in reading, he cannot understand their meaning unless he relates them in both their immediate and total context. Three passages from Shakespeare will illustrate what I mean. Have you ever noticed the difficulty that many students have in understanding these sentences from *Julius Caesar?*

> And therefore think him as a serpent's egg
> Which, hatched, would, as his kind, grow mischievous,
> And kill him in his shell.

The key that unlocks meaning here is the verb co-ordinated with *And kill*. Shakespeare provided a clue. He gave the parallel verb a parallel object: . . . *think him* . . . *and kill him.*

The second sentence is better known but, from observing students wrestling with its meaning, equally difficult.

> Here, under leave of Brutus and the rest—
> For Brutus is an honorable man;
> So are they all, all honorable men—
> Come I to speak in Caesar's funeral.

Obviously, the reader's difficulty here lies in the parenthetical nature of the second and third lines. The reader, once aware of the significance of the dashes, sees that lines one and four must be related and read as the essential element in getting meaning from what is said. To have meaning, each of these passages must be examined in the immediate context of its respective sentence.

Here is a sentence, however, that must be interpreted consistently with the total context of the play, particularly in keeping with the character of the confused but well-intentioned Brutus. If it is not, it becomes ludicrously ironical. It is so dependent upon the total context for its meaning that it can hardly be quoted alone without losing its meaning.

> And, gentle friends,
> Let's kill him boldly, but not wrathfully;
> Let's carve him as a dish fit for the gods,
> Not hew him as a carcass fit for hounds.

Gentle friends! Ah, poor Brutus, you might have been "the noblest Roman of them all," but you were far from the cleverest.

Pronoun reference, parallel structure, parenthetical words and expressions, sentence inversion are among the structural devices with which the reader of literature must come to terms if he is to succeed.

Now add a dash of metaphor to this complex of reading and watch the reader squirm. Let us go to prose for an example both masterful and familiar. "If ever a mortal painted an idea, that mortal was Roderick Usher."

A small picture presented the interior of an immensely long and rectangular vault or tunnel, with low walls, smooth, white, and without interruption or device. Certain accessory points of the design served well to convey the idea that this excavation lay at an exceeding depth below the surface of the earth. No outlet was observed in any portion of its vast extent, and no torch or other artificial source of light was discernible; yet a flood of intense rays bathed the whole in ghastly and inappropriate splendor.

This "painted idea" not only deepens the feeling of horror and fore-boding, but foreshadows the entombment of Madeline.

Immediately following this preview, Poe tells the reader by the allegorical poem, "Haunted Palace," what is to happen to Roderick Usher. Metaphor abounds. Man's body is the "fair and stately palace." The ruler of this domain is *Thought*; the hair, "Banners yellow, glori-ous, golden"; the eyes, "luminous windows"; and the mouth, "the fair palace door" which glows "with pearl and ruby."

The last two stanzas reveal what happens to the monarch.

> But evil things, in robes of sorrow
> Assailed the monarch's high estate . . .

Through the red-litten windows travellers see vast forms move fan-tastically, and a hideous throng rush out through the pale door.

Poe must have suspected the reader's difficulty with these meta-phors "because," he has the narrator say, "in the under and mystic current of its meaning, I fancied that I perceived, and for the first time, a full consciousness, on the part of Usher, of the tottering of his lofty reason upon her throne."

A painted idea—"the under and mystic current of its meaning"—metaphor, allegory, symbol, image—all converging in the creation of mood, tone, character, and action. One can hardly expect to find an example more perfect.

But have you realized what has happened since we have added a figure of speech to this complex of reading? The poor reader! Not one, but many new demands have pounced upon him if he is to read with a modicum of understanding; and, like Macbeth's show of eight kings, he might well cry, "What, will the line stretch out to the crack of doom?"

Among the host of new demands, one deserves special attention if this extended relationship between reading and literature is to be realized. Printed words come alive and reading becomes a mean-ingful, vivid experience only to the extent that the reader forms sensory images and reacts to them. The extent to which the reader "sees," "hears," "smells," and "feels" measures the extent of his understanding the events or scenes or situations in his reading. Only through sensory images can he identify himself with the time, the place, the person, and the situation. Good writers know this to be true and strive to stimulate as much as possible sensory impressions within the reader. Joseph Conrad described the process: . . . "by the power of the written word, to make you hear, to make you feel . . . before all to make you see." The result, he goes on to say, is to hold up a fragment of experience, "to show its vividness, its color, its form and, through its movement, its form, its color, reveal the substance of truth." By responding to the sensory appeal in the writing, mature readers have learned to meet writers like Conrad at least halfway.

To impress students with the tremendous importance of forming sensory images in reading, I like to take a passage from factual prose —preferably a passage with familiar words but with concepts new to the reader's experience. Here is such an example.

To see how the helicopter can do things that are not possible for the conventional fixed-wing plane, let us first examine how a conventional plane "works." It works by its shape—by the shape of its wing, which deflects air when the plane is in motion. That is possible because air has density and resistance. It reacts to force. The wing is curved and set at an angle to catch the air and push it down; the air, resisting, pushes against the under surface of the wing, giving it some of its lift. At the same time the curved upper surface of the wing exerts suction, tending to create a lack of air at the top of the wing. The air, again resisting, sucks back, and this gives the wing about twice as much lift as the air pressure below the wing. This is what takes place when the wing is pulled forward by propellers or pushed forward by jet blasts. Without the motion, the wing has no lift. [1]

I have never seen a student explain this paragraph who did not use his hands and arms to show the curve of the wing and the directions of the air currents above and below it. Frequently, he will ask spontaneously to go to the blackboard and draw quick sketches so that other students can *see* "how a conventional plane 'works.'"

Movement is the key word here. Look at the words employed to make the reader feel the motion—"deflects" . . . "motion" . . . "to catch" . . . "to push" . . . "resisting" . . . "pushes" . . . "lift" . . . "resisting" . . . "sucks" . . . "gives" . . . "pulled" . . . "pushes" . . . "motion" . . . "lift." Through responding to the sensory imagery of

[1] Frederick Graham, "The Helicopter," *New York Times Magazine,* August 17, 1952.

this paragraph, the reader comes to know "how a conventional plane 'works.'"

Now, what is it that literature does which factual prose does not do? I believe the basic difference lies in the purpose of the author. The writer of factual prose wants mainly to inform the reader. The writer of fiction, drama, poetry, and the other forms of imaginative literature wants, as Conrad said, "to make you hear, to make you feel . . . before all to make you *see*." In short, the goal of the factual writer is the end result of the reading—the knowledge—the information; the goal of the writer of literature is the emotional experience taking place during the reading—the cumulative emotional reactions and realizations. "Literature is not an abstract Science," wrote Sir Arthur Quiller-Couch, "to which definitions can be applied. It is an Art, rather, the success of which depends on personal persuasiveness, on the author's skill to give as on ours to receive." [2]

This subjective element in reading—*as on ours to receive*—is that aspect of reading which more nearly approaches art. Here is the extended concept of reading about which I have spoken—the involvement of the reader in what he reads. Once again, hear Sir Arthur:

But it is by the spark in us that we read it [literature]: and not all the fire of God that was in Shakespeare can dare to patronize the little spark in me. . . . To be Hamlet—to feel yourself Hamlet—is more important than killing a king or even to know all there is to be known about a text. . . . Shakespeare means us to feel to be—Hamlet. That is all: and from the play it is the best we can get.

The art of reading literature involves many interrelated skills, but most of all it involves the reader as a human being. So, at last, we come around to the quotation introducing this essay. And it is well to have it serve some purpose besides ornament.

> But words, if words are wise, go on and on
> To make a longer note of unison
> With man and man than living persons make
> With one another for whatever sake.

[2] Sir Arthur Quiller-Couch, *On the Art of Reading* (New York, G. P. Putnam's Sons, 1932).

14

JOHN J. DE BOER

The Concept of
Creativity in Reading

AT FIRST THOUGHT, the concept of *creative reading* would seem to be a contradiction in terms. It is the writer who creates, the reader who follows the author's lead. The good reader enters the author's world and lets that world act upon him. He may give himself over to the "willing suspension of disbelief" as the author spins a tale, or follow obediently as the philosopher expounds his doctrines—not necessarily to accept, but to understand. Indeed, the element of receptivity, which in a sense is the opposite of creativity, is essential to all good reading.

The author should have the first chance at creativity. When, in I. A. Richards' words, "views and emotions [are] already prepared in the reader's mind so that what happens appears to be more of the reader's doing than the poet's," the author is powerless to communicate with the reader. The reader needs to learn patient searching after the intention of the author.

This pliant participation in the author's thought is beautifully described by Paul Engle [1] in his poem, "Book and Child":

I

High from these printed, silent sounds, the bird
That carried Sinbad and his diamonds hangs
Out of this care of frightful phrase and word
Old tiger roars between his ripping fangs.
Down from the grassy hills of this plain prose
Indian horse and warrior surprise,
The boy hears yells of Gaul and Roman Nose
And Custer's yellow hair streams in his eyes.

JOHN J. DE BOER Professor of Education, University of Illinois. President of NCTE, 1941-1942. Editor of *Elementary English* since 1942. Member of Curriculum Commission, NCTE. Awarded Susan Colver Rosenberger Prize for Educational Research, University of Chicago, 1940. Author of *Creative Reading*, 1950. Coauthor of *Teaching Secondary English*, 1951 and of *The Teaching of Reading*, 1960. Author of textbooks in language and literature, and contributor to numerous journals.

[1] Quoted by permission. The writer is indebted to Dr. Muriel Crosby for calling his attention to these sonnets, which appeared in the Book Review section of the Sunday *New York Times,* November 18, 1956, and were reprinted in *Elementary English*, 36 (October, 1959), 374-375.

Battle comes to his bedroom. In his fright
His hands jerk back as if the book would bite.
But goes on reading, takes that book to bed,
By all that verbal violence comforted,
Happy to see, in his devoted rage,
The whole world come alive on that dead page.

II

She tries to read, but words are only jumbles
Of shapes that twist her tongue until it clashes:
Long consonants are sticks on which she stumbles,
Round vowels are muddy pools through which she splashes.
Dog is a sound that bristles like a bark,
Cat is a sound that yowls and turns up fur.
But no shape on that page is a real mark
For living animals that play with her.

She throws the book down, her feet start to stamp.
Shocked at her act, she takes it, holds it tight,
Knowing that from these pages, secret, dumb,
Her long-loved story once again will come.
Her eyes fill, not with words, tears, mad, but light.
That book glows in her like a turned-up lamp.

III

Animal stories make the world a zoo
In which the fiercest animal is you.
When the book says, "Rain fell and thunder rolled,"
They shake, and huddle down against the cold.
But when they turn the page and read, "The sun
Came out and all the clouds went," one by one,
They look up toward the light and smile for knowing
They hold the sky in their hands, blue and blowing.

No fierce ghost prowling through its haunted house,
No golden nymph turned greenly into tree,
No mouse changed into monster, back to mouse,
No spook from caves, no demon from the sea,
Has so intense and wild and lost a look
As children holding in their hands a book.

Nevertheless, the elements of creation and re-creation are indispensable in reading at the highest levels. As Emerson has said, "One must be an inventor to read well. . . . When the mind is braced by labor and invention, the pages of whatever book we read become luminous with manifold allusion. Every sentence is doubly significant, and the sense of our author is as broad as the world." [2]

Creativity in reading differs from creativity in writing, but it has in common with it one purpose: to combine and recombine the materials of language to produce a meaningful result. This means (1) that the creative reader is an active agent, not merely a passive recipient; (2) that he is a seeker and an experimenter; and (3) that he is both a builder and a leveler.

Creativity in this broad sense is present at all stages of learning. The use of clues in getting meaning in the early stages is a creative act. Creativity includes all the higher-order mental processes: perception, concept formation, seeing relationships, drawing conclusions, making comparisons, making applications. The concept of creative reading is, therefore, inseparable from that of creative thinking.

To be useful in the planning of instruction, the process of creative reading must be viewed in its more specific manifestations. Among these are the following: (1) creative inquiry, (2) creative interpretation, (3) creative integration, (4) creative application, and (5) creative criticism.

Creative inquiry. Modern education has shifted the emphasis from mere subject-matter mastery and the retention of ready-made "learning products" to the growth of a lively curiosity, a reaching-out for meaning, a re-examination of alternative "solutions" to old problems, and the discovery and definition of new problems. Techniques for such question-answering and problem-solving adventures can be taught. However, in each problematic situation the versatility and individuality required of the learner take on the quality of "creative" thinking, or "creative" reading. Such creativity is called into play in reading at various levels.

The first step in creative inquiry is the asking of the right ques-

[2] Quoted by Kathleen B. Hester in "Creative Reading: A Neglected Area," *Education,* 79 (May, 1959), 537.

tions. At a simple level, the satisfaction of curiosity, the questions may be fairly obvious ones, as in the following classroom scene: [3]

On another occasion, two boys were absorbed in the pictures in the book, *The Monitor and the Merrimac*. As the teacher strolled by, one boy asked, "What's this?" and pointed to one of the ships pictured.

"The first ironclad. Forerunner of our big ships."

"What are the splashes next to it?"

"Bullets." Ed wandered over to explain.

"Let's see, was it the War of 1812 or the Civil War?" she countered.

Ed snorted. "Well, it must have been the Civil War. See the Southern flag flying?"

"Which boat won?"

Ed answered quickly. "That's what the book's about, and about the man who got the idea for building ironclads, and how these boats were built. You should read it, Joe."

"How about letting me have it next?"

This from a boy who had complained that he could never find a book that interested him.

A somewhat more mature level is represented by the reading of the following passage: [4]

As the time dragged by, the men on the hill grew taut with tension. Many of them had contributed, in one way or another, to the building of the equipment which had made the bomb's development possible. Now the years of frustration and frantic effort were almost over. Now the moment was near when they would know whether the United States had won the race to be the first nation to release the enormous energy in the atom.

Suddenly a voice came through the darkness. The radio spoke: "Zero minus ten seconds!"

Laurence saw a green flare shoot out through the clouds, fall slowly, grow faint, and disappear. He heard the voice call again: "Zero minus three seconds!"

He watched another green flare rise and fall. Then there was a terrible stillness in the desert. Off to the east, there were the first streaks of grayness, the hints of dawn.

[3] L. Jane Stewart, Frieda M. Heller, and Elsie J. Alberty, *Improving Reading in the Junior High School* (New York, Appleton-Century-Crofts, Inc., 1957), p. 29.

[4] Robert C. Pooley and others, *All Around America* (Chicago, Scott, Foresman & Co., 1959), p. 167.

And then Laurence saw it—the most tremendous sight in the history of civilized man—the blaze of light from the rending of the very structure of matter, a fire from the core of the world's substance.

He described it later as a light "not of this world, the light of many suns in one."

One of the men near Laurence, Professor George Kistiakowsky of Harvard, said to him, "It was the nearest thing to doomsday that one could possibly imagine. I am sure that at the end of the world—in the last millisecond of the earth's existence—the last man will see what we have just seen!"

But Laurence thought it might be the dawn of a new day for mankind, not a doomsday at all. He shared the exuberance of the scientists, who leaped to their feet, and broke into a wild dance on the hill—shaking hands, clapping backs, shouting with joy.

The freeing of atomic energy on such a scale opened endless possibilities for the future—in knowledge of the universe, in power to travel to other planets, in the science of medicine, in a thousand fields of man's work. Laurence knew that this power would probably be used in war—but the war would end and the achievements made possible by atomic energy would go on for centuries, for ages to come.

In one class, such questions as these were raised after the reading of the foregoing passage: "What other modern inventions were motivated by defense and armament?" "What peaceful uses could atomic energy serve?" "Can there be other motivations than war for great scientific advance?" "What constructive things could be done if the billions spent for arms were devoted to peaceful purposes?" "How safe would it be for us to divert these billions to peaceful use?" "Can the arms race be stopped?"

These questions were stimulated, but not demanded, by the story. They arose out of experience with previous reading and discussion. They arose out of the reader's perception of the relation between what he reads and the images, problems, and situations that the reading material suggests. It is in this perception of relationships and its formulation in words that the element of creativity is to be found.

The importance of the perception or education of relationships in the process of creative inquiry has led some educators to favor the *core organization* of instruction. This plan is based on the examination of problems, either personal or social, which call for investigation in various areas, such as language and literature, the social studies, science, the arts, and numerous other subjects. Under it, the student is required to discover and formulate the questions which may lead to the understanding and possible solutions of the problems. The core curriculum stresses the active, creative approach to subject matter.

Relatively few schools have introduced courses under the name *core,* and it is unlikely that core courses will supplant any of the traditional subjects in the foreseeable future. The principle of the core curriculum, however, is now well established in both elementary and high schools. Under the labels of the traditional subjects, children and young people are studying such topics as the mass media, atomic energy, public health, boy-girl relationships, crime and delinquency, conservation, and community planning. Most of these topics are commonly considered in social studies and English classes, but the students' researches extend to the fields of mathematics, art, music, home economics, science, and other subjects. They are thus being prepared for the intelligent reading of such adult books as J. D. Bernal's *World Without War,* [5] which, although written by a scientist, deals with problems of industry, agriculture, science, economics, politics, and education; Henry Steele Commager's *The American Mind,* [6] which deals with literature, philosophy, history, law, architecture, and politics in America; or *Johnson's England,* [7] which studies eighteenth-century English life in twenty-seven of its manifestations, from the church to journalism. Indeed, much serious contemporary writing presents aspects of the human scene which bear little correspondence to the traditional subject divisions. Thus, in courses organized on the core plan, much use is made of the many new books for children and young people which deal with atomic energy, public health, conservation, urban renewal, marriage and the family, the mass media, and scores of other topics which require the discovery of relationships among the major fields of study and thereby encourage creative inquiry.

Creative interpretation. Creative inquiry is a search for answers

[5] (London, Rutledge and Kegan Paul, Ltd., 1958).
[6] (New Haven, Yale University Press, 1950).
[7] A. S. Turberville, Editor (New York, Columbia University Press, 1933).

to questions which the reader asks to meet a need or satisfy curiosity; creative *interpretation* involves an intensive effort at reconstructing the author's precise meaning. Such reconstruction is not "free" creation because it is sternly limited by the clues and symbols found in the reading matter. Nevertheless, interpretation at its best is a creative process because the ideas on the printed page must be built anew in the mind of each reader. Since minds of readers differ, and since some minds are both better informed and more creative than others, interpretations of literary materials may vary widely. Witness the conflicting interpretations of passages in the Bible or Shakespeare.

An illuminating example of interpretation on a creative level is found in the Progressive Education Association report, *Language in General Education*. [8] The authors of this report (a Committee of the P. E. A.) discuss the meaning of the expression in the Declaration of Independence, "All men are created equal." They show that the understanding of the statement is dependent on the writers' intent when they used the word *equal*. The process of interpretation then becomes one of examining many sources, including the possible lexical meanings of the word, the verbal context, and the historical setting in which the word was used. Obviously, given such complex data, and against the background of the many associations which the word evokes, the process of interpretation requires great skill and permits a considerable degree of the individuality that we commonly associate with creativity. Reading the Declaration of Independence with insight is a creative act.

The understanding of metaphorical language, too, calls for a kind of creative interpretation. When Margaret Sidney writes, in *Five Little Peppers and How They Grew*, "It was just on the edge of the twilight," can the child interpret the figure which borrows from space to describe time? What creative effort is involved in this simple translation, which the fluent reader almost unconsciously makes as he follows the sweep of the story? When an author calls his book *Out of the Jaws of Victory*, can the student quickly supply the original metaphor and relate the inversion to the political analysis with which the book deals—Truman's election in 1948? This kind of interpretation, which calls for the formation and utilization of

[8] (New York, Appleton-Century-Crofts, Inc., 1940).

mental constructs on the part of the reader, is a creative activity, although on a simple level.

In speaking of creativity in reading, we do not assume that the creative product always or usually reaches the level of art, although a literary critic reading a new novel or a scholar studying an old document may, in some cases, be considered an artist. But we speak of the first grade child's expressions in drawing or writing as creative, though they are in no sense art, because they are his own individual handiwork. So, also, creative interpretation begins when reading begins.

Creative integration. We have seen that creativity in reading means putting things together—words, concepts, images—to create something new in the reader's mind. But this "putting together" extends also to the constituent factors in a remark, a situation, a plot, or the sayings and deeds of a character. The essential moments of insight in reading occur when the reader has perceived what the various factors "add up to." The "adding up to" is, however, not a mere process of addition, but a perception, sometimes unexpected, of a central impact, a mood, a value, an attitude toward life.

To the creative reader, the "moment of insight" has value insofar as he is able to relate it to the body of his previous experience, his previous attitudes, his perception of reality, his outlook on life. Integrating what one reads (or hears on the radio, or sees on the stage or the television screen) with one's beliefs about self or others or the world or values is a process that must be unique to each individual, and is, therefore, in a true sense creative.

Let us take as an example the Biblical story of David and Goliath. The reader is moved by the story—the spectacle of a young man exhibiting great faith and courage, of the mighty defeated by the weak, of the arrogant brought low by the humble. But from this point on, each reader makes his own connections with past knowledge and experience—connections which heighten the emotional impact of the narrative, but which also give new meaning to a much broader cluster of events, issues, problems, goals, beliefs. Thus, for example, one reader, following David as he ran forward to meet the giant, remembered that he was a pastoral poet, the "sweet singer of Israel," who was not merely a military hero but also one of the towering figures in the ancient religious and cultural tradition of the Jewish people. The reminder made him see in clearer perspective the nature of the barbaric mind which harbors anti–Semitism. The reaction was not one of free association; it was a creative transference from a single dramatic episode to a generalized insight or emotion. Another reader, no less creative, would make quite different connections.

Since the wise person is an integrated person, one way of describing this aspect of creative reading is to call it "skill in the quest of wisdom," which in the view of some is the ultimate goal of education. Knowledge is an essential tool; wisdom is the end. But wisdom comes through growth. It is the distillation of many experiences and of the insights gained from them. The teacher who would cultivate creative reading tries to provide such experiences through books.

The task of guiding young people in the search for wisdom would be easier if we could agree on a description of the truly wise man. In our heritage we can find an abundance of "wisdom" literature, from the *Proverbs* to Emerson to modern books on health, sex, child-rearing, and the "power of positive thinking." Men who are honest and thoughtful have not agreed that all these books have the right formula for wisdom.

Yet, our students can be helped if we confront them with questions which are pertinent to their own lives and which they can test in their own thinking and reading:

Is it wise . . .

—to listen to others who disagree and weigh their views without passion?

—to have strong principles, but also to examine and re-examine them as new facts and new experiences challenge them?

—to change one's principles as new insights show them to be wrong or too limited in their application?

—to keep searching for new principles of action to meet the requirements of new knowledge about our complex world?

—to experiment with new ways of combating social blight, bigotry, and war?

The responses to these questions will vary, but the search for answers will call into play the abilities needed for creative reading. The task of the student is to build a structure fit for the cultivated mind to dwell in. The structure may not be a stately mansion, in the elder Holmes' phrase, but it should be a base from which new explorations can be made and from which the foundations of new structures can be planned. In a democracy, the creative reading of the many will be for the building of a house of many mansions.

Creative application. The ability to read is commonly analyzed into more specific skills. One of the skills frequently mentioned is the ability to apply what one reads. It is reasonable to question whether application is a proper part of reading itself. A closer examination of the mental processes involved in reading, however, will reveal that application is integral to creative reading. A person who undertakes to construe what he reads is handicapped in his reading unless he knows what the reading matter implies and what its possible applications may be. The good reader applies what he reads to what he has known and understood before.

The process of application of what one reads is perhaps best illustrated by the simple examples of a housewife following a recipe and of a chess addict trying to solve a chess puzzle. In these instances, the reading is accompanied by other activities, but the reading itself is focused upon the ways in which the printed words are to be applied. Considering the relative simplicity of these examples, one might hesitate to employ the term *creative* in this connection. Anyone who has sampled two cakes baked from the same recipe by different cooks could, perhaps, detect differences in creativity. The same is true when one individual's solution to a chess problem is compared with that of another. No one, however, would dispute the creative quality of applications made when the reading material is abstract or when it calls for subtle distinctions of meaning or feeling.

For example, in Harlow Shapley's *Of Stars and Men* we are given in semipopular form an abundance of information about the celestial world. For the ordinary reader the task of grasping Shapley's descriptions of the constellations is difficult enough. Nevertheless, it is possible, even for the general reader who has had no previous knowledge of astronomy, to make creative applications of many of the facts to his developing conception of the size of the universe. Speculations about life on distant planets may affect geocentric notions which have persisted among us in spite of scientific knowledge disseminated for hundreds of years. Certainly, the contemplation of the sidereal universe should give the reader an improved perspective on the petty concerns of human beings, and perhaps reduce the place which mundane conflicts of race and clan and nation hold in his mind.

To the extent that reading may affect one's thinking in general, or that an idea encountered on the printed page may reshape one's beliefs about related matters, whether they concern social organization or ethics or immortality or public health or penology, it has brought about a kind of "application" that is truly creative.

Creative criticism. Discussions of critical reading have usually been concerned with the negative aspects of the process. They have stressed analysis rather than creation. If critical reading is essentially a process of acceptance and rejection, attention has been focused chiefly upon rejection. Thus, the reader has often been encouraged to look for pitfalls and errors in what he reads. He has been taught to beware of logical fallacies, of various propaganda devices, of stereotypes and emotionalized language. Critical reading, like scientific skepticism, has too often engendered the merely defensive attitude. The fear of intellectual booby-traps has replaced the quest for a strategy of conquest.

No one will deny that American education has a responsibility for communicating to youth the ways of defending themselves against the skillful manipulators of their thoughts. The control of public opinion, often with the aid of Ph.D.'s in psychology, has become a great industry. The graduates of our schools must be more than statistics plotted in graphs by Madison Avenue experts.

But defense is not enough. Our youth must learn how to develop philosophies of their own. Reading is a seeking for answers. The creative reader accepts, rejects, puts together, raises questions, draws inferences, and comes to (at least) tentative conclusions. The reader makes a declaration of independence of the author. He is on his own, a seeker after truth. If he is creative, he will know when he can draw independent conclusions, when he must suspend judgment, and when he must trust the author.

The question of trust is crucial in creative criticism. The reader trusts the acknowledged expert with respect to facts. He is inclined to trust the innovator in the world of ideas if earlier experiences with him seem to have justified the reader's confidence. Without a degree of trust, faith, confidence in the writer, very little learning could take place through reading. But always it must be a guarded trust, a willingness to examine accompanied by a readiness to challenge.

What distinguishes creative criticism from mere suspicion or a settled attitude of skepticism is the earnest desire to use whatever is read in the process of getting at the truth. I recall a visit I made some years ago to a class of college seniors in which a controversial issue was discussed. The instructor was a brilliant young Ph.D. from Ohio State University; the topic: John L. Lewis and a coal strike. Many members of the class held no views, or no strong views, on the subject. Those who had strong opinions were about equally divided between protagonists and antagonists of Lewis.

The critics of Lewis were apparently the most vocal because the discussion soon became a recital of the nation's "grievances" against the labor leader. Our young instructor, through Socratic questioning, challenged both the facts and the arguments adduced by the critics. As the anti–Lewis participants began to retreat, the pro–Lewis members took heart. They advanced their reasons for supporting Lewis and the strike, growing bolder as they felt the instructor was on their side. But then the instructor raised critical questions about *their* facts and arguments. When the bell rang, both sides seemed subdued.

What had the students learned? Intellectual humility, perhaps. They had certainly learned that they must check their facts and sharpen their arguments. It is conceivable that this instructor followed up the experience with a more constructive approach to the problem. But if, as seems likely, the next week's discussion dealt with a new event current in the news, the students were left with no way of thinking about or dealing with John L. Lewis and the coal strike. The brilliant teacher had demonstrated the methods of finding error, but he had not helped the young people to make up their minds about issues that would not wait. Critical thinking and critical reading must lead to conclusions upon which one can act.

Creative criticism does not result in the kind of vacuum or intellectual stalemate described in the preceding paragraphs. Creative criticism is goal-oriented. The facts and the argument about the coal strike should have been subjected to the critical discipline of questions related to purposes shared by all members of the group. Among these questions, to which the remarks of members should have been addressed, are: "What responsibilities does society have for the safety and welfare of the workers?" "What social and economic organization would best meet the needs of the coal miners, the executives, the investors, and the consumers?" Critical discussion would make use of all the knowledge and ideas of the leader and the participants, and all the facts and opinions available in the library, in the effort to find answers to such questions. Critical discussion and critical reading can be fascinating, but the stakes are greater than those of a friendly game of bridge at home.

The foregoing brief suggestions are made in the hope that they will be tested and, perhaps, amplified by references to the limitless world of literature. Creative reading is a craft of a high order, but, fortunately, it is one that can be taught. The rewards in the form of personal fulfilment are great. More important, creative reading by the many is essential to the survival of the "way of life" called democratic, often erroneously associated with the Western world, but really born in the Middle East, and both developed and corrupted in Europe and the New World.

15

STELLA S. CENTER

The Hazards of Semiliteracy

THE TITLE of this article is open to challenge for there is little agreement on a definition of *semiliteracy*. The Office of Education of the United States [1] records its opposition to the term:

The term *semi-illiterate* is very seldom used today by persons working in the field of literacy education. It is too inexact a measure and requires a sort of value judgment not in keeping with an effort to be as objective as possible. Instead of using this term, authorities working in the field have developed the concept of "functional literacy or illiteracy," depending upon the circumstance in which the term is being used. *Functional literacy* is defined "as the ability to read and write at the level of the average fourth-grade pupil." A *functional illiterate* is defined "as a person who has completed less than five years of schooling." In the census of 1940, the direct question about literacy was replaced by a question about the number of years of schooling the individual had completed. It was concluded that information about schooling would prove more illuminating and reliable than the earlier question of whether an individual was able to read and write in any language.

Apparently, functional literacy and functional illiteracy mark approximately a point of meeting, the first indicating the lowest level of literacy and the latter the top level of illiteracy, the two phrases referring to a similar degree of achievement in reading and writing. From the Office of Education [2] comes another statement about the functional illiterate.

Our last decennial census counted nearly 10 million adult citizens 25 years of age and over who were functionally illiterate, *i.e.*, had had fewer

STELLA S. CENTER Reading consultant. Formerly Director of Reading Clinic of Pinellas County, Florida. Director of Reading Institute of New York University, 1936-1950. Teacher and Professor of English in schools and colleges. President of NCTE, 1931-1932. Awarded Litt. D., University of Georgia, 1929. Coauthor of *Reading and Thinking*, 1940; *Reading Today*, 1947. Author of *The Art of Book Reading*, 1952. General Editor of Junior Academy Classics. Author and Coauthor of numerous texts in English and reading, and contributor to journals.

[1] Edward W. Brice, Adult Education Section of the Office of Education, August 19, 1959.

[2] From "For a More Literate Nation," by Ambrose Caliver, Assistant to the Commissioner and Chief, Adult Education Section. *School Life* (December, 1957).

than 5 years of schooling (approximately 4 million native whites, 3 million foreign-born whites, and 3 million Negroes). The count revealed a national problem, for practically every State in the Union has large numbers of illiterates. A high proportion of them are concentrated in the ages over 45, but every year about 60,000 functional illiterates reach age 14.

The concept of literacy may be stretched from an absolute minimum to a maximum achieved by the greatest minds of the human race. Every society of human beings needs the means of communicating ideas. In a social order, the more skillful the members of it are in using and reading a written language, the greater are its possibilities of achieving a high level of civilization.

Literacy is a characteristic acquired by individuals in varying degrees from just above none to an indeterminate upper level. Some individuals are more or less literate than others, but it is really not possible to speak of literate and illiterate persons as two distinct categories. Nor is the problem solved by introducing a third category, semiliterates, placed between the literates and illiterates. The question still remains: at what point does a person pass from the illiterate to the semiliterate stage, or from the semiliterate to the literate? [3]

An Expert Committee on Standardization of Educational Statistics convened by UNESCO in November, 1951 recommended the following definitions of literacy and semiliteracy: [4]

1. A person is considered literate who can both read with understanding and write a short simple statement on his everyday life.
2. A person is considered semiliterate who can read with understanding, but not write, a short simple statement on his everyday life.

Functional literacy has been defined by Dr. William S. Gray of the University of Chicago as follows:

A person is functionally literate when he has acquired the knowledge and skills in reading and writing which enable him to engage effectively in all those activities in which literacy is normally assumed in his culture or group. [5]

[3] *World Illiteracy at Mid-Century: A Statistical Study* (New York, United Nations, 1957), p. 8.
[4] *Expert Committee on Standardization of Educational Statistics, Report* (Paris, UNESCO, 1952), p. 3.
[5] From William S. Gray, *The Teaching of Reading and Writing* (Paris, UNESCO, 1956), p. 10.

Literacy is as difficult to define as *culture,* which can mean anything from acknowledging an introduction correctly to understanding the Greek enclitic or the quantum theory. In spite of difficulties, F. R. Cowell ventures to define *culture*. His definition resembles a definition of *literacy* so closely that it is appropriate to quote it:[6]

Culture is that which, being transmitted orally by tradition and objectively through writing and other means of expression, enhances the quality of life with meaning and value by making possible the formulation, realization, appreciation, and the achievement of truth, beauty, and moral worth.

How can cultural values be created? Cowell's answer is discouraging for the vast majority of the human race, the illiterate and the semilliterate: [7]

The creation of cultural values is essentially a vast, co-operative enterprise depending for its progress upon the insight, energy, genius, and devotion of relatively very few exceptionally gifted persons whom the vast majority of the human race cannot do more than respect and follow as far as they are able to do so.

At Manchester University, on October 3, 1959, a conference on "The Teaching of English Literature" was held. Professor William Walsh of Leeds University defined *a good education* and its stabilizing effect on a world in transition. Mr. Cowell and Professor Walsh are not far apart in their concept of the highly literate man.

Professor Walsh believed that what endured from a good education was a blend of value, attitude, and assumption, a special quality of mind, a particular flavor of imagination, and he believed also that the sources of these had been contracted and enfeebled in the modern world with its insistence upon technique. Nor surprisingly, therefore, there had been a degeneration of language (that supremely humanizing influence) in our society. Only in literature would we find language most powerfully, subtly, and inclusively used, and there, too, we would discover a rich complex of "beliefs," of ideas prompted by life. [8]

[6] F. R. Cowell, *Culture in Private and Public Life* (New York, Frederick A. Praeger, Inc., 1959).
[7] *Ibid.*
[8] Reported in *The Times,* Educational Supplement, London, October 9, 1959.

One characteristic of the half-educated is a narrow view of the world, the source of bigotry, prejudice, and unreasonable hatred. William Faulkner had the vision of the *literate* which he defined succinctly in his conversation with Jean Stein in Paris: "I like to think of the world I create as being a kind of keystone in the Universe; that, small as that keystone is, if it were taken away, the universe itself would collapse." The view of the literate man is wide, but it is also intense. He may live in Yoknapatawpha County and yet be a citizen of the universe.

Vigorous efforts have been made by census enumerators to find reliable means of measuring degrees of literacy, a baffling undertaking inasmuch as there is little agreement on what constitutes *illiteracy, semiliteracy,* and *literacy.* There is an increasing trend to measure the degree of literacy of sample populations by means of objective tests, rather than by the number of years of school attendance or the individual's statement as to whether he could read and write. The percentage of illiteracy based on tests is much higher than that based on the individual's personal comment on his skill in reading and writing.

Just before World War II, the United States was predominantly a nation of eighth graders. By 1957, the national median among the adult population had risen to 10.6 years of schooling. [9] Perhaps 10.6 years of schooling is one way of designating the top limit of semi-literacy and fifth grade the lower limit. To define *semiliteracy* in terms of school attendance is unsatisfactory; unfortunately, school attendance is not necessarily synonymous with educational accomplishment. There is, however, a high correlation between the amount of illiteracy and the number of years of school completed. Nicholas Murray Butler described the United States as "the best half-educated country in the world." Another critic, Mr. R. P. Blackmuir, writing in *The Kenyon Review* (March, 1959) comments: "Americans believe in education but they distrust the intellect."

According to Dr. M. M. Lewis, "Illiteracy is important only because literacy is important. What society means by illiteracy depends upon the importance of literacy in that society. . . . To be literate is to have met the demands of society by acquiring a sufficient mastery

[9] From *Status and Trends: Vital Statistics, Education and Public Finance* (Washington, D. C., National Educational Association, 1959).

of the art of communication." The higher the standards of literacy, the more glaring is the plight of the illiterate and the semiliterate. According to Dr. Lewis, what we are really concerned about is not so much our illiteracy as the growing burden of becoming increasingly literate. [10]

The phenomenon of illiteracy is not confined to any particular part of the world or group of countries. It exists everywhere in varying degrees. As long as more than two-fifths of the world's adult population cannot read and write in any language, and are thus deprived of their full participation in the cultural life of mankind, the question of world illiteracy must continue to be of concern to all. [11]

The art of communication has become much more difficult by the invention of the telephone, the press, the radio, the cinema, and television. Dr. Lewis lists another means of communication, "nonverbal, graphic symbolization;" that is, "the use of pictures and diagrams in conjunction with the spoken word. . . . The standards of literacy are all the time rising, and this brings the illiterate more and more into the limelight."

In *The House of Intellect* by Jacques Barzun, there is a sweeping denunciation of the individual, regardless of his category, who sets a low value on intellect. His comment is a fitting description of the complacent semiliterate content with mediocrity: [12]

[He] does not want to believe in the existence of superior intellects who should be directing society. He looks to the public opinion poll to tell him what to do, and if he is to be given ideas they must be "human," unchallenging, and palatable. Nothing must be set before him which frightens, surprises, or makes him suspect that he is ignorant.

According to Matthew Arnold, "The mass of mankind will never have any ardent zeal for seeing things as they are; very inadequate ideas will always satisfy them."

Much of the confusion in educational thinking today is due to the rising tide of anti-intellectualism and the ebbing of intellectualism.

[10] From M. M. Lewis, *The Importance of Illiteracy* (London, George Harrap and Co., 1953).

[11] *World Illiteracy at Mid-Century: A Statistical Study* (New York, United Nations, 1957). Preface.

[12] The *Times* Literary Supplement, London, August 28, 1959.

It is hard to explain adequately the rising tide of anti-intellectualism. Probably it stems in part from the American pioneer tradition, where the lettered man was always suspect. In the days of the frontier, a man who could read and write with too much facility was regarded as (and indeed often was) a worthless city slicker bent on cheating the honest country-man in any way possible.

Abraham Lincoln was a great man, but I sometimes wonder whether he would have become the folk hero that he is had he been born in Boston of wealthy parents and received his education at Harvard. In himself, Lincoln was certainly not an anti-intellectual, but he has become the symbol for anti-intellectuals to flaunt before the world: The honest, uneducated country boy who by his native shrewdness bested the most highly trained minds in the nation. [13]

The concern of UNESCO is to increase literacy, which plays the primary role in social and material betterment. Approximately half the world's people cannot read and understand a newspaper, accord-ing to Dr. Luther Evans, director general of the United National Educational, Scientific, and Cultural Organization. "From my point of view," he said, "we are making too little progress against illiteracy." It should be the concern of educational systems the world over to instruct every student, elementary, secondary, college, adult, how he can achieve the highest level of literacy of which he is mentally capable. Literacy is synonymous with the skills and art of communi-cating by speaking, writing, listening, and reading. In this sense, literacy is basic to achievement in all areas of human knowledge. It is the determining factor, in most instances, in shaping the economic, social, and political aspects of society. The critical reader, however, will cite instances of nations that have achieved a high degree of literacy of a kind but have failed in that aspect which is more significant than material development; namely, belief in the rights of the individual to freedom of thought and action.

The popular conception envisions three groups, the illiterate, the literate, and the semiliterate. The three groups are not fixed, either qualitatively or quantitatively; they are constantly shifting and chang-ing according to global circumstances. What today may be defined as *literacy* may tomorrow be labeled *semiliteracy,* for the pace of

[13] Mary E. Dichmann, "The Rising Tide of Anti-intellectualism," *Journal of the American Association of University Women,* 51 (May, 1958), No. 4.

THE EXTENT OF ILLITERACY IN THE WORLD, 1950 *

CONTINENT AND REGION	ESTIMATED POPULATION		ESTIMATED EXTENT OF ILLITERACY	
	Total (all ages) (millions)	Adult (15 years and over) (millions)	Per cent of adult illiteracy	Number of adult illiterates (millions)
WORLD TOTAL	2496	1587	43–45	690–720
AFRICA	198	120	80–85	98–104
Northern Africa	65	40	85–90	34–36
Tropical and Southern Africa	134	80	80–85	64–68
AMERICA	330	223	20–21	45–47
Northern America	168	126	3–4	4–5
Middle America	51	30	40–42	12–13
South America	111	67	42–44	28–29
ASIA	1376	830	60–65	510–540
South West Asia	62	37	75–80	28–30
South Central Asia	466	287	80–85	230–240
South East Asia	171	102	65–70	68–72
East Asia	677	404	45–50	180–200
EUROPE	393	293	7–9	22–25
Northern and Western Europe	133	102	1–2	1–2
Central Europe	128	96	2–3	2–3
Southern Europe	131	95	20–21	19–20
OCEANIA	13	9	10–11	1
UNION OF SOVIET SO-CIALISTIC REPUBLICS	186	112	5–10	6–11

* SOURCE: Adapted from *World Illiteracy at Mid-Century,* p. 15

events and consequent demands are in a process of constant acceleration.

While it is readily admitted that literacy is a term applicable to a gradation of knowledge and skills related to communication by symbolic language, yet for practical purposes division of individuals into three groups is essential. This article accepts the popular conception of three categories, illiterate, semiliterate, and literate.

The study estimates that 75% of the world's illiterate population lives in Asia, 14% or 15% in Africa, 6.5% in the Americas, and 4% or 5% in Europe, Oceania, and the U.S.S.R.

In the following table, the percentage of illiterates in the population 15 years old and over since 1945 is significant in view of their contemporary history and political involvement:

ILLITERACY IN UNDERDEVELOPED COUNTRIES SINCE 1945 *

COUNTRY	Per cent illiterate
Algeria	
Muslim population	93.8
European population	8.2
Egypt	80.1
Dominican Republic	57.1
Haiti	89.5
Venezuela	47.8
India	80.7
Nigeria	88.5
Nyasaland (all ages)	
African population	93.5
Union of South Africa	
Native population (10 and over)	72.4
Iraq	89.1
Pakistan	86.2

* SOURCE: *Ibid.,* pp. 32-34

In relation to the preceding figures, the following table offers a contrast that is not surprising:

COUNTRIES WITH LOW ILLITERACY, SINCE 1945 *

COUNTRY	Per cent illiterate
United States of America	2.5
Israel	6.3
Belgium	3.3
France	3.6
Hungary	4.7
Union of Soviet Socialistic Republics	5–10
Canada	2–3
Czechoslovakia	2–3
Denmark	1–2
Germany	1–2
Norway	1–2
United Kingdom	1–2
New Zealand	1–2

* SOURCE: *Ibid.*, pp. 32-34

In spite of the high percentage of illiteracy in Africa, there are grounds for cautious optimism in appraising progress on the Ivory Coast. The handicaps, however, seem to the United States and western Europe appalling and insuperable.

While the percentage of illiteracy is low in the United States, it must be remembered that, measured by standards by no means exacting, there are approximately over nine million adults in this country who are functionally illiterate and forty-four million who have not completed the ninth grade. [14] Today, approximately one-third of the population of the United States falls into the category of the illiterate and semiliterate. During World War II, almost two million young Americans of draft age were rejected for military service because of a mental or emotional defect, and another three-quarters of a million were discharged from the Armed Forces for these same reasons while the war was still under way. [15] The basis of rejection was not only mental and emotional defects, but crass illiteracy as well.

[14] Ambrose Caliver, "Government's Concern for Adult Education," *School Life* (June, 1957).

[15] From Eli Ginzberg, *Human Resources* (New York, Simon and Schuster, Inc., 1958).

In the world-wide battle against illiteracy and ignorance, much credit should be accorded missionaries who have reduced many oral languages to writing. Among the most famous of the missionaries is Frank Laubach. He recognized the necessity of crusading for literacy and devised written forms for dozens of Asiatic and African languages in order that he might teach illiterates how to read the Bible.

The grave concern about illiteracy, or, rather, a greater degree of literacy, has long rested heavily on society's thinkers. William James gave voice to the growing need to "live in a world without walls." To do so, he said, "takes a head for the risks and a sense for standing on the perilous edge."

Facts Indicative of Literacy or Semiliteracy

Each of the three groups—the illiterate, semiliterate, the literate —lives, moves, and has its being in a cultural climate of its own creating, made manifest by its activities and interests, but especially by its identification with forms of *re-creation* in its hours of leisure, the true index of the individual's cultural level. The following facts are relevant more or less to some phase of intellectual accomplishment in the United States:

Recreation

1. During the week ending August 7, 1959, 82,300,000 persons entered a drive-in or motion picture theatre.
2. In 1959, there were approximately 50 million sets of television in the United States and the number is steadily increasing.

Average Number of Hours Spent Weekly
in Televiewing [16]

	Boys	Girls
Grades 1–6	17.33	18.56
Teen-agers	21.31	20.23

Once a week one fourth, perhaps one half of the children of our nation spend an hour or so in a church or synagogue where they learn of kind-

[16] *Television and Youth,* reporting a scientific study by Professor T. C. Battin of children in Grades 1-12 (Television Information Committee, National Association for Radio and TV Broadcasters, Copyright, 1954).

ness, sympathy, love, co-operation, and the preciousness of human life. On the same day, most of these same children view television programs of hate, violence, and murder for several hours—and for every day of the week, year after year. They find these programs more exciting and interesting than what they heard in church or synagogue. . . . It is the children from 2–6 for whom television is the longest and most frequent baby-sitter. [17]

READING

	Circulation	
	Daily	Sunday
New York News	2,014,542	3,564,865
New York Mirror	834,066	1,424,886
New York Times	633,106	1,291,134
New York Journal-American	580,006	818,012
New York World Telegram & Sun	473,732	———
New York Herald-Tribune	377,400	567,265

2. MAGAZINES [19]

	Circulation
Reader's Digest	11,390,918
Life	5,961,154
Ladies Home Journal	5,614,599
TV Guide	5,470,177
Saturday Evening Post	5,449,193
True Story	2,625,967
Time	2,172,230
True Confessions	1,371,924
Newsweek	1,154,011
Modern Romances	1,098,435
Motion Picture	848,139
True Romance	701,817
Secrets	659,503
True Love Stories	410,703

[17] Garry Cleveland Myers, Editor, *Highlights for Children.* From an address at 10th Anniversary meeting of National Association for Better Radio and TV, May 21, 1959.

[18] *World Almanac, 1959.* Publishers' statements to Audit Bureau of Circulation as of March 31, 1958. Daily circulation figures based on Monday to Friday average.

[19] *World Almanac, 1959.* Latest publishers' statements to Audit Bureau of Circulations available to September 1, 1958.

2. MAGAZINES   *Circulation*

Revealing Romances	361,986
Personal Romances	302,553
Confidential Confessions	275,519
True Life Stories	241,677

One of the encouraging proofs of advancing literacy can be found in the circulation figures of *The Atlantic Monthly,* covering the past decade, 1948–1959 (first six months).

Year	Subscriber	Newsstand	Total
1948	134,259	35,699	169,958
1959	223,693	44,564	268,257

Mr. Edward Weeks, editor, attributes the increase to two factors: the foreign supplements and the efforts that went into the Centennial issue of November, 1957.

FURTHER ENCOURAGING STATISTICS [20]

	1949	1959
Saturday Review	88,958	218,939

These figures show a gain of 146.1 per cent.

Harper's Magazine	135,000	200,000

3. It is estimated that 90 million comic books are published each month in the United States; the number of readers far exceeds the number of sales.
4. Newspapers, especially the Sunday edition, cite the number of pages of comic strips as an inducement to persuade adults to subscribe.
5. Not more than 25–30 per cent of the national population reads one or more books a month, according to Lester Asheim, dean of the Graduate Library School of the University of Chicago; he stated recently: "The book audience is the smallest of all audiences for media which might be considered in any way to be mass media."

EVIDENCE OF PROGRESS

While it is generally conceded that the forces that combat illiteracy are not moving fast enough, yet there is evidence of sober, con-

[20] Certified by Audit Bureau of Circulation, 123 North Wacker Drive, Chicago.

scientious effort to increase the ranks of the literate in the United States. [21]

	1954	1956
School population 5–17 years of age	34,540,052	37,262,000
Average daily attendance	25,643,871	27,760,000
Enrolled	28,836,052	31,145,000

Current expenditures per pupil in Average Daily Attendance (ADA) show an increase of 72 per cent in the past ten years:

1948–1949	1958–1959
$197.65	$340

The variation among states is great, from $164 in Alabama to $535 in New York. The ADA average per pupil is $332.

At least 49 per cent of our population has the mental ability to complete 14 years of schooling with a curriculum of general and vocational studies that should lead either to gainful employment or to further study at a more advanced level.

At least 32 per cent of our population has the mental ability to complete an advanced liberal or specialized professional education. [22]

The total enrollment in higher education institutions in the fall of 1958, according to the United States Office of Education, 1959, was 3,258,556, or 6 per cent above 1957, and 54 per cent over 1951. About 59 per cent of the students were in publicly controlled institutions. All young people are entitled to such opportunities as will permit them to develop and achieve according to their potentialities. But only recently has the 32 per cent been identified. Even today, society has a divided mind as to the right provision for their education. This group represents the best resources of the nation for developing leadership. There is much concern about stockpiling material resources in the interest of national safety, but unless there is stockpiling of intellectual resources, the *material* will be as effective as the Maginot Line. It is even more essential to strengthen the educational system than the military establishment.

[21] *World Almanac*, 1959, p. 487.
[22] *Higher Education for Democracy*. President's Commission for Higher Education, December, 1947. (Washington, D. C., U. S. Government Printing Office).

In Krakow, in one of Europe's oldest universities, the Jagellonian University, Copernicus was once a student. In the courtyard of the university stood a statue representing him as a young student, not as the great astronomer and thinker. On the pedestal were engraved these lines from Lucretius: *"Et extra processit longe flammantia moenia mundi*—(He sent his mind beyond the flaming ramparts of the world)."

Lucretius' words should be a challenge to every student in college today, for we live in what has been called "an expanding universe," in "a dangerous age," "an era of destiny." Like Copernicus, modern youth must go boldly beyond the walls. [23]

It is not possible to estimate the possibilities of youth. It was Cuchulainn, the epitome of youth, who said, "Though the span of my life were but a day, little would I reck of that if but my noble deeds might be remembered among men." In this age of a contracting world and an expanding universe, youth will be challenged to enterprises of dangerous moment.

In the Interest of Literacy

In 1916, during World War I, the war that was to end war, Blasco Ibáñez wrote *The Four Horsemen of the Apocalypse*. In this novel, four horsemen, in their mad, devastating course, gallop over the lands of terrified humanity. War, Famine, Disease, Death—they are seated on white, red, black, and pale horses, respectively. The four horsemen are still galloping, especially in those countries that have a high percentage of illiteracy and are, therefore, undeveloped. It is oversimplification of global problems to claim that their solution is a matter of raising the level of literacy in the trouble spots of the two hemispheres. Our foreign policy, however, in rendering aid, stresses the value of instruction in various areas of knowledge and the skills to communicate with other countries on a higher cultural level.

Illiteracy is decreasing gradually, but not rapidly enough to meet increasing demands upon adults. No longer can we afford to wait upon

[23] Ethel Sabin Smith, "The Perilous Age," *Journal* of the American Association of University Women (March, 1953).

time either to eliminate the adult illiterate or to bring us a generation of adults free from illiteracy. The nature of the problem is such that we must seek a solution *now*—and seek it in a co-ordinated nation-wide effort. [24]

A little more than a century ago, the Europeans came to West Africa for a variety of reasons, some of them beneficent and some of them reprehensible. Eventually, all Europe took part in opening up the Dark Continent. They established the beginnings of a modern system of communications; they attacked disease; they introduced modern techniques of agriculture; and, best service of all, they attacked the enormous problem of education, according to Austen Kark. [25]

The last two or three years have seen a fantastic acceleration, with African states almost unheard of except in geography lessons becoming politically important. Ghana and Guinea have joined Liberia as sovereign and independent states. Next year, Nigeria, with its population of more than 34,000,000, the largest African state, will, like its predecessor Ghana, take its place as an independent nation within the British Commonwealth. The French mandated territories of Togoland and the Cameroons will advance to complete independence, to be followed later by the British colony of Sierra Leone. The states of what used to be called French West and Equatorial Africa are now members of the new French Community, their Prime Ministers sitting with the President, the Prime Minister, and other Ministers of France, on the Executive Council of the Community. They have the constitutional position of autonomous republics, responsible for the government of their own territories, with certain powers being reserved to the community as a whole, such as defence, fiscal policy, and foreign affairs. Even the Belgian Congo, which seemed until recently to be isolated from the prevailing spirit of dynamic African Nationalism, has been promised eventual independence.

The whole picture of Africa has radically changed and that of West Africa, most of all. Against the historical time scale, before you have had time to turn a page, all the textbooks are obsolete: West Africa has changed overnight from a territory of 60,000,000 people ruled by a few thousand Europeans to a series of African states governed by Africans.

[24] Ambrose Caliver, "For a More Literate Nation," Adult Education Section, *School Life* (December, 1957).

[25] Austen Kark, "Democracy in a Hot Climate," *The Listener* (July 2, 1959).

The eighth annual assembly of the World Confederation of Organizations of the Teaching Profession that met in Washington, D.C. (August, 1959) urged that the time had come to turn away from school systems borrowed chiefly from England and France. The trend now is to devise for the emerging and underdeveloped nations in Africa, Asia, and Latin America school programs suited to the special needs and interests of given areas. [26]

Whatever is done to increase literacy, qualitatively and quantitively, levels semiliteracy and stark illiteracy up, not down. The teacher, the preacher, the priest, the rabbi, the social worker, the bar, public-spirited men and women, at times view with discouraged alarm the millions of half-educated, the semiliterates, who determine the standards, political, social, cultural, in virtually every community. While every area must cope with decreasing illiteracy and semiliteracy according to the nature of the community, there are certain factors that have a universal significance. The semiliterates by the sheer impact of numbers alone, approximately one third of the population of the United States, wield powerful influence on the nation.

Universal education in a literate world must banish national myopia and narrow parochialism. Twentieth-century complexities in the interplanetary space age can be resolved only when the skills of linguistic communication can be practiced by all the people, as they engage in international activities: sports, trade, finance, travel, education, political negotiations, and jurisprudence concerning legal questions as to the use of outer space. The skill of reading has top priority if civilizing tendencies are to be continuous and progressive. "The spoken word," wrote John H. Fischer, "has no equal for prompt and easy communication through space, but, to communicate across time, man's best invention is still the printed page. This is the most reliable means any generation has to build on the experience of its forebears, to tap their wisdom, and avoid their mistakes."

THE RESPONSIBILITY OF EDUCATION

On October 5, 1957, somewhere in Russia, Man entered the Age of Space.

[26] Reported by Leonard Buder, *New York Times*, August 9, 1959.

The highly literate group must find a way to channel the age away from the realm of mass destruction into beneficent service of mankind. The jet-propulsion plane makes every place on the globe accessible in a few hours. As the world contracts and the universe expands, Man's destiny will be the outcome of a race—the competing rivals, catastrophe and education, according to H. G. Wells. The race can be won by education if all nations create opportunities favorable for each individual to achieve his potentiality in literacy and apply the skills of literacy to making life a good life for everyone.

In *The Anatomy of Freedom,* Judge Harold R. Medina has emphasized that we value freedom because it respects individual integrity and values man's capacity for growth. The individual can realize his potentiality only in a climate of freedom. In a dictatorship, he surrenders as an individual and conforms to the mass group. What promotes freedom provides an essential factor in developing progressive literacy. Conversely, progressive literacy creates a climate of freedom.

The most serious threat in modern life is the threat to destroy the dignity, the independence, and the value of the individual person. In the totalitarian states, the destruction of the individual is accomplished directly by force. In the Western World this destruction may come about by more subtle, but equally deadly, processes. The pressure for conformity, the leveling power of the group, the demand for the organization man, these and like forces threaten to erase the person who stands out as an individual. [27]

It is readily conceded that the fundamental responsibility of raising the intellectual standards of the community rests upon teachers, administrators, and boards of education, a threefold responsibility. It is not unusual to find communities more concerned at election time about the political affiliation of a prospective board member than about his qualifications to serve as a member of the Board of Education. Reporting on the successful operation of a high school, Dr. Conant stated, "Without a good school board, the situation is almost hopeless." [28] If the number of highly literate is to be increased

[27] Athens Clay Pullias (president of David Lipscomb College, Nashville, Tenn.), "The Individual is in Peril Despite 'One World'," *The Peabody Reflector* (July-August, 1959).

[28] From James B. Conant, *The American High School Today* (New York, McGraw-Hill Book Co., Inc., 1959).

and become a determining factor in raising the level of constructive intellectualism, much responsibility rests on members of boards of education. It is encouraging that among members there is very real doubt as to how intelligent they can be in directing the destinies of our modern, increasingly complex school systems.

Many of them are saying, in effect, "In nearly every board meeting I am asked to make decisions regarding matters which I sense can have far-reaching educational significance. Yet I understand very little of what is involved. That bothers my conscience." "How can I get above the details and emergencies of board meetings to take a look at the total enterprise and where we are going?" "Why talk to me about policy? That's no concern of mine. Just let me see to it that there is no dirty work in spending the tax-payer's dollar." Just how widespread such feelings of insecurity in the job are, no one knows. [29]

The fact that board members entertain real doubts argues well for the possibility that they may accept the challenge to become leaders in jolting communities out of their apathy and indifference to the quality of education provided for children. If communities were even more concerned about the quality of education in the public school system, we should witness a beneficent circle: communities electing board members who spend more time discussing educational problems, and board members informing communities how to improve their schools and convincing them that education costs much money. According to Plato, "Children are a man's riches, the greatest of his possessions, and the whole fortune of his house depends on whether they turn out ill or well." When school boards are more aware of their responsibility and when communities are less irresponsible in their selection of board members, the ranks of the semiliterates will be considerably depleted.

If the sciences and the humanities are to be welded, the scientist must learn to write. If he cannot write, then science has the obligation to find someone who can serve as a scientific scribe, able to clothe equations and formulae in words that widen the intellectual horizon of even the semiliterate. Too often the run-of-the-mill working scientist deserves the charge of using words unnecessarily long, involved syntax, clichés, even jargon. The great writers of science

[29] From Daniel R. Davies, "The Challenge of School Board Membership," *Teachers College Record* (Columbia University, February, 1950).

tower like peaks above the traditional level of writing. The scientist must find the facts and truths of the physical world, but, in addition, he must communicate his findings if practice does not continue to lag decades behind the theory.

What the colleges—teaching humanities by examples which may be special, but which must be typical and pregnant—should at least try to give us is a general sense of what, under various disguises, *superiority* has always signified and may still signify. The feeling for a good human job anywhere, the admiration of the really admirable, the disesteem of what is cheap and trashy and impermanent—this is what we call the critical sense, the sense for ideal values. It is the better part of what men know as wisdom. [30]

Since knowledge can grow only by a free exchange of information and experiences, the cause of literacy can be greatly advanced by the interchange of technicians and scholars in all areas of the sciences and the humanities, and especially the exchange of students. It is imperative that this interchange of men and women take place on college and university levels.

For interchange of ideas, it is essential that the study of foreign languages be made more effective the world over. The public school systems of the United States are weak in their foreign language program, a decided structural defect. Much time is wasted on the secondary level because a student's knowledge of a foreign language too often stops short of being functionally useful. In recent years, the barrier of an interpreter has often blocked international understanding and negotiation. Literacy in the United States includes the skillful use, not only of English, but of other languages as well, in the interest of universal education and communication—a goal that is remote but not impossible of attainment. Dr. James B. Conant in his recent report deplores the practice of permitting students to get a smattering of one or more languages without mastery of any. He found that students as well as teachers feel that two years of study do not provide a working knowledge of a language. Dr. Conant's recommendation of four years of study would yield large dividends.

If adults were not so complacent about their educational systems, they would be more concerned about the high school and college

[30] From William James, *Memories and Studies* (New York, Longmans, Green & Co., Inc., 1911).

students who leave school or college, the "drop-outs" whose leaving should be construed as a challenge to the efficiency of the school system and the cultural climate of the community. Certainly, there are many reasons why students end their formal schooling. Of the eight million or so of high school students, probably 25 per cent may be classified as "bright"; that is, they are potential college material, yet not half of them enter college. Not one student in six finishes high school. These statistics deserve the sober thought of educators if the ranks of the literate are to be increased and the millions of the half-educated reduced. A report of the United States Office of Education (March, 1958) states that one out of four students drops out of college in the first year of enrollment. More than one-fifth of those who quit permanently are in the top 20 per cent of their high school graduating class. Lawrence G. Derthick, Education Commissioner, described this as a "distressing waste of talent, particularly when the number of eighteen-year-olds in our population is very low." He added that this was the population group the country would look to for leadership twenty to twenty-five years from now. [31]

CALL FOR ACTION

If it is conceded that less than a high degree of literacy involves hazards affecting the well-being of the human race, then a peremptory call to action deserves top priority in all countries everywhere now. To implement the call for action, certain trends should be accelerated.

1. Literacy is virtually synonymous with education on all levels from the preschool age to adulthood. Improvement in education should begin in the local area, extending to wider and wider areas until it becomes a global enterprise. Communities should shake off their apathy to the quality of education provided for all age levels, demanding better teaching and administration, and providing funds to subsidize quality.

   Communities should face the fact that a high level of literacy demands better holding power of secondary schools. The conditions that prevail in New York City are true more or less through-

[31] *New York Times*, March 2, 1958.

out the United States. One of every three pupils entering a New York City high school drops out before attaining his diploma, according to Dr. Morris Krugman, assistant superintendent in charge of guidance in the New York schools.

The holding power of our 54 academic high schools is 74 per cent thus far. That of the 31 vocational high schools is only 45 per cent. The combined holding power of our 85 high schools is 66 per cent.

Predicting that the final figures will run even lower, Dr. Krugman reported that boys and girls leave school because of failure in their studies, particularly in reading and arithmetic; low educational motivation; excessive absence and lateness; poor health; difficulties at home; and poor personal relationships. [32]

2. Synonymous also with literacy are skills in reading, the habit of reading widely in the sciences and the humanities, taste and discrimination in selecting what to read, and, especially, judgment in appraising the value of what is read. The best criterion for measuring the efficiency of a school is its program of reading instruction. According to Carlyle, "All that a university, or final highest school can do for us, is still but what the first school began doing, teach us to read."

3. Society must set a higher value on "the individual man, not the organization man, not the mass man of modern manipulations, the individual man multiplied by his millions through the nation, but always the individual man journeying toward fulfillment." [33]

It is futile to indulge in a jeremiad about the future of the human race. The hazards can be removed if the intellectual and spiritual resources are mobilized on local, national, and international levels. Where there is vision, the people need not perish.

[32] Report made at the regional meeting of the American Association of School Administrators, in Cleveland, April 6, 1955.
[33] From Jack Schaefer, "Desert Where the Spirit Flowers," *Think* (July, 1959).

16

LUELLA B. COOK

The Search for Standards

T WO DIFFERENT but equally important concepts clash unceasingly in our minds, creating a dilemma which is the source of educational confusion:

The concept of *growth and development* of the individual to his highest capacity.

The concept of *achievement*—the intrinsic worth of which is to be rated or judged.

The producer and the product; the person and the "thing" outside himself which he has brought about—these are the two poles of concern between which we swing. This is the root of the philosophic dilemma which underlies that unfortunate slogan, popular but a few years ago: "Teach the child, not the subject." This is the false dichotomy which split our ranks and set two equally important ideas at odds with one another. This is the Humpty-Dumpty which somehow must be put together again as we search for a new concept of "standards."

To teach the child obviously refers to that particular orientation of teaching, especially appropriate at the elementary level, which seeks to nurture growth of the individual. It puts development of the child's native abilities as the central aim and uses the study of a subject as a means to that end. It recognizes that fumbling is a legitimate phase of learning and that the premature insistence on specific requirements may not only retard growth but may actually block achievement. It faces the fact that people learn not only at different rates but to different degrees—along any scale of values— and that in intellectual growth, as well as physical, nature cannot be coerced. There is not only a right and wrong *way* to apply pressure; there is a right and wrong *time* to set fixed standards for achievement. Human beings mature gradually, and growth of the individual is

LUELLA B. COOK Formerly Consultant in Curriculum Development in the Public Schools of Minneapolis, Minnesota. Classroom Teacher of English, Central High School, Minneapolis. President of NCTE, 1955-1956. Recipient of Distinguished Achievement Award, University of Minnesota, 1953. Citation, Minneapolis Citizens' Committee on Public Education, 1955. Chairman NCTE Committee on Evaluation of Pupil Performance. Author and coauthor of literature textbooks.

uneven and spasmodic. "Teaching the child" may, for this reason, be regarded as good husbandry in the classroom, and education under this banner considered less like the building of a house and more like the careful tending of a plant.

Except as it disregards another point of view, equally important, this orientation of teaching cannot be assailed. It is one of the outstanding advances in thinking which mark our age. Yet there is a time and a place, also, *to teach the subject*—if we may let the phrase stand for a quite different orientation of teaching, appropriate at all levels of education, though in increasing proportion in high school and college. Whenever attention is turned outward to the task at hand with the child or the student expected to adapt himself to its requirements, rather than expecting the task to be adapted to his needs or preferences, we have obviously shifted our focus of attention. Our difficulty with standards arises when we fail to see that both approaches are important, and that neither one should be sacrificed to the other.

Roughly dating from Sputnik, our reaction against "teaching the child" has been sharp, and at times, violent. At least, there has been widespread criticism of what is called "soft pedagogy" and a persistent clamor for a return to "teaching the subject." While it was but a short time ago that we discarded the so-called philosophic absolute—that concept of a fixed standard by which to judge success—now with equal fervor we seem ready to abandon the concept of relativity, as applied to judgment of pupil performance. We seem to long for the old certainties that make evaluation easy and uncomplicated. The new danger that faces us is that instead of harmonizing the two concepts—those of growth and achievement—we shall but support anew the dichotomy that has plagued us for so long, and but trade one set of errors for another.

If we accept the dual responsibility of the school—*to the individual* (to provide for his growth) and *to society* (to train those capable of being trained in specific competencies)—then it follows that we must also recognize two different, but equally valid, concepts of evaluation: the concept of relative judgment, when we are evaluating growth, or development; the concept of objective measurement when we are judging specific achievement. It is the intermingling of these two concepts in our evaluation of pupil performance that has created confusion and hampered us in our search for standards. By what criteria shall we judge progress? Standards are applicable only to the concept of achievement; yet growth is in itself a kind of achievement which should be recognized—though not in the same terms as scholastic achievement. There's the rub! The very word *standards* connotes different meanings to different people.

Critics of modern education say we have "lost" or "lowered" our standards, while defenders of modern education react to the word with hostility because of the many sins against individual growth committed in its name. What do we mean by standards? What is it that we are supposed to have lost?

To some, the loss of standards seems to refer to a loss of firm content, to the washing away of a fixed body of subject-matter in a flux of "experience," and to a less and less clear-cut image of what achievement in English is. In our zeal to apply the old adage, "experience is the best teacher," perhaps we did yield too easily our teaching prerogatives to select and guide classroom experiences so that they would result in significant learning. Under the banner *teach the child* it is easy to lose track of what, specifically, we are trying to accomplish—just as it is easy, under the banner *teach the subject* to lose track of the individual pupil's growth. *Teaching the child* lost some of the definiteness which is associated with *teaching the subject*. Our aims became more diffuse, more ephemeral, and our content seemed to slip away from us as we wrestled with the terms in which our teaching responsibilities should be expressed.

Some educators seemed to say that the activities we provided for pupils constituted our content. *What pupils did* became easily confused with *what was learned* (as a result). It is quite possible that current reaction against methodology can be traced to this source.

Others equated content with materials, and we weathered a sharp reaction against so-called "textbook teaching," that method of teaching which failed to recognize the need to use different materials to suit different purposes and different levels of ability. And so again our basic content seemed to elude us, in the sense that it became less and less apparent *what* we taught *in common* for *all* pupils.

It is at this point that the source of our confusion becomes clear: while it is possible to identify what it is that all pupils should seek to learn to the best of their ability, it is not possible to identify a specific degree of mastery which can be expected from all pupils. Some provision for individual differences in ability, therefore, must be made.

This fact has long since been accepted as a truism by the teachers of America, and in part been built into our curriculum guides—a glance at which, the country over, will reveal the fact that our English content has been reinterpreted in terms of goals and objectives: *what* it is we seek to accomplish through activities and by means of varied materials: the specific knowledge or understanding, the skills and attitudes, we seek to develop. This is our firm content; these are the values we seek; this is the end in view.

But such a content, firm and definite though it can be, does not fully answer all those who say that we have "lost our standards," though it does pave the way for a resolution of our conflict by identifying content in terms that permit diversity within unity, that recognize both the need for common goals and the fact of individual differences in the ability to attain those common goals. Content expressed in such terms is roughly analogous to a through highway over which many different makes of cars travel at different rates of speed to different destinations. The highway must be well conceived and built to withstand the diverse traffic, but the problems of regulating speed and determining destination involve other factors.

So, in the management of classroom learning: while the need for a firm content impinges on the problem of standards, it does not of itself solve it.

To still others the loss of standards seems to refer to a loss of respect for excellence and a worship of the commonplace. In our zeal to measure growth by the many statistical devices now available, we have, perhaps unconsciously, come to accept the median as our standard of value. What the majority of pupils at any age *can* do with ease by and large is what we aim for. Value has come to be judged not so much on the basis of intrinsic or ideal worth, as on the basis of prevalence or popularity. Polls and statistical ratings have conditioned us to the unexpressed, but firmly held, belief that "whatever is, is right." Since Sputnik, however, we are beginning to question this point of view, as though we vaguely realized a kind of betrayal of that innate respect which unconsciously we hold for a hierarchy of values—a belief in a *better* and a *best* as well as a *good*;

a value that is not to be found by studying the normal curve; something which science can measure but not create. That value, or those values, belongs to our subject-matter field, and are not to be found by looking at our pupils. Instead, we must look at our subject, study it well, to discover the many possibilities it offers to those who seek to learn its secrets.

It might be said in passing that along with the tremendous increase in knowledge about child growth and development over the past fifty years has come also a tremendous increase in knowledge about the nature of language itself and the part it plays both in personal growth and social development. Similarly, our understanding of the role of literature in life has deepened with the result that the values we now seek in the teaching of English have become less obvious and matter of fact and more intricate and subtle.

If, then, we think of these values to be sought (our content) stretching from *A* to *Z* along a horizontal line (figuratively referred to earlier in this article as a highway) we must also, to complete our picture, think of vertical lines intersecting that horizontal line, each one representing the *degrees of success* to which our content (or values) may be learned. Such a scale will be built not only out of a knowledge of our subject, but also out of a knowledge of the learning process as it relates to language and literature. Such a scale will range from the first visible attempts to recognize or apply any of the values identified along our horizontal line to complete understanding and skilled performance. Not yet, however, has such a scale been put widely into use, and only now are we returning to the idea of identifying various levels of performance in each of the language arts, against which to measure an individual's success.

What is *good writing? good reading?* Against what scale shall we measure the intrinsic worth of a particular product? Pupils at all ages need to acquire a sense of what excellence means, of what, in any situation, mastery is. This is not to say that they must achieve excellence in order to appreciate it. Indeed, the more subtle task confronting us is to help pupils of all ages distinguish between what is *good in itself* (as judged by stated criteria) and what is *good for them* (under varying circumstances). Teachers, too, need to distinguish constantly between improvement and significant achievement. The balance is a delicate one, taxing constantly our ability to hold fast to two important concepts which are interrelated but not mutually exclusive.

How shall we, ourselves, recognize and help pupils to understand that what may be "good" performance for them at their particular state of development is not good enough to qualify them to undertake tasks that call for a higher level of ability than they have as yet attained? How can we help them to recognize and respect degrees of excellence which lie beyond their own powers to achieve, at the same time to maintain faith in themselves? This is our problem as we search for some new concept of standards that will serve fairly both the individual and society.

What, then, are *standards*? At this point we may well ask the question again, as we search for a more definitive answer. Presumably, they refer to a particular place on any scale of values below which scores are looked upon as disqualifying a person—from what? In common practice, from receiving a "passing grade" or—in the opinion of the teacher—a "satisfactory" rating. Standards for "passing" vary widely from teacher to teacher, and the only constant seems to be the marks we use to designate degrees of success: *A, B, C, D–F.* These marks have long since lost their common denominator and in actual practice seem to refer both to growth and to achievement. Satisfactory performance, in other words, may refer either to expected *improvement,* or it may refer to the *quality* of a particular product, or it may refer to a blend of both.

The solution to our problem of standards, then, is not to be found merely in a return to the use of these standardized symbols of judgment but in a clarification of the question just posed: If a standard is, in truth, that place on a scale of values below which one is disqualified, we need a better answer to the question: *From what* (disqualified)? than is at present to be found in the conventional reply: "from passing."

Outside the classroom, standards are determined by the necessities inherent in any given situation, to meet which a person seeks to qualify himself. For example, all drivers of automobiles must measure up to a specific "standard" of competency. They must pass a driver's test which has been set up to measure that minimum degree of skilled performance required for safety on the road. That "passing" grade, in other words, is determined by factors inherent in the traffic situation. Not all people of any age group must pass the test; only those who wish to drive automobiles. Those who cannot pass the test are not allowed to drive cars.

The responsibility of driving a car is but one of hundreds of responsibilities, both large and small, which life imposes on those who are able and who wish to assume them. Those who cannot meet the standards imposed by such responsibilities quite obviously should not be entrusted with them.

In school as well as out of school this principle holds: the principle that to do certain things one must "have (or develop) what it takes." At all levels of education, in other words—elementary, secondary, and college, there are situations which, in themselves, make legitimate demands on those who are to be entrusted with the responsibility of meeting that situation, or of qualifying themselves for meeting it later on.

It is not teachers or adults who arbitrarily set up standards; it is rather circumstances. While it is beyond question that the calibre of our students must be taken into account before they are expected to meet particular standards, it is not their calibre as such that determines standards; it is, rather, the nature of the responsibility which they are expected to assume. Pupils of limited ability should not be expected to assume responsibilities beyond their powers. But neither should pupils of great ability be expected to meet standards solely for the purpose of demonstrating their ability to do so. Such aimless contests of skill may be exciting, sporting adventures. It is difficult to defend them as *education*.

Not all "superior" students are college-bound, nor is superior ability, as statistically measured, the sole prerequisite for success in college. Average ability, plus a high degree of interest and industry, is likely to go farther than superior native ability bogged down in apathy and laziness.

What we so obviously need at the moment is a concept of standards that will operate effectively for all levels of ability; which will hold in high esteem the job-well-done regardless of its size: the lowly task perfectly performed, as well as the large, complex responsibility skillfully executed. Quality applies to small things as well as to big. In our efforts to recapture our concern for quality, we run the new danger of worshipping, not significance, but size.

A clue to such a concept lies close at hand: in most schools the curriculum includes both Required Courses and Elective Courses— Required Courses (subjects) for all pupils; Electives, for some—in many cases only those who can qualify. English is a Required Course in every grade—at least up through Grade 11. Common Electives in English are: Creative Writing, Speech, Commercial (or Business) English, Modern Drama, and, more rarely, the systematized study of grammar. This does not exhaust the possibilities for other English Electives, but it does illustrate a curriculum organization that might be used to accommodate the two differing, but equally important, responsibilities referred to earlier—to the individual and to society. It might be assumed, for example, that in Required English, common goals would be sought (those values identified along the horizontal line referred to on page 243, and representing our content) and pupil-performance judged on a relative basis; that in all Electives, specialized goals would be sought and standards maintained: that is, a particular level of performance in relation to the four language arts (as indicated on the *vertical* line referred to on page 243) would be indicated as a minimum degree both for acceptance into the course and satisfactory performance within it.

Not only would Electives be organized differently from Required English, and students oriented to them differently, but admission to them would be based on careful teacher guidance as well as on student preference. The name itself might change. It is used here merely to refer to an organizational plan that already exists in many schools of America and could, therefore, serve as the basis for a new organization designed to provide more adequately for both growth and achievement. Required Courses might be oriented around the concept, "Teach the child;" Electives, around the concept, "Teach the Subject." When we "teach the child," we may assume, we pursue goals; when we "teach the subject," we maintain standards. It is the unconscious intermingling of the two concepts that has clouded the whole problem of grouping.

In Electives, standards might be set up on the basis of what degree of proficiency in the four language arts the special subject calls for; or, what degree of interest or aptitude is essential to success or satisfaction; or, yet again, what special demands the subject makes upon the pupil.

In Required English attention would center not so much on common achievement relating to the subject being studied, as in individual growth in the four language arts. Here, in other words, the content might be regarded more as a means to an end than as an end in itself.

Obviously, the marking system used in Required Courses would justifiably be different from that used in Electives; whereas, in Required Courses there would undoubtedly be occasions for the objective appraisal of the worth of a product in relation to a particular set of criteria—by and large, performance would not be rated A, B, C, D–F. These marks have meaning only in relation to a fixed standard of achievement and only confuse the issue when used to indicate individual improvement. While they might serve well in Electives, where students study a subject, and the degree of mastery of that subject is an important consideration, they do not serve as well in Required Courses, where students seek to develop language power.

The teaching approach would also be different in the two types of courses. The point can be well illustrated in relation to the study of grammar: in Required English, the functional approach seems the more appropriate; in an Elective, in Grades 11 or 12, a systematic study of grammar as a subject is justified.

For years we have been complaining that at the completion of Grade 12 pupils do not "know their grammar." *What* pupils? we might ask, and, in what manner, *know*? Not all pupils know their grammar equally well, or as well, perhaps, as they should, but many know more than we give them credit for; however, they "know it" in a way that must be deduced from the way they use language in speech and writing, rather than from a test on grammar as such. For many pupils, perhaps, this way is sufficient, and before we repudiate that way, we might well reflect on how grateful we ourselves would be if we "knew" the grammar of a foreign language in this very same way—as knowledge absorbed unconsciously, and used, rather than learned consciously.

Like other phases of our English program, grammar can be regarded both as a subject to be studied thoroughly, and as a tool in the development of language power. For many pupils, it is important to study grammar formally, *as a subject*. For others, it is less important. For the latter, a knowledge of grammar will become internalized (as it does for most adults, including many teachers) as a part of their speaking and writing equipment. For many students it is less important that they know the parts of the sentence than it is that they can express their thoughts clearly. To the extent that a knowledge of the parts of a sentence will help them improve their expression, grammar should be taught, and is taught, *functionally*— a term which might well be applied to other phases of the English program in Required Courses as well.

Although no contrasting term has as yet been coined to indicate the teaching approach more appropriate to Elective courses, we might call it the "objective approach." By *objective approach* is meant the direct pursuit of special knowledge as contrasted with the development of language power. The two approaches are not exclusive, consistent entities, but the broad difference in orientation they suggest offers a clue for relieving that common frustration in the classroom which comes from confusing these two broad, general aims—a confusion which stems from the manner in which we state our aims or objectives. Here, for example, are some of the common goals set up for Required Courses, chosen at random:

To *understand* the structure of the English sentence.

To *appreciate* the form of a play.

To *respond* to the mood of a poem.

Understanding, appreciating, responding, are relative terms. Some students' "understanding" will be deeper than others and their "response" will be more intense, or more verbal. While the goals (or aims or objectives) are the same for all pupils, achievement will vary.

In the study of a subject, goals might be stated quite differently so as to accommodate the concept of standards, for in an Elective our aim is the conquest of a field of study. Aims corresponding to the above, therefore, might be expressed as follows:

To distinguish accurately between the parts of a sentence: subject, predicate, modifiers.

To define a plot.

To distinguish between a lyric and a ballad.

When objectives are stated in this way, it is obvious that partial knowledge is of little or no value. One must know all three parts of a sentence if he is going to understand sentence structure. One can tell a ballad from a lyric or he cannot, and if a student fails to master too many of such items of subject-matter content, he has obviously failed to fulfill the purpose of the course.

True, the pupil may not master all these concepts at once; he may move gradually, in several steps, from vague ideas to clear, concise expression of them. Still, the ultimate goal when one studies a subject is to arrive at a specified point, and judgment of whether one has or has not is simple and unconfused. It is when we intermingle the two concepts, referred to by the words *goals* and *standards,* that we run into difficulty and become "tough" or "soft" in the wrong places. It is impossible, for example, to demand or to insist upon *understanding* or *appreciation* or *response* without running the danger of defeating our purpose. Nor should we grow "tough" about the right things in the wrong places. Some pupils should never be held to distinguishing between a lyric and a ballad, albeit they should be helped to a kind of appreciation of both—an appreciation based more on *emotional response to,* however, than on *intellectual understanding of.*

Briefly, then, it seems reasonable to suppose that in Required English, goals would be set up in terms of what we wish to accomplish in the way of development: to improve reading skills, to appreciate literature as an art form; to improve writing and speaking ability, and so on; and that, in Elective (or assigned) Courses, aims would be expressed in terms of results expected—those results determined by the nature of the subject and the student's purposes in studying it: distinguishing features of the one act play; style of writing appropriate in business letters; five requirements of good reporting, and so forth.

It follows that teaching methods would also be different in these two types of courses. Just as grammar can be taught both functionally and as a subject, so can Shakespeare or News Writing or any other course set up within our field. In an Elective in Shakespeare, we may assume a minimum of reading competency and proceed accordingly. The reading of a Shakespearean play in a Required Course, however, permits no such assumption, and teaching methods would take this fact into consideration. The free use of films and recordings and simplified versions of the text would all aim at helping the slow student to follow the plot, understand the characters, and grasp, as well as he is able, the theme or significance of the play as a whole. Our disappointment in pupil performance frequently arises from our own failure to gear our expectations to a valid purpose. We look for mastery instead of growth and unconsciously measure our own success in those terms.

I have been suggesting an organizational clue that will break the deadlock between two equally important concepts of education and permit us to fulfill a dual teaching responsibility—to the individual and to society—without conflict. To build upon this clue requires the nurture of two basic attitudes, both within our students and within ourselves: a respect for excellence, and a respect for the task to be done. We face daily the problem of playing fair both with our pupils and with our subject; of dealing understandingly and compassionately with the immaturities of our pupils, yet also of retaining our own loyalty to the subject that we teach, recognizing its true worth, despite the many flagrant violations of its disciplines. But our pupils are caught in the same tension: to hold on to a belief in themselves, regardless of their failures in accomplishment, at the same time that they seek to move closer to the goals we have set for them.

How, then, do we build in the minds of our pupils a respect for the excellence which they themselves cannot attain? By the process known as "ability grouping?" That's one way, but it is questionable whether it is the best way to develop in *all* our pupils both a respect for excellence beyond their powers to achieve and a respect for the task at hand—no matter how humble.

In building the first attitude, perhaps we can take a leaf from the sportsman's creed; we can differentiate between amateur and professional standing. In sport the amateur—even the dub—is in good social standing. Yet, how enthusiastically he applauds the achievement of the champion! He knows what championship is and exults in mastery—from the sidelines, to be sure, where most of us must sit. But in a democracy the "sidelines" are important, and to the degree that the masses support their leaders intelligently, is democracy secure from the hazards of social explosions caused by the accumulated resentment of those who have learned secretly to envy but never to admire openly.

The inculcation of such an attitude might conceivably be one of the goals of Required Courses, an attitude that would aid in the selection of students for Elective (or assigned) Courses. But there is another attitude even more basic to the maintenance of standards in Elective Courses: as previously referred to, it is respect for the job at hand, a belief in its priority over and above one's own immediate inclination. The success of a subject-oriented course will depend upon the study habits of the students who elect or are assigned to the course, and the development of these, in turn, might well be one of the goals sought in all Required Courses. Too frequently, it is merely assumed that students *should* be able to accept responsibility for an assignment, without appropriate steps being taken to develop a sense of responsibility.

Even elementary pupils are familiar with the concept, "The play must go on," or "The school paper must come out on the day promised"—regardless of the personal convenience of leading man or editor. In countless activities, we stress this need and in so doing help to build in the minds of our students a pride in the enterprise itself. We have only to apply the same insight more widely to problems of individual study. When, for example, is one just learning (by experience), and when demonstrating what one has learned or performing publicly on that basis? When is it permissible to make mistakes in a trial and error type of learning; and when is it legitimate that we should be held to account? What is the difference between private writing (for practice) and public communication? And what are the special responsibilities one automatically assumes in the latter which he need not heed in the former?

These are distinctions rarely made in our judgments of pupil performance, and the two concepts have become confusingly intertwined, with the result that we are fair neither to our students nor to our subject but dangle helplessly between two major considerations, both of which deserve our allegiance.

It is to the clarification of such issues as the foregoing that we must look before we can settle the problem of standards. Our "search for standards," in other words, leads us out in many different directions that embrace the whole curriculum. Yet the issue itself may serve us well in this time of public debate on education—as a lens through which we may re-examine our entire English program.

The issue brings to mind a grand piano that stands awkwardly in the middle of the room into which a newcomer's furniture has just been moved but not yet placed. There it is, blocking all progress in the settling of the room. But once its position has been decided, all the other pieces seem to fall easily into place.

Just so does the problem of standards seem to interfere with the solution of many other curriculum problems. Could we but clarify for ourselves this issue, many other problems would automatically be solved.

17

MARK A. NEVILLE

Custom Serves for Reason

T HE TEACHING and learning of English have been criticized from generation to generation. Criticism will continue as long as those responsible for the teaching of English dare not disobey what Custom has ordained. The blind following of Custom has created false ideas of values and, too frequently, has made English an unpopular academic subject.

Custom has decreed that "English," or the "English Language Arts," now a popular and more precise designation particularly on the elementary school level, should be taught only by a "specialist" in English. *Reason* suggests that all teachers who communicate in the English language should be well versed in grammar and rhetoric, oral and written composition, and the mechanics of style. But little attention is given by educators to the voice of *Reason*.

Laymen are forever challenging the schools to teach sentence structure, grammar, punctuation, and spelling. Many specialists in the English teaching and learning process contend that the traditional approaches have failed to produce a people confident in their oral and written expression. The layman and the specialist have a right to be concerned: the speech behavior of American children, youths, and adults leaves much to be desired. Reading ability is considered, generally, to be poor; and personal written expression by the average man is becoming obsolete.

For far too many students, English is a stumbling block on the path of academic progress. They see no reason to master what English teachers pronounce "correct" in language structure, and fail to see the "obvious beauty" in a selection of literature highly praised by the teacher who frequently accepts the word of the textbook author. The causes of student reactions are obvious. Teachers of English are unable to agree on what English *is* and what English *is not*. For

MARK A. NEVILLE   Professor of English, Indiana State Teachers College. Formerly Headmaster and Teacher of English, The Latin School of Chicago. Head of the English Department and Director of Public Relations, John Burroughs School, St. Louis. President of NCTE, 1949-1950. Editor of Book Lists, NCTE *Your Reading, Books for You.* Author and editor of numerous texts in literature and language arts for elementary and secondary schools.

255

example, some teachers of English insist that a knowledge, understanding, and command of the traditionally accepted principles of
English grammar are absolutely necessary as a foundation for appropriate expression, oral and written, and for an appreciation of
literature. Some other teachers question many of the accepted principles, suggest that traditional grammar is false, and emphasize function and usage rather than a formal study of a well-organized traditional "course" in grammar. Still other teachers have no ideas of their
own, are blown about by every wind of fashionable doctrine, consider the latest textbook the best, and so follow blindly the "new
approach" which they do not prepare themselves to understand.

Some teachers believe in *intensive* courses in literature; some in
extensive courses. Some would defend the teaching of *Silas Marner*
as a great exposition of inevitable progress caused by change; some
would prefer to teach *Catcher in the Rye* as an introduction to adolescence seeking security; and some few might possibly wish to express their academic freedom by teaching *Lady Chatterley's Lover* as
a classic example of the decadence of the English middle class, the
down-to-earth awful honesty of the bewildered transitional man, and
the dogged stupidity of the lower class.

There are many approaches to the teaching of English; there are
many ways of organizing content to be taught and learned; there are
so many resources from which content may be selected, that it is
little wonder there are so many differences among English courses of
study in public schools and course outlines in independent (private)
schools. The result is that, to too many students, English means little
more than confusion.

Every teacher of English, every teacher of other subjects, every
parent, and every student must be taught the fact that the definite
purpose of the teaching of English is to help the student to say, to
hear, to read, and to write a simple idea, observation, or experience in
a simple or plain way. *Reason* says, "This is a consummation devoutly
to be sought." And it can be attained; but not through any present-
day organization for the teaching and learning of English with which
I am familiar. Only by redefining the role of English in education as
a whole, by giving teachers of English a new direction, by setting up
a plan for the instruction of all teachers in the teaching of practical
English, and by planning activities that are fundamental to the

teaching-learning process in every curriculum area in the school will the basic aims of the teaching of English be realized. English is the language of the American people, the language through which they send and receive ideas and impressions. It is one common basis of our common culture.

Our reasonable plea is for a distinct and thoroughgoing reorganization of educational administration so that approaching English as a "content" subject competing for time with other subjects each day be recognized as an impracticable organization. The point we stress is that English should be made a condition of school life, and that part of the responsibility of every teacher should be to see that it is. English should be the framework which makes it possible for all subjects to attain the heights of humanness. English content is derived from all patterns of the culture and is contrived in the light of student personal needs as reflected by societal demands. Many young minds do not accept as important an "English-Class English" that apparently is not the concern of non-English teachers.

The plight of teachers of English is to be pitied. They are an uncertain people, dedicated to "they don't know what," but bitterly critical of the place of English in American education, and most intelligently concerned about the "English" background of some administrators and fellow teachers.

The teacher of English, the 1960 active expounder of the faith, has inherited professionally: 1. a specious ancestry, 2. an apathetic parentage, and 3. a weak culture. These unstable foundations have standardized a fallacious framework within which English courses of study circulate. Reason has spoken many times; and each time has asked, "What is Truth?" and jesting teachers of subjects other than English would not stay for an answer.

We do not need, it may be said, to be taught English; to write and to read, in Dogberry's opinion, comes by nature. This view is, perhaps, not likely to be now so crudely stated, but it has long been acted upon by many who are engaged in education, and is acquiesced in by many who control it. . . . It is an instance of the divorce of education from reality, which we have already found to be a main cause of failure in the past. English may come, by nature, up to a certain point; but that point is soon reached, and thenceforth the possibility of mental development, in whatever direction, is seriously diminished for those who have not achieved mastery of their mother tongue. What a man cannot clearly state, he does not perfectly know, and, conversely, the inability to put his thought into words sets a boundary to his thought. [1]

From time to time, new approaches to educational planning have been labeled "the teacher-centered school," "the parent-centered school," "the child-centered school." Each has had its day. Each failed because it was not based on the assumption that a sound educational system must have as its keystone the conviction that human speech, the spoken and written word, is the foundation of communication. So we now propose to disobey Custom and plead reasonably for an organization which we shall call, *The English-Centered School*.

The English-Centered School must be based on the fact that all children, youths, and adults in the United States are born in a culture or come into a culture in which English is the instrument of thought and the means of communication. It is the instrument through which individual capacity is released. It is the pattern through which we learn. Every teacher is a teacher of English because he teaches in English, and it is necessary that his general education be sufficiently pertinent to ensure unceasing instruction in the English language!

Teachers of English have not failed. As a matter of fact, it is surprising how well they have done in the light of little or no help from curriculum specialists, administrators, and fellow teachers. If the learning of English is to be highly efficient, conception of the teaching of English must be changed, and courses of study liquidated. Not only must there be recognition of the insufficiency of nation-wide English programs but also the so-called subject matter of English courses must be faithfully, carefully, and honestly studied; and the trivia must be excluded no matter how long they have held a place of importance.

As the core of American education, English must be recognized as the most important humanizing influence. And what we choose to call *English* should never have been a specialized subject for teaching in secondary schools. Almost all teachers who do not teach English in secondary schools have had no English course beyond the required

[1] *The Teaching of English in England,* Board of Education: Committee on the Position of English in the Educational System of England (London, H.M. Stationery Office, 1921).

"Freshman English." The awful fact seems to be that the departmentalization of education experiences into subjects has created specialists in science, mathematics, foreign languages, social studies, art, music, drama, speech, physical education, and English. Each specialist has been recognized as an expert in his field and slowly and surely has acquired a vested interest in it. But the part English plays in national education has not been made clear. And it never can be made clear under the present directions "core courses" and "humanities courses" are taking, for the obvious reason that English is not a subject-matter specialty as is history, mathematics, and science. English is a condition! It transcends all other subjects because upon it all other subjects depend. The English teacher, as a lone specialist to teach students the social-practical aspects of communication (speaking, listening, reading, writing, and studying), has been ineffective because his assignment has been impossible.

We have come to the realization that, when the English teacher was created, his spiritual, symbolic inimical "non-English teacher" was also created. The non-English teacher is a specialist in an area that can well be defined. He understands that English is difficult to define and, therefore, because he is uncertain, is likely to belittle the importance of English. In other words, departmentalization absolves him of all responsibility to teach his students what they need to be taught in order better to compose ideas in oral and written expression, and, as a defense for his ignorance, he is hypercritical of teachers of English because, "he (the student) just don't know the King's English. He don't know how to spell; he can't footnote. What good is all this poetry stuff anyway?" So non-teachers of English have been developed (unwittingly, I am sure) in many college level institutions. And many of these teachers become administrators who take pride in their admitted opinions that English is unimportant. Something has to be done!

The teacher must exist before the student. If we are to make the education of the American youth and adult better than it is, teachers must be taught the ideals of a liberal education which is founded on the practical and esthetic bases of communication. Although we recognize the importance of a liberal education as the foundation for teaching as a profession, we must also insist that students who desire to teach prepare to teach before they take on the responsibilities.

State regulations control the practice of medicine, law, and other professions. Certainly the most important of all professions—teaching —should be under the careful scrutiny of the state, not as a police action, but as a helpful endeavor to raise standards for teaching and for preparation for teaching in public and independent schools. I know there are many who will object to this point of view, but I have never been willing to accept the occasional Mr. Chips, who does not come up to accepted professional standards, as representative of the quality of all substandard teachers. I hold that, unless practical standards which all teachers must meet are set up, teaching will merely consist of jobs held by some competent teachers whose professional attitudes, spirit, and even income will continue to be down-graded by those teachers who take pride in never having taken a course in "Education," and furthermore never intend to take one.

To realize our purpose, which is to place qualified teachers in all schools—and we hold that any teacher who cannot teach the practical aspects of English is unqualified—we must state emphatically that colleges of liberal arts, colleges of education, and colleges of technology that are preparing students to teach should require a stated number of practical English courses of all prospective teachers. After the completion of the required content courses, all should take another required course in which the principles and practices of the teaching of English in the English-centered school will be propounded and discussed. Following such courses the teacher will be ready to fulfill the required apprenticeship or practice-teaching assignment which will call for lesson-planning to include the teaching of the aspects of practical English related to the concepts and content under discussion. Naturally, such a plan will serve to decimate the number of other education courses, required and elective; but, I am sure, the added quality of content and instruction will fully compensate for the diminished quantity. And more important, English will be related to education as a whole.

This plan means that the teacher of English in the old tradition will become expendable. This idea is based on the assumption that what we call English has a two-fold function: first, English is social-practical, that is speaking, listening, reading, writing, and studying about the past, present, and future in everyday affairs; second, English is social-esthetic, that is creation, participation, and enjoyment of literature in its many forms of fiction and nonfiction expressed in prose and verse. We can train any person of average intelligence to teach phonics, spelling, vocabulary, sentence structure, grammar, usage, punctuation, capitalization, paragraphing; and possibly unity, coherence, and emphasis. (If he cannot learn these things he should not teach; he has no more right to teach than the person interested in law but not a member of the bar has a right to practice law.) But the teaching of literature is something else.

The enjoyment of literature means an experience in creative reception. In the fine sense, literature cannot be taught. And because of this fact the attempt to expose students en masse in schools has not produced a population educated to select literature discriminatingly for leisure time reading. Teaching is usually associated with acquiring knowledge, information, and discipline. In this sense, the teaching of literature has been a failure. Literature must not be thought of as a lesson to be mastered; rather, it is something alive, timeless, a supreme experience in understanding and enjoying the results of the process of man talking meaningfully and enthusiastically to man through the centuries. Literature consists of the voices that represent all peoples, and the harmonies they produce can never be heard by the average man until literature is recognized as an art and taught as such. The teacher of literature should be endowed with the ability to transmit his enthusiasm and to help students to recreate another's experiences. *The literature teacher should have some controlled histrionic ability.* He must be able to discuss intelligently and discreetly the motivations that cause tragedy and comedy; and he must know his students well enough to select, with and for them, literature of recognized excellence for study that will challenge their intellects and provide a continuity of experience in their cultural growth. His students must become his partners in greatness.

A university degree, simple or complex, is not a guaranty that one can teach literature. Therefore, we cannot entrust the teaching of literature to a person merely because he has majored in English. It may well be that some of our most effective teachers of literature are in mathematics or fine arts. At least, we should find out. Of course, we must keep in mind the fact that in order to assign a literature course to one not trained to teach literature (as if one can be trained to do so), we must convince the state departments of education that literature is not a measurable subject, such as mathematics, and that academic distinction may be a warrant for a fine mind but not for a spirit that motivates appreciation. The way to recognize a true teacher of literature is a discussion in itself; therefore, I shall now return to the teaching of the social-practical aspects of English which is the business of every teacher because he teaches in English.

We must retain the present-day teacher of English, but because we have eliminated the traditional pattern for teaching English, he must be given a new direction. His old responsibility should be questioned because he was assigned the impossible, and although he tried valiantly, suffered immensely, and died gloriously, he did not succeed. What is his descendant's new direction? His new direction is to initiate the teaching of English in the English-centered school. He will gradually work out the plans to modify the present-day organizations and work toward the reasonable point of view suggested in this discussion. He will really be a supervisor of the all-school (meaning *all-teacher*) approach to the teaching and learning of practical English.

Our newly directed teacher of English would be responsible for the in-service training in practical English activities for all teachers; for setting up minimum essentials of English-language competence from kindergarten through grade twelve (we would break down the artificial barriers between elementary and secondary school English programs by training our supervisor of practical English to cover the entire range); for direct teaching of students who are not developing at a normal rate; and for evaluating the teaching-learning success in the English principles, techniques, and skills outlined for each grade, kindergarten through twelve.

We must assume that the administrative head of the school is in sympathy with the new approach to the teaching of English. He will outline for assistants in administration and teachers the new direction the teaching of English should take, and will ask the chief supervisor of English to express in detail the formulation of the proposed organization.

The representative of the teachers of English will suggest that the English language-arts in the elementary school and English in the secondary school are not actually subject-matter courses. He will emphasize that English is comprised of patterns of experiences developed through activities that are common to every class meeting of every subject in the curriculum. He will state that the isolated class in English as the only organized group to which the techniques and skills of English are directly taught and to which literature experiences have been suggested has proved to be inadequate. He will assume that only when all teachers accept the responsibilities for teaching and helping students to improve their abilities to communicate and to receive impressions within every area—history, mathematics, literature, foreign language, the fine and practical arts—will full-purpose education in our American democracy be realized. Although specialist teachers of English have done their utmost, they have, unconsciously, but fortunately, proved that *English,* as the word is used in this discussion, cannot be mastered in isolated classes at isolated times.

Teachers of English are not asking help from nonteachers of English; rather, they are assuming a new role and are ready to supplement the work of other teachers. The absurdity of "English Week" has been quite well demonstrated, and the "asking for assistance, 'please, oh, please,'" concept, is false. With the foregoing statement as background, teachers will hold that: 1. the study of English is fundamental to the mastery of all content subjects, and 2. what English is, is debatable. He will then make clear that at the request of the administration, committees will study the practical English needs of students, kindergarten through grade twelve, in Speaking, Listening, Reading, Writing, and Studying. The chairman of each committee will be appointed by the principal of the school. *The chairman will not be a teacher of English;* but a teacher of English will be a member of each committee.

I believe that the following assumptions would come from the above "new directions" study.

1. *The content of English study is derived from societal experiences and student needs as expressed through all activities and studies that require oral and written participation and reading for meaning.*

English is the language with which Americans communicate. Its content is everything expressed and interpreted. English is what is said, written, heard, and seen. Our newspapers, magazines, radio programs, and television shows are English. The Broadway and touring plays are English, for good or bad, that people hear and see. It follows, then, that most human experiences in the United States are in English; and English is, fundamentally, what is understood, not necessarily, what is said. And what is thought about and understood is expressed in language appropriate to the occasion and situation, for instance, "When you call me *that,* smile!"

2. *Standards of appropriate English in speaking and writing should be defined as conditions for in-school and out-of-school living, and should be fostered in all school activities.*

There is no such thing as "correct" English. Correct English is that which English teachers teach, but do not speak. They (the teachers) are controlled by textbook authors who do not always practice what *they* preach. Appropriate English is English for the occasion, yet, there must be standards, and they must be adhered to. *Standards* mean only that one knows when to use "I" or "me"; "who" or "whom"; "apt" or "likely"; "sit" or "set"; "lie" or "lay." Regardless of the "structural linguistics" claim that English grammar is false, all teachers, English and non-English, must learn the "false" before they know what is the true! *They must learn what not to teach*—the essence of good teaching! Although Lord Chesterfield was a "heel," he was a good adviser to his son: "Acquire the graces!"

3. *Any lesson requiring communication through speech and writing should always be a lesson in spoken and written English.*

The English teacher cannot teach magnificently under existing circumstances. One period a day, five days a week, a student studies language and literature with a teacher. The language the English teacher uses has not been mastered by his non-English colleagues. He loves to initiate "English Day," "English Week," and even "English Month," as ways to make other teachers "co-operate." It is high time that *all* lessons be guided in appropriate English. There is one and only one interpretation to this statement—every teacher, who accepts his vocation as a profession, must also accept this golden rule of instruction: I *shall* teach my students art, music, arithmetic, social studies, and science; but *will* teach them how to communicate intelligently, cogently, and gracefully. (I, the writer, am not at all interested in those unprofessional opportunists who "for their bellies sake/ creep and intrude and climb into the fold!/ Blind mouths! that scarce themselves know how to hold/ A sheep-hook, or have learned aught else the least/ That to the faithful herdsman's art belongs!")

4. *Teacher and student knowledge, understanding, and mastery of present-day English grammar and usage are fundamental to effective communication.*

Grammar, as generally thought about and taught about, is a well-defined pattern of principles and rules to be memorized with the hope that the principles and rules will function at some remote time. As a result, classification is emphasized, and immediate function is slighted. Usage is not well defined; and, the fact is evident, that what is acceptable is quite vague.

To be an effective instrument in acquiring communication technique and skills, grammar must be taught as a living and lively experience in thinking. In English, the following is good grammar, but bad construction: "Why, in hell, should I reside when I can dwell in heaven?" When grammar means definitions to be memorized and words and word-groups classified as ways to gain mastery of appropriate English expression, then it is no wonder that almost all students dislike grammar with a single-minded intensity. *Grammar is not* nouns, pronouns, adjectives, verbs, adverbs, conjunctions, prepositions, and interjections! *Grammar is* predicates, subjects, complements, modifiers, connectives, and absolutes *as they function now! The grammar-functions now* are linguistically sound and must be invoked by all teachers as pertinent parts of all subjects, connotative and denotative, as basic for good instruction.

5. *A program of sequential activities, kindergarten through grade twelve, should be set up in speaking, listening, reading, writing, studying, and the induction to literature.*

To insure mastery in listening, speaking, reading, writing, studying, and the induction to literature, I incline toward Admiral Rickover's generalizations, although not to his specifics. The program should be based on minimum essentials determined by faculty observations of student language needs in a particular school. Some persons recognized as specialists in the teaching of English state that students' needs are so varied and different that minimum essentials cannot be prescribed; yet these same critics, who are authors of and editors of textbooks, certainly set up minimum essentials in their basic outlines for the books they publish. If minimum essentials are not stated for a given school other than those in textbooks, then I hold that there is not a thoughtful and dynamic program in practical English for the school.

6. *Needs should be determined in the light of the stated standards for each grade, and the techniques and skills to be taught and re-taught will be specifically outlined as a scope and sequence growth pattern, kindergarten through grade twelve.*

Although there is no standard English, there are standards for English, and they must be recognized as pertinent to all class instruction. The teacher who is not cognizant of the meaning of appropriate English just should not teach. There is no such person as a first, second, seventh, or twelfth grade teacher! Whoever teaches is a teacher of first, second, seventh, or twelfth students; and he teaches *in* English; therefore, he should be a teacher *of* English. He should know that sentences are statements or questions, including *always* predicates and subjects, and usually modifiers and complements. He should know that punctuation is a guide to intelligent reading, and that spelling is quite well standardized. He should know that "lying down" is reclining, and that "laying down" is putting oneself or another object into a place different from where he is now. He should know that his responsibility is to inculcate the concepts of decent and graceful speech.

7. *An all-school recommended reading list should be compiled by English teachers and teachers of other areas. Outside reading must become a condition of school life, and not merely a requirement of the English department.*

Although this essay is not dealing with the teaching of literature as a classroom activity, literature as an experience in creative reception must be considered as a practical matter. The reading of literature is not a daily demand of English teachers; rather, it is a condition of human growth and progress. We propose, therefore, that reading literature be made an extra-learning project of all areas of instruction. The "reading lists" will then become a condition of all-school requirements, and will include readings in all patterns of the culture. Thus, we shall place books in their proper perspective and take the onus off the English teachers.

As an introduction to the new program, we should keep in mind that the learning activities for all grades are the same. The difference is in degree. In the kindergarten, children are taught (we hope) to speak as distinctly as possible, and as they progress from grade to grade their teachers continue to help sharpen their sensitivity. Students are willing, but teachers are not always impressed by the need for graceful speech, nor are the parents of students. For example, if teachers and other adults would stop calling children and youths, "kids," the tone of our social behavior would improve immensely. Undignified name-calling results in undignified action.

There are skeptics, custom-lovers, who will object to my proposals. Yet, I am in good company which calls attention to my point of view. Dr. George F. Homer is reported as saying: [2]

Beginning students in the University of North Carolina achieved very poorly in . . . sections of the test: (1) organization, and (2) sentence structure and style; and (3) most of their difficulties in this subtest (grammar and usage) were with the principal parts of irregular verbs; number of *each* and *one*; the use of *this* and *these*; the use of *who* and *whom*; the use of *it's* and *its*, and so on as has been reported in the *English Journal* from time to time for forty years or more.

And the *Saturday Review*, January 23, 1960, quotes Dr. Edmund S. Morgan, professor of history at Yale as saying to the 1959 freshmen,

Many people suppose they know something if they can stammer out an approximation of what they mean in speech. They are mistaken. It is extremely unlikely that you have thought clearly if you cannot express yourself clearly, especially in writing. Writing is more than an instrument of communication. It is an instrument of thought. You should have acquired some competence in its use by now. *I suspect from past experience that you have not* (author's italics). But even if you have, you have a great deal more to learn about it. And if you do not know much more about it four years from now, it will again be a sign that we have failed in our part of the job, the job of making you communicate clearly.

I submit that the teaching of English is everybody's job! If it is not, the likes of Dr. Homer and Dr. Morgan will be quoted as authorities fifty years from now.

[2] "This World of English," *English Journal*, XLVIII (November, 1959), No. 8, 484.

18

JOSEPH MERSAND

The Teaching of Literature in American High Schools 1865-1900

PREFACE

THROUGHOUT the length and breadth of the land English is taught in the high schools five days a week for four years. It was not always so, and the story of the attainment of English into the pivotal place in the secondary curriculum which it now occupies is a fascinating one. Regardless of the criticisms expressed today about many aspects of English instruction and the outcomes of such instruction, few critics would reduce the time now devoted to the subject. It has been estimated that today the English course of study contains twenty-odd areas ranging from grammar (the first area to be taught) to TV appreciation. Each area had to justify itself before becoming generally accepted, and even today controversy is still carried on over some of them.

Only one area will be considered in this paper—that of teaching literature—itself a topic of debate for almost a century or more. We shall draw a distinction between the teaching of reading and the teaching of literature appreciation and understanding. The former has been well handled in numerous monographs and treatises as part of the history of methodology in reading.

We shall be concerned with some of the following aspects:

1. What was the nature of the literature studied?
2. What types of textbooks were utilized?
3. What methods of teaching were employed?
4. When and where courses in literature were introduced into the high school course?

Our study must of necessity be limited in the number of schools to be studied. Finney states that between 1861 and 1890, the founda-

JOSEPH MERSAND   Chairman of the English department, Jamaica High School, Jamaica, New York. Formerly curriculum co-ordinator, academic high schools, New York City; Principal, James K. Paulding Junior High School. President NCTE, 1958-1959. Chairman, Committee on the Playlist, NCTE. Chairman, editorial board for *Guide to Play Selection,* second edition, 1958. Author of *Chaucer's Romance Vocabulary,* 1939; *Traditions in American Literature,* 1939; *American Drama, 1930-1940,* 1941; *American Drama since 1930,* 1949. Author and coauthor of texts in language and literature and contributor to numerous journals.

tions of the American high school were laid. By 1870, there were 160; by 1880, 800; by 1890, 2800. [1] It is obvious that any generalizations made in this paper could be based on only a small sampling of these many schools of the period being considered.

Some studies have already been made of the high schools in certain areas and might hence be considered as representative for that area. Thus it might be assumed that James Fleming Hosic in his *The Reorganization of English in the Secondary School* speaks for the New England and Middle Atlantic States area. [2] Hertzler writes specifically of the high schools in Connecticut. [3] John E. Stout writes principally of the North Central States. [4] Occasionally a reference is made to the situation in the far West. [5] Further research will obviously uncover new information as courses of study from the high schools in existence from 1865-1900 are obtained, and as statements from teachers, administrators, board members, and students of the time are ascertained. It is significant that in all the sources consulted for this paper not a single reference was found to a statement by a student of the literature of the time. No doubt that with time and effort, such opinions could be obtained, so that we would know how the literature course which is being discussed really affected the recipients of instruction.

---

[1] Ross L. Finney, *A Brief History of the American Public School* (New York, The Macmillan Co., 1927) p. 153. Cf. Edwin Grant Dexter, *A History of Education in the United States* (New York, The Macmillan Co., 1904, [1911]), p. 173.

[2] *Bulletin, 1917, No. 2*, Department of the Interior, Bureau of Education.

[3] Silas Hertzler, *The Rise of the Public High School in Connecticut* (Baltimore, Warwick and York, 1930).

[4] John E. Stout, *The Development of High School Curricula in the North Central States from 1860–1918* (Chicago, University of Chicago Press, 1921).

[5] Elmer Ellsworth Brown, *The Making of Our Middle Schools*, 3rd rev. ed. (New York, Longmans, Green and Co., Inc., 1910), p. 423, n. 1.

I

LITERATURE STUDY BEFORE 1865

L ITERATURE—at least in the form of extracts from the works of great authors—appeared in the educational program with the very first American reader, Noah Webster's *An American Selection of Lessons in Reading and Speaking* (1785), two years after the signing of the treaty of peace. This "was largely made up of the patriotic orations of Hancock, Warren, Ames, Livingston, and other American orators, with the Fourth of July oration of Joel Barlow at the North Church in Hartford." [6] Two competitors of Webster's volume likewise included extracts from the works of famous authors in their books. These were Caleb Bingham's *The American Preceptor* (1794), his *The Columbian Orator* (1797), and Lindley Murray's *English Reader* (1800).

Of Lindley Murray's *Reader*, Lincoln is reputed to have said, ". . . it was the best school book ever put into the hands of an American youth." [7] Caleb Bingham's *The Columbian Orator* has the distinction of being the earliest of a long list of books containing selections from both prose and poetry for reading and declamation as well. Since the tone of these early books of literary extracts was to be adopted by many other similar collections for almost a century, it might be interesting to read Bingham's reasons for his omissions as well as for the extracts included. In the preface to his three-hundred-page book he states that it is "a new selection of lessons for reading and speaking in American schools." He admits that preference has been given to works of American genius; that no place has been given to romantic fiction and that "tales of love have not gained admission. . . . Nor is there to be found a word or a sentiment which would raise a blush on the cheek of modesty." [8] Lindley Murray, like-

[6] Elwood P. Cubberley, *Public Education in the United States*, rev. ed. (Boston and New York, Houghton Mifflin Co., 1934), p. 291, n. 4.

[7] George R. Carpenter, Franklin T. Baker, and Fred N. Scott, *The Teaching of English in the Elementary and the Secondary School*, (New York, Longmans, Green & Co., Inc., 1905), p. 43.

[8] Cubberley, *op. cit.*, p. 292, n. 2.

wise, emphasized the piety and virtue that would be inculcated by the selections in his *Reader*. [9] Several other anthologies appeared, such as those by Cobb, Parley, Pickett, and Pierpont. Because they suited the American democratic spirit of the times, they became popular.

John Pierpont's readers (1820-1830) added the new literature of the rising romantic school of Washington Irving, Bryant, Scott, Byron, and Campbell. In his preface to the first edition of the *American First Class Book* [10] he reveals the patriotic fervor which pervades the book:

Our country both physically and morally has a character of its own. Should not something of that character be learned by its children while at school? Its mountains and prairies and lakes and rivers and cataracts; its shores and hill-tops that were early made sacred by dangers and sacrifices and deaths of the devout and the daring; it does seem as if these were worthy of being held up as objects of interest to the young eyes that from year to year are opening upon them, and worthy of being linked with all their sacred associations to the young affections, which sooner or later must be bound to them, or they must cease to be what they now are —the inheritance and abode of a free people!

H. H. Reeder recounts the development of the readers to the end of the nineteenth century. [11] For purposes of this study it is significant that, although all of these books were essentially New England productions, they were carried westward by New Englanders and utilized in the schools they established in their new locations.

With the appearance of William H. McGuffey's *First Reader* and *Second Reader* in 1836 in Cincinnati, a new element was added— gradation as to difficulty. [12]

[9] Lindley Murray, *The English Reader: or Pieces in Prose and Poetry. Selected From The Best Writers. Designed To Assist Young Persons To Read With Propriety and Effect; To Improve Their Language and Sentiments, and To Inculcate Some of The Most Important Principles of Piety and Virtue.* (Philadelphia, S. Probasco, 1831), Title page. A summary of some of the contents is found in John Swett's *American Public Schools* (New York, American Book Co., 1900), p. 139.

[10] Carpenter, Baker, and Scott, *op. cit.*, p. 43, n. 2.

[11] Cf. H. H. Reeder, *The Historical Development of Early School Readers*, Columbia University, Contributions to Philosophy, Psychology, and Education, VIII (May, 1900), No. 2.

[12] A glowing tribute to McGuffey's *Readers* is paid by Herbert Quick in his *One Man's Life: An Autobiography* (Indianapolis, The Bobbs-Merrill Com-

The books mentioned above had as their essential aims the improvement of reading and declamation. Moral or spiritual values were to be derived from the content. However, the treatment of literature as a belletristic subject came later. By 1865, the beginning date of this study, students were studying English and American literature, not in order to declaim it or to perfect their reading voices, but to develop taste in appreciation and to acquire the facts of historical development of both English and American literature.

II

THREE STAGES OF DEVELOPMENT, 1865–1900

Stout, in tracing the development of instruction in literature per se in the North Central states, refers to the emphasis on select readings as the first stage of development. [13] There were many short selections from a relatively large number of authors. Charles D. Cleveland compiled such a compendium in English literature as early as 1849 [14] and another in American literature in 1859. [15] These readers were used for training in oral expression, declamation, and acquainting students with good literature. Long before courses in "literature" had been introduced into the high school curricula in English, declamation was almost universally required. Emphasis in these books was still on the mechanics of oral reading, rather than on appreciation of literature as we understand it. For example, McGuffey's *Sixth Reader* has sixty pages on articulation, inflection, accent, emphasis, reading verse, voice, and gesture. [16]

---

pany, 1925), pp. 156-59, and reproduced in Edgar W. Knight's and Clifton L. Hall's *Readings in American Educational History* (New York, Appleton-Century-Crofts, Inc., 1951), pp. 516-517.

[13] Stout, *op. cit.*, p. 130.

[14] Charles D. Cleveland, *A Compendium of English Literature Characterized and Arranged from Sir John Mandeville to William Cowper Consisting of Biographical Sketches of the Authors, Selections from Their Works, with Notes, etc.* (Philadelphia, E.C.J. Biddle, 1849).

[15] Charles D. Cleveland, *A Compendium of American Literature Chronologically Arranged with Biographical Sketches of the Authors and Selections from Their Works* (Philadelphia, E.C.J. Biddle, 1859).

[16] Stout, *op. cit.*, p. 130.

As to the literary quality of these readers and the number of selections, the following figures may be considered as representative:

McGuffey's *Sixth Reader* had 400 pages, with 150 selections from 100 authors.

William Swinton's *The Student's Reader* had 419 pages, with 113 selections. Some of the titles are: *Expulsion of the Arcadians, The Man Without a Country, The Universal Prayer, Washington, The Bridge of Sighs, Scene from Henry VIII, Lay of the Last Minstrel, Pied Piper of Hamlin, Faithless Sally Brown, Contest with a Cannon, The Tempted Scholar, Cicero's Impeachment, Thanatopsis, Lycidas, L'Allegro, Alexander's Feast, Intimations of Immortality from Recollections of Early Childhood.*

George R. Cathcart in his *Literary Reader* has 179 selections of 68 authors. Cathcart differs from McGuffey and Swinton in the respect that he has more American literature and some scientific writing. [17]

However, the reading of extracts for elocutionary purposes was by no means the only form of literary study during this early period (1865–1880). We have the evidence from W. J. Rolfe that, as early as 1867, an annotated edition of *Julius Caesar* was used in the Cambridge, Massachusetts, High School, and undoubtedly was used in others. [18] Rolfe, who was later to become a prolific editor of his own editions of Shakespeare's plays, as well as the poems of Gray and Goldsmith, was adapting for his own students an edition previously prepared by Professor George L. Craik of Queen's College, Belfast. It is interesting to note that in 1869–1870 Harvard University required that candidates for admission should be examined in reading aloud. *Julius Caesar* and Milton's *Comus* were the works listed from which the reading was to be done. [19] It is to the fine glory of Boston that in its public high school which opened in 1821—the first in the

---

[17] George R. Cathcart, *Literary Reader: Typical Selections from Some of the Best British and American Authors from Shakespeare to the Present Time* (New York and Chicago, Ivison, Blakeman, Taylor, 1875).

[18] W. J. Rolfe, *The English of Shakespeare: Illustrated in a Philological Commentary on His Julius Caesar by George L. Craik* (Boston, Ginn & Co., 1867, [1869]).

[19] John Fleming Hosic, Compiler, *Reorganization of English in Secondary Schools*, Bulletin, No. 2 (Washington, Government Printing Office, 1917), p. 12. Hosic was Secretary of the NCTE and Chairman of a joint committee representing the National Education Association Commission on the Reorganization of Secondary Education and the NCTE.

country—English literature was one of the subjects in the curriculum. [20]

That other classics in their entirety were studied, or would probably be studied, at Harvard University is evident from the following extract from the English Composition requirement for entrance at that university in 1873–1874:

English Composition: Each candidate will be required to write a short English composition, correct in spelling, punctuation, grammar, and expression, the subject to be taken from such works of standard authors as shall be announced from time to time. The subject for 1874 will be taken from the following works: Shakespeare's *Tempest, Julius Caesar,* and *Merchant of Venice;* Goldsmith's *Vicar of Wakefield;* Scott's *Ivanhoe* and *Lay of the Last Minstrel.* [21]

Carpenter, Baker, and Scott, authors of one of the first textbooks on methods in English, consider this a milestone in the English instructional program of both secondary schools and the colleges. Writing apparently with only limited knowledge of the conditions in the almost 200 high schools which existed by 1875, they state, "Up to about 1876, then, there was scarcely to be found, in the United States, any definite, well-organized system of secondary instruction in the mother tongue." [22] However, from evidence that has appeared since this book appeared in 1903, we know somewhat more about the teaching of literature in the United States before 1875.

That there was opposition to the teaching of literature, or, at best, a halfhearted attempt to teach it, can be assumed from an understanding of the difficulties many subjects of the high school curriculum have had before they were accepted and taught capably. Writing about the distinguished Dr. John Seely Hart, who was setting a very high standard of instruction at the Central High School in Philadelphia about the middle of the century, Elmer E. Brown [23] states:

[20] Elwood P. Cubberley, *Readings in Public Education in the United States* (Boston, Houghton Mifflin Co., 1934), p. 230. Cf. Alexander J. Inglis, *Principles of Secondary Education* (Boston, Houghton Mifflin Co. 1918), p. 421.

[21] Hosic, *op. cit.,* p. 12.

[22] Carpenter, Baker, Scott, *op. cit.,* p. 46. Cf. A. S. Hill, L. B. R. Briggs, B. S. Hulburt, *Twenty Years of School and College English* (Cambridge, Mass., Harvard University Press, 1896) for a complete discussion of this topic.

[23] Elmer Ellsworth Brown, *The Making of Our Middle Schools,* 3rd ed. (New York, Longmans, Green & Co., Inc. 1910), p. 422. Cf. John Seeley Hart, *A Manual of English Literature: A Textbook for Schools and Colleges* (Philadelphia, Eldridge & Brother, 1872).

Dr. Hart laid strong emphasis upon a study of the history of the English language and literature, and this subject soon came to be the dominant branch of instruction in English. Dr. Hart prepared textbooks for use in this study, and other works of a similar sort appeared about this time, and within the years next following.

Of the difficulties encountered in introducing literature study in the Far West, Dr. Brown [24] relates this interesting incident of 1872 in the high school in Oakland, California:

Mr. J. B. McChesney, for many years principal of the high school at Oakland, California, has given me an interesting account of his early efforts to introduce a study of English masterpieces into that school. The matter was discussed with Edward Rowland Sill, then a teacher in the Oakland High School, with such editions of the desired works as could be got. Within a few years thereafter, many school editions of such masterpieces became available.

Dr. Brown, who was later the U. S. Commissioner of Education and eventually Chancellor of New York University, agrees with Carpenter, Baker, and Scott on the effect of the Harvard requirements for study of English classics upon high school practices. "It was not, however, until the colleges began to make definite requirements in this field," he writes, "that the literary study of English masterpieces became at all general in the schools or took on a definite scholastic character." [25]

Stout has made an intensive study of the changes in emphases in teaching literature in the high schools in the North Central area. By studying his data we get a picture of circumstances in many midwestern cities. Basing his generalizations upon a study of the printed courses and catalogues of these communities, reports of the Boards of Education and similar documents, he concludes that the most important changes from the standpoint of amount and character of subject matter between 1860 and the later period occurred in literature. Just as was the case in New England, selections from various authors were almost universally studied.

A shift in emphasis from studying literature to the history of literature occurred in this area. Stout cannot give the approximate date.

[24] *Ibid.*, p. 423, n. 1.
[25] Brown, *op. cit.*, p. 423.

Yet it was the biographical facts, rather than the true history of litera-ture which were studied. Although a textbook in the history of Eng-lish literature was available in 1868, it was not widely read or used. [26] Dissatisfaction with the status quo led to changes in this area of English study as it has led to many others. In the Annual Report of The Board of Education of 1873, the Superintendent of Schools of Chicago complains about the emphasis upon the facts of litera-ture, rather than upon the writings. [27]

By 1885, says Stout, the emphasis in literature was upon whole works, rather than small extracts, and this constitutes the third phase of instruction in literature in his opinion. How much this was due to the college entrance requirements in Harvard and/or North Central colleges and how much to the realization of master teachers and to the demands of parents and members of Boards of Education, it is not easy to ascertain. Several factors combined to bring out the intensive study of selected classics.

Returning to New England of the 1870's, we find that "the exam-ple of Harvard was followed by other colleges and led, after a time, to the creation of The Commission of New England Colleges on Ad-mission Examinations, which undertook the task of formulating from year to year the requirements in English. The custom of prescribing certain masterpieces of English literature as the basis of tests in writing was followed and became firmly established." [28]

III

EARLY ANNOTATED TEXTBOOKS, 1867–1889

Naturally, the textbook writers would edit those texts which were prescribed, with full critical apparatus for use in the schools. It has already been stated that William J. Rolfe, master and later Head-master of the High School in Cambridge, had issued an American adaptation of Craik's edition of *Julius Caesar* in 1867. Later he edited school editions of most of Shakespeare's plays, and the poems of Gray, Goldsmith, Milton, Browning, Macaulay, and Wordsworth. Since

[26] William Spalding, *The History of English Literature with an Outline of the Origin and Growth of English Literature* (New York, D. Appleton & Co., 1867).
[27] Stout, *op. cit.*, p. 133.
[28] Hosic, *op. cit.*, p. 12.

the publishers claimed in their advertisements that the popularity of this edition of Shakespeare was extraordinary and that it was used more widely, both by schools and colleges, than any similar edition ever issued, it may be fruitful to examine one of these volumes. In this way, one can ascertain what actually confronted a high school pupil of 1879 as he opened his copy of Rolfe's edition of *Romeo and Juliet.* [29]

The "Contents" reveals that there were an Introduction, The History of the Play, The Sources of the Plot, Critical Comments on the Play (pp. 9-34), the play itself, and Notes (pp. 137-218), and an Index of Words and Phrases Explained. Rolfe admits that he was heavily indebted to H. H. Furness's New Variorum edition for most of his notes. Some time after 1907 all of his Shakespearean editions were brought out by the American Book Company in revised editions. [30]

Contemporary with W. J. Rolfe as an editor of Shakespeare's plays was the Rev. Henry N. Hudson, whose 1879 edition of *King Lear* will serve as an example. [31] This pocket-size volume of 231 pages has an Introduction on pages 3-54. His notes, unlike those of Rolfe, which follow the play, are at the bottom of each page in smaller type than the text. Pages 213-231 are discussions of textual emendations. How many of these notes were designed to be for the instructor rather than for the student is not indicated, but they were certainly exhaustive.

A new aspect of annotated editions of Shakespeare's plays is discovered in Brainerd Kellogg's edition of *The Tempest* (1882), [32] in which (pp. viii-ix) he presents a Plan of Study for Perfect Possession. This is an early example of methodology in the study and teaching of Shakespeare. At the time when he edited *The Tempest,* Kellogg was Professor of the English Language and Literature in the Brooklyn Collegiate and Polytechnic Institute and had already written a *Textbook on Rhetoric* and a *Textbook on English Literature,* as well as

---

[29] William J. Rolfe, *Shakespeare's Tragedy of Romeo and Juliet* (New York, American Book Co., 1879, 1898, 1907).

[30] Publisher's announcement to the above.

[31] William Shakespeare, *Tragedy of King Lear,* edited by the Rev. Henry N. Hudson (Boston, Ginn & Co., 1879). These editions have been revised, given more attractive covers, and are still in use in high schools today.

[32] Published by Maynard, Merrill & Co., New York.

coauthoring Reed and Kellogg's *Graded Lessons in English*.[33] It is of interest to note, therefore, what, in the New York City metropolitan area in the 1880's, was expected of youths with respect to their understanding and appreciation of Shakespeare.

At the end of the book are examination papers on each of the five acts of *The Tempest*. Since Kellogg admits that "Some of the questions [were] taken from Papers of the English Civil Service Commission," they are doubly interesting.[34] For the first act, these questions are asked:

1. Give the substance of the story told by Prospero to Miranda.
2. State the parts played by Ariel and Caliban.
3. State by whom, to whom, and on what occasions, the following lines were uttered:
   (*a*) We are *merely* cheated of our lives by drunkards.
   (*b*) In the dark *backward* and abysm of time.
   (*c*) From the *still-vex'd Bermoothës*, there she's hid.
   (*d*) To do *me business* in the veins o' the earth.
   (*e*) He's *gentle* and not *fearful*.
   (*f*) A *single* thing, as I am now, that wonders.
4. Explain the words in italics in the above.
5. Explain Shakespeare's use of the following words and phrases:
   (*a*) *Play the man*; (*b*) *incharitable*; (*c*) *god of power*; (*d*) *The very virtue*; (*e*) *holp*; (*f*) *from such a deed*; (*g*) *closeness* (*h*) *a hint that wrings mine eyes*; (*i*) *grand hests* (*j*) *capable of*.
6. Give some instances of Shakespeare's peculiar grammar, in the use of double comparatives, and such phrases as *I were best*.

It can be seen that the student was asked to summarize (Question 1), identify and give the actions of characters (2), identify lines spoken (3), explain meanings of word (4 and 5), and explain some of the peculiarities of Shakespeare's grammar (6). Since the particular copy under discussion bears an identification of the New York City Board of Education, we may reasonably assume that such questions were asked of Metropolitan students in the 1880's. This volume is one of a series of 120 published in handy pocket-size at twelve cents (!) each by Maynard, Merrill & Company.

Another series of classics, on which publishing began in 1886, was

---

[33] Cf. *ibid.*, title page.
[34] Cf. *ibid.*, p. 135.

the *Riverside Literature Series,* by Houghton Mifflin Company of Boston. These appeared in paper covers at fifteen cents a copy or $1.25 for a year's subscription of nine numbers. Number 32 was issued in January, 1888, and is typical. The publisher's announcement is of interest because it reveals the purpose of one of the most widely used series of classics. The original editor (1886–1901) was Horace E. Scudder, to be succeeded by Bliss Perry of Princeton and later of Harvard. [35] The volumes in the 1890's were often edited by distinguished teachers in colleges and secondary schools.

IV

EARLY COLLEGE ADMISSION REQUIREMENTS AND THEIR EFFECT UPON THE ENGLISH PROGRAM

The Harvard admission requirements and those of the Commission of New England Colleges on Admission Examinations prescribed certain masterpieces of English literature as the *basis of tests in writing* (author's italics). This lasted for almost twenty years until, in 1894, Yale University introduced questions on the knowledge of literary masterpieces for their own sake. The Commission of New England Colleges on Admission Examinations favorably considered this innovation in 1895, and it soon became general.

Whether the colleges in the North Central area were influenced in their admission requirements by the practices of Harvard and the Commission of New England Colleges on Admission Examinations or whether they developed independently along parallel lines of thinking has not yet been established by the writer. The similarities are striking, however. Stout states that when the colleges in the area covered by his study required little by way of English, the college preparatory courses gave little attention to the subject. For example, in 1867, the University of Illinois entrance examinations were given only in orthography, reading, and grammar. In 1899–1900 the University required training in composition, rhetoric, and literature for entrance and the statement in the catalogue specifies: "two years of high school work with five recitations per week will be necessary for

[35] *The Gettysburg Address* by Abraham Lincoln and *An Essay on Lincoln* by James Russell Lowell (Boston, Houghton Mifflin Co.), January, 1888.

the above preparation." Similar requirements were made by Indiana University, the State University of Iowa, Cornell College (Iowa), and De Pauw University. Prior to 1873, there was no requirement specified except grammar. [36] Stout, after studying the English curricula in many cities of the North Central area from 1860 on, noted three changes in the treatment of English as a subject (not literature only). These were: [37]

1. An increase in the amount of time devoted to English.

2. Increasing importance of English as evidenced by the tendency toward greater uniformity among the schools.

3. The relative amount of attention given to grammar and rhetoric decreased while that given to literature increased.

The changes in the attention to literature were not only quantitative but also qualitative. For example, as far as Stout could ascertain, between 1860 and 1865 American literature was not included in the schools of twenty cities whose records he examined. Thirty years later (1896) the University of Illinois required nine classics to be studied, of which six were English and three American.

As was the case in the Harvard entrance requirements, until 1894 a knowledge of the classics was required, not for appreciation of their beauties, but for written expression. Thus, in 1893, the University of Illinois entrance requirements read as follows: [38]

In 1893 longer essays will be required (except for those offering Greek) upon subjects drawn from the following works: Shakespeare's *Julius Caesar*, Scott's *Marmion*, Webster's *First Bunker Hill Oration*, Goldsmith's *Deserted Village*, Irving's *Sketch Book*. . . .

In 1894, the following works were required: Shakespeare's *Merchant of Venice*, Scott's *Lady of the Lake*, Emerson's *American Scholar*, Longfellow's *Evangeline*, Macaulay's *Second Essay on the Earl of Chatham*.

Almost coetaneously with Yale University's requirement of 1894 and that of the Commission of New England Colleges on Admission Examinations in 1895, Illinois established an examination on the con-

[36] Stout, *op. cit.*, p. 124.
[37] *Ibid.*, p. 124.
[38] *Ibid.*, p. 134.

tents of certain assigned classics. For 1896 these were: Shakespeare's *Midsummer Night's Dream,* Defoe's *History of the Plague in London,* Irving's *Tales of a Traveler,* Scott's *Woodstock,* Macaulay's *Essay on Milton,* Longfellow's *Evangeline,* and George Eliot's *Silas Marner.* For 1897, the Defoe, Irving, Longfellow, and Eliot items remained, while Shakespeare's *As You Like It* and Hawthorne's *Twice-Told Tales* were added. A totally new group was required for 1898, including Milton's *Paradise Lost* (Books I & II), Pope's *Iliad* (Books I and XXII), *Sir Roger de Coverley Papers,* Goldsmith's *Vicar of Wakefield,* Coleridge's *Ancient Mariner,* Southey's *Life of Nelson,* Carlyle's *Essay on Burns,* Lowell's *Vision of Sir Launfal,* and Hawthorne's *House of Seven Gables.* It can readily be understood why the various publishing houses issued annotated texts to fulfill the needs of students in the secondary schools who had to meet the requirements for college entrance.

Other colleges in this area specified texts similar to those indicated above for Illinois. In 1893–1894, De Pauw University required Longfellow's *Courtship of Miles Standish,* Irving's *Sketch Book,* and Dickens's *David Copperfield,* in addition to some already listed for Illinois. A time minimum in English was also specified, three semesters in English. [39] Indiana's requirements were similar to those of De Pauw and Illinois.

It has long been a subject of dispute as to what influence these college entrance requirements of the 1890's in literature had on both the selection and manner of teaching English and American classics in the high schools of the time and afterward. Stout, [40] speaking for the North Central area, feels:

To what extent the entrance requirements in English were influenced by what was actually being taught in the high schools is not easily determined. It is entirely clear that some high schools were offering work in literature consisting of material very similar to the entrance requirements above cited several years before the higher institutions adopted the requirements. It is not improbable, therefore, that the agreement on the part of the higher institutions in the general plan was determined somewhat by what the high schools were already doing. On the other hand,

[39] *Ibid.,* p. 135.
[40] *Ibid.,* pp. 135-136.

the lack of uniformity in the details of entrance requirements shows that the work was not standardized by the high schools and that the higher institutions had not yet worked out uniform requirements.

Just as high schools in New England (for example, Cambridge, Massachusetts, in 1867) had been teaching entire classics before Harvard required them for entrance in 1874, so there were high schools in the North Central area which presented entire classics in place of extracts which had formerly been used in the study of literature before these were required by the universities in the 1890's. The course of study of Milwaukee, Wisconsin, included classics in 1877. At the same time, Laporte High School in Indiana in 1883 was still concentrating on the study of extracts, except for one of Shakespeare's plays. From 1886–1890, says Stout, the printed courses of study show conclusively the tendency to substitute classics for abstracts. Examples are given from Lawrence, Kansas; Kankakee, Illinois; Genesceo, Illinois; Evansville, Indiana; Fairburg, Indiana; Grand Rapids, Michigan; and Richmond, Indiana. [41]

What were students reading most frequently in their English classes in the North Central states from 1886-1900? Stout compiled the following statistics; in more than 25% of the schools the following works taught were the most popular:

1. *The Merchant of Venice*
2. *Julius Caesar*
3. *Bunker Hill Oration*
4. *The Sketch Book*
4. *Evangeline*
4. *The Vision of Sir Launfal*
5. *Snowbound*
6. *Macbeth*
7. *The Lady of the Lake*
8. *Hamlet*
9. *Deserted Village*
10. Gray's *Elegy in a Country Churchyard*
10. *Thanatopsis*
10. *As You Like It*

The Merchant of Venice was taught in more than 70% of the schools studied. Of the fourteen most popular texts, five were Shakespeare's plays. Eight works were by English authors; six, by Americans. In more than 10% of the lists of high schools of the North Central area but in less than 25% of these schools, the following classics were used:

[41] *Ibid.*, pp. 136-137.

1. *The Courtship of
   Miles Standish*
2. *Il Penseroso*
3. *Paradise Lost*
3. *L'Allegro*
3. *Lycidas*
4. *Ivanhoe*
4. *Sir Roger de Coverly Papers*
4. *David Copperfield*
4. *Silas Marner*
5. *In Memoriam*
5. *Enoch Arden*
5. *Behavior*
5. *Marmion*

5. *Tales of the White Hills*
5. *Lays of Ancient Rome*
5. *A Midsummer Night's Dream*
5. *The Vicar of Wakefield*
5. *Iliad*
6. *Henry VIII*
6. *Among the Hills*
6. *Cotter's Saturday Night*
6. *The Chambered Nautilus*
6. *Comus*
6. Bryant's *Favorite Poems*
6. *The Princess*
6. *Saul*
6. *King Lear*

In addition, there were almost two hundred other works of English and American authors studied in these North Central schools.

V

Movement for Uniform College Entrance Requirements in English

This lack of uniformity in the selection of texts to be studied must have obtained in other areas of our country in the 1890's. Even though the New England Commission endorsed Yale University's entrance requirement of a knowledge of literary masterpieces, the college admission requirements in English (and their effects upon high school instruction) did not become uniform even throughout New England. In 1893, Wilson Farrand, principal of the Newark Academy in New Jersey, read a paper on "English in the Preparatory School" before the Association of Colleges and Preparatory Schools of the Middle States and Maryland which met at Columbia College. In this paper he deplored the lack of uniformity in the college entrance requirements in English. A committee was appointed to prepare a report on the subject. A short time before (1893), the Committee of Ten of the National Education Association, which had been appointed to study secondary education, published a report in which it made certain recommendations about uniform college entrance requirements. These recommendations were endorsed by the committee of the Association of Colleges and Preparatory Schools of the Middle States and Maryland, [42] and they added a few recommendations of their own. Three of these recommendations pertain to entrance requirements in literature:

1. That any examination set should be based upon the reading of certain masterpieces of English literature, not fewer than those at present recommended by the Commission of Colleges in New England on Admission Examinations.
2. That certain of these books should be of a kind to be read by the candidate as literature; and that others—a limited number—should be carefully studied under the immediate direction of the teacher.
3. That each of the whole number of books should be representative, so far as possible, of a period, a tendency, or a type of literature, and that the whole number of works selected for any year should represent, with as few gaps as possible, the course of English literature from the Elizabethan period to the present time.

The committee of the Association of Colleges and Preparatory Schools of the Middle States and Maryland proposed a joint conference with other associations having to do with the problem of college entrance in English. In 1894, the Conference on Uniform Entrance Requirements in English was organized. The Conference selected lists of books for reading in the secondary schools, and appended certain aims of English study and directions concerning the examinations.

VI

THE VOGUE FOR ANNOTATED CLASSICS

Publishers of editions of these books referred to the College Entrance Requirements, ostensibly for sales purposes. Thus, an edition of Macaulay's *Essay on Addison* by Houghton Mifflin sometime after 1901 listed on its inside cover:

A List of the Issues of the Riverside Literature Series
Containing College Entrance Requirements in English.

These were under the categories "Required for Careful Study" and "Required for Reading." A specially bound volume of numbers "Re-

[42] Hosic, *op. cit.*, p. 13.

quired for Careful Study" for the years 1903–1908 was issued. [43]

Longmans, Green published its own list of classics, carefully edited by such distinguished professors as Barrett Wendell and George Pierce Baker of Harvard; Brander Matthews, George Edward Woodberry, George R. Carpenter (the general editor), and William T. Brewster, all of Columbia; William Lyon Phelps, Albert S. Cook, Charles Sears Baldwin, all of Yale; as well as some teachers in secondary schools such as Huber Gray Buehler of Hotchkiss School, Percival Chubb of the New York Ethical Culture Schools, James Greenleaf Croswell of the Brearley School, Edwin L. Miller of Englewood, Illinois, High School, and D. O. S. Lowell, Roxbury Latin School.

In these texts, too, reference was made to the books in the series which were prescribed for reading and for study for the examinations of 1899, 1900, 1901, 1902. [44]

A third series put out by Scott, Foresman & Company under the editorial supervision of Lindsay Todd Damon of the University of Chicago in the late 1890's indicates by asterisks and other symbols those of its edited texts required for reading and study in the College Entrance Examinations for 1900. For this series, distinguished college teachers and secondary school instructors were secured. The edition of Scott's *Marmion* had an introduction by the poet-playwright-teacher, William Vaughn Moody, and a glossary and notes by Mary R. Willard of the Jamestown, New York, High School. [45]

Robert Morss Lovett, who, with William Vaughn Moody, co-authored one of the most widely used textbooks on the *History of English Literature* (Charles Scribner's Sons, 1902, 1918, 1925, 1935), included the following "Suggested Examination Questions" at the end of his edition of *Marmion*:

1. *Explain:*
   "The leaden silence of your *hearse* [Introd. to Canto I., 199]."
   "Sober he seemed and sad of *cheer* [V., 56]."
   "Wealth of winter *cheer* [III, 47]."

43 Thomas Babington Macaulay, *Life and Writings of Addison*, William P. Trent, ed. (Boston, Houghton Mifflin Co., 1896).

44 Sir Walter Scott, *Marmion*, Robert Morss Lovett, ed. (New York, Longmans, Green & Co., Inc., 1898 [1896]).

45 Sir Walter Scott, *Marmion*, William Vaughn Moody and Mary R. Willard, eds., (Chicago, Scott, Foresman & Co., 1899).

"Well dost thou *brook* thy gallant roan [I., 149]."
"And well could *brook* the mild command [VI., 121]."
"Such *buxom* chief shall lead his host [Introd. to IV., 202]."
"St. George to *speed* [III., 429]."
"That spear-wound has our master *sped* [VI., 867]."
"When joins yon host in deadly *stowre* [IV., 679]."
"On the warp'd wave their death-game played [Introd. to Canto III., 92]."

2. *Define: wassail, beadsman, pursuivant, trews, bratchet, sewer, wager of battle.*
3. Who was Brunswick? What justified Scott's extended reference to him in the Introduction to Canto III?
4. Compare Scott's treatment of Pitt with that of Fox, in the introduction to Canto I, and account for the difference.
5. Discuss briefly Scott's defence of his choice of subject matter and literary method as outlined in the Introductory Epistle to Erskine. Describe the influences by which Scott was impelled to this choice.
6. Write a short essay on one of the following topics:
   "The Influence of Scott's Private Life upon His Literary Career."
   "Scott's Feeling for Nature as Illustrated by *Marmion*."
7. What descriptive value have the following passages: IV, 605-611; IV, 628-634.
8. Criticize VI, 293-310 and VI, 798-818. Which passage do you like better and why? [46]

We note that, just as in 1882, the pupil is asked to define difficult words both in context and out of context, and discuss the action of certain characters. However, the difference in type between a play and an essay account for differences in questions. He is asked to appreciate descriptive writing, as well as compare Scott's treatment of two characters.

The student of 1896—like the student of today—was expected to do "research." Therefore, the following topics are given for further study:

1. Compare *Marmion* with *The Lady of the Lake* as specimens of narration.
2. Compare the characters in *Marmion* with those in one of Scott's prose works, *e.g.*, De Wilton with Ivanhoe, Marmion with Bois-Gilbert, Constance with Rebecca, Clare with Rowena. What general

[46] *Ibid.*, pp. 267–268.

conclusions can you draw in regard to Scott's selection of characters and methods of portrayal?

3. Why was Scott, in the opinion of the British public, surpassed as a poet by Byron?
4. [Discuss] The Homeric spirit in Scott's poetry.
5. Are Carlyle's strictures on Scott justified?
6. [Discuss] Scott's friends and their influence upon him.
7. [Compare] Scott and Wordsworth as poets of nature.
8. The verse of *Marmion* compared with that of *The Lay of the Last Minstrel.*
9. [Discuss] The use of color in *Marmion.*
10. [Describe] The Political atmosphere in which *Marmion* was written.

In addition to the three series of edited English Classics already referred to, other publishers entered the market in the 1890's, evidently hoping to reap the golden harvest by pointing out that they, too, were printing classics which were required for the College Entrance Examinations. Of these, the following series are worth mentioning:

Maynard's English Classic Series, represented by an edition of Walter Scott's *The Lay of the Last Minstrel* (1898). [47] Its advertisement on the last pages was headed by "Literature for College Entrance Requirements Met by Maynard's English Classic Series." Then follows a statement of these requirements, together with a list of the works required for 1901–1905 and provided by this publisher.

Standard English Classics, published in Boston by Ginn and Company, as exemplified by Albert S. Cook's edition of Tennyson's *The Princess* (1897), [48] and Charles Lane Hanson's edition of *Representative Poems of Robert Burns* (1897).

English Classics for Schools, published by the American Book Com-

[47] Sir Walter Scott, *The Lay of the Last Minstrel* (New York, Maynard, Merrill & Co., 1898). This firm had published Brainerd Kellogg's edition of *The Tempest* in 1882 and other texts.

[48] Alfred, Lord Tennyson, *The Princess,* Albert S. Cook, ed. (Boston, Ginn & Co., 1897). It is interesting to note that Professor Cook was the author of *A Summary of the Meetings of the Conference on Uniform Entrance Requirements in English,* 1894–1899. It is to be presumed, then, that his edition of the classic would agree with the opinions of the members of the conference. Charles Lane Hanson was an instructor in English at the Mechanics Arts High School in Boston. His edition represents the views of a high school teacher in a vocational high school. In 1911, Hanson was one of three authors who wrote *An Introduction to the English Classics,* evidently to accompany the series published by Ginn & Company.

pany, as exemplified by an edition of *The Sir Roger de Coverly Papers*. [49] No editor is indicated by name.

The Academy Series of English Classics, published in Boston by Allyn and Bacon, represented in H. W. Boynton's edition of Tennyson's *Idylls of the King* (1903). [50] This series followed the editions of certain classics as far back as 1891, when the distinguished teacher, Samuel Thurber, brought out *Select Essays of Macaulay.* Thurber took issue with the detailed editions then in use and had his own idea of what an editor should put into an edited classic text. He was a frequent speaker at educational meetings and wrote in the educational magazines [51] on the teaching of literature.

English Readings, published by Henry Holt & Company, Inc., as exemplified by Henry A. Beer's edition of *Selections from the Prose Writings of Samuel Taylor Coleridge* (1893). [52]

The Appleton English Classics, published by D. Appleton & Company, as represented by Franklin T. Baker's edition of *The Sir Roger de Coverley Papers* (1899). Since Baker occupied the first chair of the teaching of English in Teachers College and was coauthor of one of the earliest textbooks on English methodology, his edition possesses more than usual interest. An innovation in his edition is the printing at the end of his books of some actual examination questions set by various colleges from 1895 on. [53]

[49] Addison, Steele, Bodgell, *The Sir Roger de Coverley Papers* (New York, Cincinnati, Chicago, American Book Co., 1892).

[50] Alfred, Lord Tennyson, *Idylls of the King,* by H. W. Boynton, ed. (Boston and Chicago, Allyn and Bacon, Inc., 1903). In 1891, Samuel Thurber, a distinguished teacher and editor, issued an edition of *Select Essays of Macaulay* (Boston, Allyn and Bacon, Inc., 1891).

[51] Some of Mr. Thurber's ideas were expressed in the following articles: "Some of the Main Principles of Secondary Teaching," *Addresses and Proceedings of the National Education Association* (1898), p. 671; "Aims and Methods in the Study of Literature," *Education,* XVI, 449.

[52] Samuel Taylor Coleridge, *Selections from the Prose Writings,* Henry A. Beers, ed. (New York, Henry Holt & Co., Inc., 1893). The *Dial* called this series "One of the best series of annotated school texts that have ever been produced."

[53] *The Sir Roger de Coverley Papers from the Spectator,* Franklin T. Baker and Richard Jones, eds. (New York, D. Appleton and Co., 1899). In addition to individual examination questions concerning this classic, Baker's edition also contains the entire Entrance Examination in English for Amherst in June, 1898; University of California, August, 1898; Johns Hopkins University, June, 1899; The Leland Stanford Junior University, May, 1899; and Vassar College, June, 1898. In this regard, Baker's edition was the forerunner of the multitudinous Regents review books which reprint examinations of several preceding years and enjoy a wide sale today.

Macmillan's Pocket American and English Classics, as represented by Charlotte Whipple Underwood's edition of *The Merchant of Venice* (1899). [54]

VII

CO-OPERATION
BETWEEN HIGH SCHOOLS AND COLLEGES

While many of these texts kept referring to the College Entrance Examinations as one of the justifications for purchase and use, it must not be assumed that the colleges alone were responsible for the program in English literature in the secondary schools. A powerful influence for change came from the schools themselves. The National Education Association had long shown a great interest in the teaching of English and the publication in 1894 of the Report of the National Committee of Ten on Secondary Schools gave a new basis to instruction in English at this level. The subcommittee dealing with English was composed of secondary teachers from high schools and preparatory schools as well as college teachers. Their job was to prepare a curriculum in English that "should serve the interests of general education, for the benefit of the many, and not merely that of the few who go to colleges. Their admirable report was the first attempt, in England or America, to systematize secondary instruction in English." [55] The praises of this report were still being sung twenty-four years later by Alexander J. Inglis in his *Principles of Secondary Education.* [56] Since some of the recommendations this committee made in 1894 are still being discussed as desiderata in 1960, it may be profitable to examine the main points as summarized by Carpenter, Baker, and Scott:

1. It made of English instruction in the secondary schools a complete organism. Through it, the schools came to realize for the first time that instruction in English means, not a group of disconnected studies

[54] William Shakespeare, *The Merchant of Venice,* Charlotte Whipple Underwood, ed. (New York, The Macmillan Co., 1899).

[55] Carpenter, Baker, and Scott, *op. cit.,* p. 51.

[56] Alexander J. Inglis, *Principles of Secondary Education* (Boston, Houghton Mifflin Co., 1918), pp. 422-423.

in grammar, rhetoric, English literature, and elocution, but one constant current, as it were, of work, running throughout the whole period of instruction.

2. The committee was convinced that secondary education in English can be properly systematized only when it is considered in direct connection with elementary instruction in the same subject. It proceeded, therefore, to lay down certain principles and plans for the teaching of English from the earliest grades of the elementary schools through the highest classes in the high schools. [57]

This co-operative enterprise between college and secondary teachers has been duplicated in the English field on later occasions with good results. Thus, the National Joint Committee on the Reorganization of English in Secondary Schools (1917) and the Commission on the English Curriculum of the National Council of Teachers of English (1947 on) both had and now have representatives of the secondary and collegiate levels.

VIII

NEA COMMITTEE ON COLLEGE ENTRANCE REQUIREMENTS

Five years after the Committee of Ten had published its report, the National Education Association attempted to follow up its work by appointing a committee on college entrance requirements in English which issued their report in 1899. It will be recalled that the National Conference on Uniform Entrance Requirements was a *conference* of various interested institutions, but it was not an official body, appointed either by the U. S. Department of Education, the National Education Association, or any other authorizing agency. Those high schools and preparatory schools which implemented its recommendations did so, not necessarily because they felt that these recommendations actually met the needs of their students, but primarily because they wanted to be certain that the graduates from their schools who wished to enter the colleges represented by the conference could do so by meeting their requirements.

Those who looked to the Conference on Uniform Entrance Re-

[57] Carpenter, Baker, and Scott, *op. cit.*, p. 51.

quirements for help in setting up a good course of study in literature for their schools were looking to the wrong agency. For the National Conference never really attempted to deal with secondary education as such. It was concerned with college education and the ability of their incoming students to master the college program. As a matter of fact, the reports of the proceedings of the Conference show that it "sedulously avoided the appearance of dictating the high school course in English and did not suggest any definite organization of the subject matter which it approved." [58] It must be remembered that 1895 was not 1960 when almost every city of considerable size has its own course of study in English, prepared by its own people, and designed to meet the English needs of the majority of students, who will definitely *not be going to college.*

Evaluating the contributions of the Conference to secondary instruction in English in the mid-nineties, it may be stated that the books listed were almost always worthwhile from the point of view of the student of English literature. Some of the books, however, were too mature for students in their teens.

Yet there were complaints from the high school teachers, assuming the following forms:

1. The examinations given for college entrance tended to over-emphasize historical and other facts of literature.

2. They fostered mere memory work.

3. They encouraged writing which was based entirely on literature.

It is still a debatable question how much these ill effects were due primarily to the uniform examinations, to the lack of definite educational standards in the secondary schools themselves, and/or to the ignorance of the principles of high school instruction on the part of high school teachers. It was not until 1896 that the first native American textbook on methodology in English appeared and this was not concerned with literature at all. [59] For a complete American manual on method in all phases of English, high school teachers had to wait until 1902 for Percival Chubb's *The Teaching of Eng-*

[58] Hosic, *op. cit.*, p. 13.
[59] B. A. Hinsdale, *Teaching the Language Arts* (New York, D. Appleton and Company, 1896).

lish [60] and 1903 for Carpenter, Baker, and Scott's *The Teaching of English in the Elementary School and the Secondary School.* Secondary teachers had to wait until 1910 for a methods book written entirely by a high school teacher of English. [61]

Returning to the 1899 Committee on College Entrance Requirements set up by the N. E. A., we note that this was a quasi-official body, and that its "Report," issued in July, 1899, was a quasi-official report. What did it contribute to the improvement of instruction of English in secondary schools?

1. Unfortunately, by definition of purpose, the Committee was interested primarily in preparation for college, and not in an English course that would meet the needs of all high school students regardless of their college destinations.

2. On the positive side, the Committee contributed the following:
   (a) It distributed a list of books for four years of high school only partly identical with that provided by the National Conference on Uniform Examinations in English.
   (b) It outlined the studies which should accompany these books.

This outline, proposed in 1899, was in existence to a considerable extent in Boys High School, Brooklyn, New York, in 1920–1924 when the writer was a student there, and may still be observed in many high schools today. Basically, it recommended the following:

1. In the first half of the first year, *narration* was to be studied in both literature and composition. In the second half, it was *description*.

2. In the sophomore year, *exposition* was to be the main object of study.

3. In the junior year, composition was correlated with the novel and drama.

[60] Percival Chubb, *The Teaching of English in the Elementary School and the Secondary School* (New York, The Macmillan Co., 1902).

[61] Charles Swain Thomas, *How to Teach English Classics* (Boston, Houghton Mifflin Co., 1910). Thomas, who was Head of the English Department of the Newton, Massachusetts, High School, eventually enlarged this pamphlet of 132 pages into a full size book in 1917, and he revised it in 1927. For many years, it was the most popular methods book in English for high schools.

4. In the senior year, the history of the English language and English literature was studied. Compositions were to be longer and more mature. [62]

Commenting on the effects of these prescriptions, James Fleming Hosic, [63] then Secretary of the National Council of Teachers of English, and compiler of the report on *Reorganization of English in Secondary Schools* says:

The rhetorical element was . . . unduly emphasized in the outlines of literary study, while, on the other hand, the close correlation of composition with certain typical literary forms could result in nothing but excessive emphasis on composition essentially literary in purpose or in subject matter. Like the preceding commissions, the committee on college entrance requirements made a report that tended to foster a type of English study that practically ignored oral composition and subjects of expression drawn from the pupil's own experience, and that constantly applied in the study of literary masterpieces formal rhetorical categories.

The twentieth century has been one of inquiry, revolt, and reorganization of the course of study in English, which is still going on today. In 1952, the National Council of Teachers of English published *The English Language Arts*, the first of a series of five volumes of reports of its Commission on the English Curriculum. Discussion has been widespread all over the land. In 1954, *Language Arts for Today's Children*, which was concerned with the elementary grades, appeared. *The English Language Arts in the Secondary School* followed in 1956. The following volumes will treat respectively the English program in college and in teacher education.

IX

Some Innovations of Methodology, 1865–1900

As has been mentioned earlier in this paper, attempts at indicating a methodology in teaching literature had already appeared as early as 1882 in Kellogg's edition of *The Tempest*. We have some evidence

[62] Hosic, *op. cit.*, p. 14.

[63] *Ibid.*, p. 15. Cf. Herbert G. Lull, *Inherited Tendencies of Secondary Instruction in the United States*, III, 3, University of California Publications in Education (Berkeley, 1913), pp. 227-233.

of how a distinguished teacher suggested the study of prose non-fiction in Samuel Thurber's edition of *Select Essays of Macaulay* (1891). Thurber spoke about his theories of teaching literature at educational gatherings and wrote about them in educational magazines. His views in his edition of Macaulay's essays may be considered typical of his views on method generally. Thurber emphasizes, first, the need of research on the student's part to master all the allusions of the author studied. He does not approve of overannotated classics which give the student all the information he needs. Rather he would prefer them to find out things for themselves.

"An English piece," says Mr. Thurber, "must be read and got through with. . . . Work in English should be vigorous and rapid, taking many things for granted. The skillful teacher surmises when his pupils fail to understand a point rightly, and halts the column of march only on such occasions. [64]

Mr. Thurber did not forget the preparation of the teacher of literature. "The teacher," he says, "should look over a few pages in advance and note the points at which special difficulties of any kind will arise. These points, as they require more elaborate investigation, he will separate from the text when he assigns the lesson, and he will exempt the class en masse from giving them attention. The text, thus temporarily cleared of the chief difficulties, is prescribed to all the class, who must work it out and be prepared on it at the next lesson. At the same time the special points of difficulty are dealt out to individuals, one to each, to be looked up and reported on. The interest of a class exercise is much enhanced if the individual pupils bring different contributions, so that each is listened to with curiosity on a fresh topic. [65] This method has a contemporary ring, except that we now call it "individual research" and "reports to the class." The rapid reading of the whole text rather than little niblets is also quite the vogue today. Even in the recommendation for a classroom library of reference books, he was decades in advance of his day. "If all alike are required to make the same investigations, the reference books may not suffice to go around," he wisely states.

It is not enough for the English teacher to hand out topics for research, but he must "say where the desired matter can be found.

[64] Thurber, ed., *op. cit.*, p. xi.
[65] *Ibid.*, p. xi.

He must know whether the books that will have to be used are in the school library or must be looked for in the public library of the town." Sometimes, Mr. Thurber admits, the teacher has to give the information himself. "In such a case it is the teacher's privilege to present as a downright gift the matter which, in better circumstances, it would be more proper to let pupils work for and earn the right to possess."[66] Mr. Thurber realized that there were some things that the teacher was better equipped to present than the students.

His remarks on the vitiating effect of cramming for examinations might well serve as a guide today. "The school should prepare for life," he writes (long before Dewey said this), "and not for examinations." The memorizing method, the cram method, the note method, is good only for examinations. The English that pupils are destined to read for their entertainment and culture as mature men and women will not be annotated." [67] It can readily be understood why Carpenter, Baker, and Scott say of Dr. Thurber, "Teachers like Dr. Samuel Thurber—to name one of many—realized, as did men of the same rank and importance in France and Germany, the duty of the schools of the people in teaching the language of the people, and used every effort to put the study of English in the secondary schools on a firm basis." [68]

Another secondary school teacher who did a great deal of editing of English classics and who left his mark on the school system of New York City was Herbert Bates, who came to Manual Training High School, Brooklyn, New York, after being an instructor at the University of Nebraska. In addition to editing several English classics, he wrote a blank verse translation of Homer's *Odyssey* which is still used in our courses (including the writer's). In 1895, he edited Coleridge's *The Rime of the Ancient Mariner* for Longman's English Classics. Since we have seen Kellogg's suggestions for teaching a Shakespearean play in 1882 and Thurber's suggestions for essays in 1891, it may not be inappropriate to read what Bates has to say about teaching students about a long narrative poem. [69]

[66] *Ibid.*, p. xii.
[67] *Ibid.*, pp. xii, xiii.
[68] Carpenter, Baker, and Scott, *op. cit.*, pp. 48-49.
[69] Samuel Taylor Coleridge, *The Rime of the Ancient Mariner*, Herbert Bates, ed. (New York, Longmans, Green, & Co., Inc., 1895, 1905), pp. xxvii-xxx.

First he tells us what not to do. "Do not study the poem as a piece of English to be parsed." Obviously this must still have been a practice in some schools in 1895. "Do not," he continues, "if you are a teacher, make your pupils rewrite into prose. It is not meant to be written in prose. Poetical ideas are meant for poetry; in prose they are out of place—as awkward as the poor albatross must have been if he tried to walk the ship's deck." Until recent years the New York State Regents Examinations in English were giving poems to paraphrase into prose in the form of a précis.

Finally: "Do not make of the poem a combined edition of grammar, spelling-book, dictionary, rhetoric, and encyclopedia." [70] Thus, by pointing out what the teacher should *not do*, Bates was indirectly criticizing the teaching of poetry as it must have been practiced by many of his colleagues in 1895. Bates also warns against excessive time spent on the words in a poem. "Point out," he says, ". . . words that are suggestive, picturesque, poetic—words that suggest a whole clause of description. Do not, however, think that the poetry lies in these particular words. They are suggestive *here*. In another place, they would be, very likely, as prosaic as any others." He was advanced in his caution against over-analysis which, in his language, "will merely kill the goose, and get not a golden egg for your pains."

Bates's positive suggestions are as follows:

1. Gather some idea of the individuality of the man who wrote the poem (this, by reading his introduction).

2. Get, incidentally, an idea why he told the story.

3. Read the whole poem through, rapidly, at one sitting.

4. Then the student will be ready to study it.

By *study* Bates wished to avoid the ugly connotation of the word in connection with the Latin or Greek classics. Bates compared the study of a poem like this to an excursion through an art gallery. Some race through it hurriedly and get a hazy glimpse of the whole collection. The more careful viewers study each canvas to get the meaning which the artist tried to convey. Bates considers each stanza in Coleridge's poem a picture. Hence, slow study and sympathetic

[70] All quotations, *ibid.*, p. xxvii.

repetition will bring out beauties of which the hasty reader has no inkling.

In order to achieve this, Bates advises the student:

1. Resolve to see each scene distinctly.

2. Try to see some good illustrations (e.g., Doré's).

The teacher's job here is to question his pupils with regard to each scene, and have them compare the mental pictures that they see. "This will suggest to each much that would otherwise have passed unnoticed." [71] Bates constantly urges students to visualize each scene accurately and compare it with their own experiences.

The appreciation of the poet's art should be attempted, [72] as well as realizing an emotional experience. His suggestions sound very modern. "Try to appreciate, too, the poet's art. Ask constantly what artistic impulse prompted him to select this word, this incident, this metrical form. Why could it not, just as well, have been otherwise? Think of all the possible means of expression, all the possible turns of the story, and try to decide why, of all these, he settled on those before us." [73]

Bates' final advice is almost fatherly:

For method, take a few stanzas at each lesson, dwelling on each till, if possible, you have absorbed it into your memory—not only in its words but in its spirit—till its poetry has become part of you, without the aid of printed letters. Try to enjoy without scorning study, and to study without missing enjoyment. Poetry, without pleasure, is profitless.

How widespread Bates's ideas on the teaching of narrative poetry were, it is difficult to say, but he was certainly in advance of many teachers in earlier decades.

Not to omit the contributions of the distaff side to the methodology in English literature at the end of the nineteenth century, the views of Charlotte Whipple Underwood, Instructor in English in the Lewis Institute in Chicago, will be discussed. In 1899, she edited *The Merchant of Venice* for Macmillan's Pocket American and English Classics. [74] In her preface, she states her concept of the

[71] *Ibid.*, p. xxix.
[72] *Ibid.*, p. xxx.
[73] *Ibid.*
[74] Cf. footnote 45.

teacher's aim and her method in teaching Shakespeare to classes of boys and girls in secondary schools.

The aim of the teacher of fiction, Miss Underwood states, is "to secure from pupils a thoughtful, accurate interpretation of an author's words, and at the same time to arouse an enthusiastic interest in the characters portrayed." She feels that pupils need to give more thought than they often do to the author's language. She frequently required from a student the paraphrase of a difficult passage. She recommended memorizing of many quotations and reading many passages aloud. [75]

The practice of reading aloud from the play is always to be commended. Far more valuable to the pupil often than any explanation and study is the hearing of some passage appreciatively read by the teacher. When the play has been carefully worked over line by line, when its characters have been discussed in all possible relations and from every conceivable point of view, even when long quotations have been committed to memory, still the class has not come fully into its inheritance until the whole play, or most of it, has been read aloud—whole scenes and whole acts at a time —and that by pupils who have previously rehearsed their parts with spirit and expression.

To this very day, teachers and students do a great deal of reading aloud from Shakespeare.

Her notes of 1899 differed somewhat from Rolfe's and Hudson's in 1879 in the respect that she frequently asks questions rather than states all the facts as her predecessors had done in their editions of Shakespeare. In this regard, her practice is followed to this day.

Whereas the writers on methodology discussed in this section were all in the front line of teaching, as it were, and expressed their views in their editions of classics—drama, essays, and poetry—there was one writer on method who used more general terms and wrote in belletristic fashion. In 1895, Arlo Bates delivered a series of lectures to the Lowell Institute on *Talks on the Study of Literature*. [76] These were printed in 1897 and the book is frequently listed with the methods books of the early twentieth century. How much influence Bates's views had on the teaching of literature is difficult to determine, although there can be no doubt that his lectures were attended by

[75] *Ibid.*, p. viii.
[76] Arlo Bates, *Talks on the Study of Literature* (Boston, Houghton Mifflin Co., 1897, 1901).

secondary teachers and his book was probably read by many others.

It remained for Percival Chubb, Principal of the Ethical Culture High School, to present in 1902 the first organized account in America of the teaching of literature from elementary school *through* the high school. In the 1930's he revised his book which had become one of the standard texts on the subject. In 1903, Carpenter, Baker, and Scott, all professors in colleges and prolific writers of secondary school texts, issued their rich volume, *The Teaching of English in the Elementary School and the Secondary School*. This was a fairly complete compendium of the good practices at the beginning of the new century and for many years guided the practices of teachers of English in high schools.

X

Summary and Conclusions

We have traced the course of the teaching of literature in our high schools from 1865 to 1900. We have seen that in this period literature came into its rightful place as an important subject in the secondary curriculum. The changes in the textbooks, in courses of study, and in methodology, as far as could be ascertained, were indicated. As students in the high schools faced the twentieth century, they were in a far better position than the generation before them. Books were more complete, better edited, and based on sounder principles of selection. Teachers were better prepared to present the literature and to make it the dynamic stimulus for growth and better living. Constant questioning and challenging of the status quo made for improvements all along the line: materials, courses of study, methodology, and evaluation. The millennium in the teaching of literature had by no means been attained by the turn of the century, but teachers had come a long way from the chaos that prevailed before 1865.

19

HELENE W. HARTLEY

The Continuing Education
of the
Teacher of English

THE SIGNING of one's first contract to teach is for most who enter the teaching profession a significant moment. If it has come as a result of thoughtful choice of a vocation, it represents a kind of culmination of what seems a long period of preparation, and it is lighted by a sense of elation and achievement. The prospective teacher who has chosen English as his major subject because of particular pleasure in it looks forward with happy anticipation to transmitting to others—his students—his own delight and the knowledge he himself has gained. Equipped with a baccalaureate degree, perhaps also with the designation of "Master," with an accumulation of course credits representing a major in English carried with satisfactory scholarship, inducted into the professional aspects of his work through courses in education and through practice in teaching, he feels a not unwarranted confidence of success.

The first chill may come when he receives a copy of the course of study he is to use, or when he talks with experienced teachers about what they are doing. Gradually he senses what seem to be serious lacks in his preparation.

"All that grammar!" he exclaims. "Why, I haven't done anything with it since I was in high school, and I've forgotten most of that." —"Biography, drama, the short story as literary forms? But I had just one course in types and that was the novel."—"A whole year's work in American literature? I concentrated on English literature with special emphasis on the eighteenth century."—"You use much contemporary literature, you say. But how does one select and evaluate it?"—"Modern books of particular appeal to boys and girls of junior high school age? Of course, *Alice in Wonderland* and *Little Women* are too young for them. What books do you mean?"—

HELENE W. HARTLEY Professor of Education, Emeritus, Syracuse University. Formerly teacher of English and Latin in New York State schools and a supervisor of English. In charge of professional preparation and graduate work of teachers of English, Syracuse University. Summer session lecturer at many colleges and universities. President of NCTE, 1945-1946. Chairman, NCTE Committee on English in Small Schools. Member of the Curriculum Commission, NCTE. Author of *Tests in the Interpretative Reading of Poetry* and of research studies; author and coauthor of textbooks in literature for high schools, and contributor to many journals.

"Speech as a regular part of the English course, the arts of communication, the use of the mass media, structural linguistics! I must need a dozen courses at least that I have not had. Perhaps I'd better think again about teaching English."

It is not only the beginner who experiences a shock of discovered inadequacy for what he is expected to do. An experienced and successful teacher may find himself in a similar predicament. It was not long ago that the boundaries and requirements for the study of English in high school were clearly defined and fairly limited in scope. College professors and representatives of secondary schools (the function of which was in the main college preparatory) had agreed upon selections from literature and points of emphasis in composition and language to be expected. But that is now a matter of history. From the presses and mimeographing machines of cities, school-district offices, state departments, and small rural communities the country over, new courses of study in English have been coming forth for more than a decade. They represent a deepening realization of the challenge of universal education, a more penetrating understanding of the nature of language and literature as media of education, and advancing scholarship in the subject itself. In these newer courses of study familiar content has been supplemented, new aspects of the subject introduced, less familiar approaches and organization devised, and the boundaries of English as a subject in the curriculum vastly widened and interlocked with other areas.

However sound the changes, however commended and generally accepted these new courses may be, no one who visits schools extensively can fail to observe a disparity between such courses and the actual classroom work. Delays in adoption are, of course, necessitated for administrative adjustments, need for new materials, requisite interpretation to the public; but another more serious problem intervenes. A sincere and capable teacher stated it frankly: "I think our new course of study is excellent, but I am using very little of it. I am simply not prepared to teach according to it. I think I shall accomplish more for my students if I continue to teach what I am prepared to do well. I am too far along now to go back to college for further preparation. Besides I have my master's degree, and I have taken all the additional in-service work for which our school system gives credit and advancement."

In the dismayed reflection of the beginner and in the frank statement of an able and experienced teacher lies, insofar as they represent typical instances, an indication of a need generally recognized
and often stated, but rarely sharply defined as a necessity to be met
with thoughtfully considered procedures.

This need is, in the first place, for a clearer recognition that the
very nature of our subject—its richness and scope, its potentialities
as an educational medium, its advancing scholarship, and a discovery
of its interrelations with other disciplines—precludes teaching it,
save in the narrowest sense, with the kind of mastery of content and
skill possible to a greater degree in many other areas of the curriculum.
To be sure, our understanding of the processes of education makes
less possible for any teacher a sense of mastery such as it was
reasonable to expect under an earlier concept of learning. Teachers
no longer devote themselves to a mere transmitting of what they already know to young people who are expected to acquire it in toto
and even verbatim. In any subject, the teacher constantly reaches
out for new developments in his field, fresh and immediate experiences for his students, and an enrichment of subject matter to induce
understanding, inquiry, and eagerness for learning, such as rote
processes over well-worn routes rarely secured, or even sought to
secure.

If this is true of all teaching, it is especially so in the many-faceted
study of language and literature in "English" as a basic requirement
in secondary education. For the teacher of English, a pleasant and
ego-bolstering sense of mastery must be replaced by the ever-exciting
pursuit of his subject and the art of teaching it. As one teacher re-
marked: "I choose to teach English because I know I shall die un-
satisfied!"

Beyond this recognition of the challenge to continued study that
lies in the very nature of our subject, a second need is imperative.
It must be realized—and early in the process of preparation—that
no mere dependence on "taking courses" can meet the requirements
of the teacher in this field.

Characteristically in this country, for reasons understandable in
the early development of our educational system, much stress has
been laid on accumulation of credits from academic courses as evidence of competence for admission to any profession. Controversy

often arises as to the number of credit hours that should be required
in a subject major for teachers and the proportion of courses to be
given in professional education. Certification to teach rests, in the
main, on a numerical count of stipulated credits-in-course. School
systems, too, seeking to improve instruction, offer inducements in
salary or other advancement to teachers to continue to "take courses."
Extension classes, summer sessions, workshops, in-service courses are
offered for them, often with stiff competition among neighboring
higher institutions to attract them by a studied offering of "something
practical" to meet immediate needs in the schools.

Under such stress on courses as the route to certification for the
prospective teacher, and upon more courses for advancement once he
is launched on his work, it is not strange that the individual teacher
tends to rely upon them as his major, almost exclusive, resource,
and that he may throw up his hands despairingly if he is asked to
go beyond what he has been so taught.

Certainly there can be no sound disparagement of continued study
in advanced courses in strong institutions of higher education, where
the stimulus of direct contact with scholarship, representative of
both classic and modern, the established and the theoretical, can be
renewed and maintained. The inaugurating of postdoctoral programs
in some of our universities indicates such a continuing necessity. But
there is a regrettable aspect, twofold in its effect, of an overemphasis
on taking courses.

In the first place, a pressure builds up for departments in colleges
and universities to organize and match their offerings too narrowly
to the specific needs represented in the requirements of secondary
school curriculums. This can result in a diluting of collegiate work
similar to what took place in the earlier normal schools, where, in
successive courses, teachers studied in the main what they themselves
would teach in each grade of the elementary school. It tends to
obscure the more important goal of college courses to lay a foundation
in knowledge, to open up enticing areas of scholarship, to arouse
interest and inquiry, and to leave the student with ability and resources that will make possible a confident pursuit of the subject
long after the final examination is taken and the course, in its
academic sense, completed.

A second related aspect of overemphasis on course-taking and credit-acquiring for the teacher is to obscure the inescapable necessity for continued independent study throughout his teaching career. A program of planned independent study can be not only the most important means for meeting the requirements of his work but one of the richest rewards of teaching in an area that makes such study readily possible and personally satisfying. For no matter how much one profits from and enjoys academic offerings in organized courses taught by scholarly and inspiring instructors nothing can yield the delight of discovery that we can give ourselves superior courses also, organizing them to our liking; pursuing them with the aid of many scholars whose writings are abundantly available to us in libraries and increasingly in inexpensive paperback editions, utilizing the power to do-for-ourselves developed in the period of greater dependence upon instruction by others. A beginning teacher expressed her surprise at discovering her own ability to proceed independently when she said: "I am using a novel in my class that I had never read in any course I had taken. In getting ready to teach it I found that I could analyze, understand, and appraise it without a professor's doing it for me. Now, when do you suppose I acquired that ability?"

Reference was made above to the necessity for a *planned* program of independent study. Such a program goes far beyond the desultory and sporadic effort that too often constitutes an individual's continued self-education. Recently a teacher decided that he was using the traditional English poets almost exclusively in his courses because, as he frankly admitted, he did not know how to read modern poetry. A trip to the library, a few pleasant hours spent in investigating the files, examining current reviews, critical journals, and recent volumes on the shelves yielded a bibliography. Starting with John Ciardi's *How Does a Poem Mean?*, he was launched on a zestful experience of reading and learning that lasted, as he said, from September to Christmas. Much that he gained he could not use directly in the junior high school in which he taught. It was too mature, too scholarly. *But it was personally satisfying.* And this is perhaps the most important result of a teacher's independent study—that he feels himself continuously in communication with mature minds in his field, that he replenishes reservoirs of his own understanding and delight, that his own knowledge grows beyond his teaching so that he never approaches the limit of what he has to give.

Another young teacher discovered that she had missed many of the classics, as well as more recent literature for the young. Her preparatory courses had not included literature for adolescents. With the aid of published guides and of the school librarian, she prepared a reading list for her own relaxed, recreational use. She found that she was not reading down at a child's level. Her artistic delight in *Wind in the Willows* was that of the mature reader. With Salinger's *Catcher in the Rye,* Mary Stolz's *To Tell Your Love,* and Dorothy Canfield Fisher's *Understood Betsy* she gained further adult understanding of the process of growing up as revealed in effective fiction. Fresh enjoyment of the familiar and a pleasurable discovery of the new came with May Arbuthnot's *Time for Poetry.* She made the acquaintance of Johnny Reb and Johnny Tremaine, along with heroes of older tales she had missed. The humor of folk literature and the tall tale gave her fresh enjoyment. The program she planned and followed enriched her as a reader and, in this case, was directly usable with those she taught.

In some instances, groups of teachers of English explore together some particular aspect of their field. In one school a drama-study and play-reading group meet once a month, with husbands and wives participating in the experience of further learning.

Many experienced teachers are eager to know more of the advancing scholarship in language. Unable to go to graduate centers where such work is available, they nonetheless find that they can gain knowledge and understanding of structural linguistics and of language as human behavior with the aid of many writers. Books, periodicals, articles in abundance provide material for a solid course of planned study.

Incentive to undertake a rigorous course of study of this sort may come from intellectual curiosity and interest alone. It may be stimulated by practical considerations after reading claims for the advantages of teaching structural linguistics in high school, such as were outlined by W. Wilbur Hatfield in the *English Journal* for December, 1958, or by teachers whose success in using this approach has been reported in other issues of the *Journal.* Charlton Laird's *The Miracle of Language* may have awakened a zestful eagerness for further study.

The background of a teacher of English often starts with a traditional course in the history of the language, taken, perhaps, as a somewhat perfunctory fulfillment of a major requirement before more recent scholarship brought fresh interest to the subject. It may have included a newer type of course in "The English Language" or in "American English." In a course in methods of teaching English, many teachers will have read *Teaching English Usage* by Robert C. Pooley, gaining understanding of the distinction between usage and grammar, a concept of levels of usage in contrast with earlier doctrines of correctness, and some appreciation of the function and development of language in communication. Some will also have met the work of Charles C. Fries, at least his *American English Grammar*, and will have been introduced to the newer descriptions of language and the methods used to arrive at more accurate analyses.

With a general background such as this, resources appropriate for the less advanced linguistic student will be needed as a beginning for a program of independent study. Use can well be made of the National Council of Teachers of English since over a period of years the Council has been promoting linguistic scholarship among teachers through its publications and the programs of its annual meetings. *The English Journal, College English, College Composition and Communication, Abstracts of English Studies,* and *Tools for Teaching English* will contribute helpfully to the building of a bibliography. So, too, will *Readings on Applied Linguistics,* edited by Harold B. Allen, and his article in *College English* (February, 1960) on "Books about Language". These latter guides will aid also in selecting points for emphasis on specialized aspects, such as language as structure, the nature of usage, or, perhaps, the broader aspects and implications—psychological, anthropological, social—of language in communication.

Whatever direction one's program of study may take, however far it may lead, the basis will doubtless be laid in the work of the structural linguists. In the bibliography, such books as *Patterns of English* by Paul Roberts, *The Structure of English* by Charles C. Fries, and Harold Whitehall's *Structural Essentials of English* will be included. The goal of preliminary study should not be to adopt any one system of description, but to become familiar with points of view, methods of work, directions of research, and the present status of scholarship in a rapidly advancing field.

Obviously, this brief sketch merely illustrates some of the approaches and procedures that may be useful in planning a self-directed course of study in the language area of our subject. Exacting as such an undertaking may be, its rewards will be great, not alone through keeping us as teachers abreast of current scholarship, but in the intellectual stimulus to us as individuals to thinking with exactness and scientific precision, balancing the more customary philosophic and aesthetic concern with our field.

In 1949–1950, the appearance for several weeks of a book on style in writing [1] among the then current ten best-selling books of nonfiction must indicate that many people desire to achieve greater understanding and skill in this aspect of communication. An often neglected part of the preparation of teachers of English, the fine art and craftsmanship of writing might well constitute another phase of a program of continuing self-education.

Fortunately, much has been written about their work by classic and modern authors—the nature of the creative process, the sources and use of experience, essentials of style, and its relation to personality. With little effort even a busy teacher, once his attention turns in this direction, can draw together a rich program of reading that will enhance his critical judgment of his own writing, that of his students, and that exemplified in literature.

Reading of the sort can draw upon authoritative literary criticism. It will also include periodical articles addressed to the general reader, for example, "A Sane Approach to Style" by Charles W. Ferguson in *Saturday Review* (September 26, 1959). The delightful book by Mary J. J. Wrinn, *The Hollow Reed,* written on the craftsmanship of poetry for "the young in heart", the enlightening *Story of a Novel* by Thomas Wolfe are examples of writing that will deepen insight. If one's own college education preceded recent experiments in integration of the humanities, it is still not at all impossible through independent study to gain a more penetrating understanding of the art of writing through study of composition in other fields—in music, painting, or the dance. *Literature as a Fine Art,* edited by Donald J. McGinn and George Howerton (Row, Peterson & Company, 1959), can launch such a venture with delighted discovery.

[1] William Strunk, Jr. and E. B. White, *The Elements of Style* (New York, The Macmillan Co., 1959).

Needless to say, some practice in writing should accompany reading as an important part of a program of continued education—writing done alone, or as one of a friendly group of "scribblers," or, even, on occasion, as a member of one's own class, joining with them in a co-operative effort towards improvement. Through such a program of reading and writing, a teacher can escape from composition as a dreary process of proofreading and correcting and can penetrate into the delight of participating in the appreciation and practice of a fine art, both as a student and as a teacher.

If programs of planned, independent study are to become more frequent supplements to traditional courses, encouragement is needed from such organizations as the National Council of Teachers of English, and from state and local groups, for school systems to accept such programs, under well-defined conditions, as bases for advancement in evidence of growing scholarship, as some already do. In meeting obstacles the individual teacher, too, must take an active part. To find time to do so, he often has to take his conscience in hand. A sense of duty to some familiar procedure may stand in the way of larger values. A brief study of the problem may reveal possible short cuts in lesson planning, desirable substitutes for some of the red-inking of written exercises. An occasional neglect of self-established routine may be a reasonable price to pay for one's own continued growth. Not out of barrenness, but out of ever-deepening richness, we must teach. Of all good teachers it can truly be said: "His cup runneth over." This is the challenge that teachers of English must meet, not alone through traditional study, but through self-initiated, self-directed, *zestful* pursuit of the subject itself and the art of teaching it.

20

BRICE HARRIS

The Pedant and
Some Other Characters
in His Profession

T HE EIGHT PARTS OF SPEECH are his servants," observed Sir
Thomas Overbury of the seventeenth-century pedant. "He
treads in a rule," and it would never occur to him to question
"that the nominative case governs not the verb." Sir Thomas was
using the word *pedant* of course in its now obsolete sense of schoolmaster or teacher, but even in its heyday the word connoted its
modern sense because most schoolmasters were pedants as we understand them today. They were preoccupied with the rules, with grammar, with a show of learning, with technicalities and a rather comic
intent to moralize, or "teach," at the expense of everything else.
Seemingly, they had small time for grace and clearness and charm
and effectiveness and wit. Fortunately today most teachers are not
pedants, nor is pedantry any longer isolated in the profession of
teaching. Some of our loudest critics are pedants of the first water
even though they may never have faced a classroom.

The "Character" writers for a hundred years after Sir Thomas
Overbury continued to amuse themselves with witty and acrid comment about grammar school teachers, scholars from the universities,
and practitioners of and pretenders to learning. Thus, John Earle
wrote of a "Downright Scholar" that time had "got a vein of making
him ridiculous, and men laugh at him by tradition." Every unlucky
absurdity "is put upon his profession." "He names this word *college*
too often, and his discourse beats too much on the university." He
knows so little about the levels of language that he could not "speak
to a dog in his own dialect." But Earle offered some welcome con-
solation: "Practice him a little in men, and brush him o'er with good
company," and he will outshine all of his scorners as gold does gold
lace.

Addison even gave his pedant a name, Tom Folio, the universal

BRICE HARRIS Professor of English, The Pennsylvania State University;
Chairman of Department, 1947-1957. Visiting Professor, University of
Zaragoza, Spain, 1957. President of NCTE, 1957-1958. Chairman, College
Section, NCTE, 1952-1955; Director, Commission on the Profession since
1958. Research Fellow, Huntington Library, 1936-1937. Grant for study in
England, 1934, American Council of Learned Societies. Author of *Sackville,
Earl of Dorset*, 1940. Editor, *Restoration Plays*, Modern Library, 1953.
Numerous articles and reviews in learned journals.

scholar. Tom knows the title-pages of authors, the editions through which they have passed, and their reputations in the learned world. A literary discussion with Tom consists of the name of the editor, the year in which the book was printed, the excellence of the paper, the diligence of the proofreader, and the beauty of the type, but nothing of the beauty of the style of writing or the justness of the thought. And a contemporary of Addison, an anonymous lady, voiced the old complaint about pedants that they are not at home in their own time and place. Mention Assyria, Persia, Greece, or Rome, and they answer like oracles. Certainly, they must have been confidants of Semiramis, tutors to Cyrus the Great, cronies of Solon, advisers to the twelve Caesars. But talk about the present or their native country, "and they hardly speak the language of it, and know so little of the affairs of it, that as much might be reasonably expected from an animated Egyptian mummy."

Now the "Character" had pretty well disappeared as a literary type by Addison's time. The "Character" approach was appearing in the informal essay in a much more personalized vein, and it was soon to be incorporated organically into the novel by Fielding and his successors. But the charm and fragrance (and sometimes odor!) which it diffused for a hundred years are not easily forgotten. The brief, concise, objective summation of the typical properties of a person in a special category is memorable in this approach. The wit, satire, and moral are inescapable. The method of beginning with a sentence of definition and continuing with a series of phrases beginning with "he" is effective. The concluding thought, wrapped up in an epigram or a conceit, may be devastating. But the Character device can never be taken personally because it calls no names and it deals with types alone. [1]

Would it be feasible to compose a series of twentieth-century Characters concerned with the pedants and scholarly folk of today, many of them in the profession of English teaching? Let us try.

The *Department Character* belongs to a rapidly disappearing genre, but he is still present on almost every English staff. He barks

[1] Were there a reader unfamiliar with the seventeenth-century "Character," let him consult Gwendolen Murphy, *A Cabinet of Characters* (London, Oxford University Press, 1925), with its charming introduction and its tasteful selection of representative Characters.

at students who enter his lair, and he insults them in the lecture room. He allows no questions or discussions in his classes because his statements are all ex cathedra. He infuriates his student audience by announcing at the first lecture that they are stupid and lazy and that a mere minimum of them may expect to pass his course. He orates at length (when he should be explaining the details of his subject) about the sad plight of youth and education in these post-millennial years. He questions their right to be members of the university community and casts aspersions on the registrar for admitting them. He scorns any intimation that a student does his best work when it is made interesting and challenging to him, believing rather that there is no royal road to learning. If a student commits the unpardonable sin of visiting his office during an office hour, he appears extremely busy for ten minutes and then spends the period of forced consultation opening his second-class mail (which he has carefully hoarded in a side drawer for that purpose) and intimating in obvious ways that the interloper's time is up. He fancies himself Mr. Chips; actually he is Simon Legree in cap and gown. His students despise him and secretly ridicule him; the alumni spin yarns about him at commencement drinking bouts; and the board of trustees names a new humanities building for him on his retirement.

The *Scholar-Teacher* is the Happy Warrior of the profession, what every college English teacher should wish to be. He is master of a "field," as he fondly and somewhat slyly puts it, and he has demonstrated his mastery by writing one or more superior books about it, a sheaf of articles, and a respectable list of reviews. He writes and continues his studies because he believes that only as a scholar can he offer the best to his students. He would be deeply pained, nay, incensed, if anyone accused him of using scholarly pursuits merely to achieve promotion or to impress the dean or his fellow scholars. He is just as surely dedicated to the profession of teaching. He sees his students as people, not as cabbages or pawns, and he charts their intellectual level early in his classes so that he may raise it. When he teaches Keats' *Ode on a Grecian Urn* to undergraduates or to graduates, he makes it live forever in their minds. He would never think for a moment of wasting part of his valuable hour in pointing out a textual emendation in line 13, or, for that matter, of listing all the pertinent bibliography on the subject of urns from Sir Thomas

Browne to the present. He believes fervently that a critical appreciation of literature and a crisp, modern style of writing are the most
precious possessions he can will his students. His classes are packed
year in and year out, and his reputation as a teacher and a scholar will
long outlive him.

The *Drifter-In* just happened to become an English teacher. He
had planned to enter the ministry but had lost faith somewhere along
the way. Faced with embracing some profession he fell into teaching
English. On Career Day he had heard a high functionary in his
college proclaim that the profession of English teaching placed few
demands on its followers. An English teacher might expect to spend
a long life pursuing his own ends, working slowly, if he liked, with
scholars like himself. He would be highly respected in the community though he would be paid poorly, and he would be assured of
being able to go his own way without much tampering from the
administration. He liked the sound of this rosy dream. He rather
supposed that he liked to read, and, of course, anybody could teach
English anyhow because everybody spoke and read it. He was almost
deterred from his glorious ambition by his freshman English teacher,
who reminded him that he must publish, that the college library had
small research facilities, and that at his own expense he might have
to visit the Folger, the Huntington, or even the Bodleian. But he
visited the functionary and was reassured—materials for research
were all around him: the daily papers, magazines, telephone di-
rectories. And so he drifted into English teaching. He teaches poorly
and publishes not at all, but he has become an expert dry-fly fisher-
man, a popular speaker on science fiction, and the owner of a superb
collection of phonograph records.

The *Disappointed Novelist* had not planned to teach English in
the first place. On graduation, he envisioned a brisk and illuminating
year on a New York magazine or trade journal while he put the
finishing touches to his *Opus One* (in C minus). But no New
York offer worthy of his genius turned up. He grudgingly and rather
sullenly deigned to accept a position teaching freshman English at
his alma mater. Within a year *Opus One* would be off the press and
his worries over. Three years later, after six refusals, the novel appears under the imprint of a second-rate publisher and is reviewed
adversely, cavalierly, or not at all. Fifteen hundred copies are re-

maindered at thirty-five cents each. He becomes a full-time English teacher, but he will still write novels; he will take no advanced degrees. He considers writing the Great American novel, but eventually settles for a new field of fiction, the "different" college novel. Ten years later he is competing rather bitterly with the Disappointed Poet and the Disappointed Short-Story Writer for the advanced courses in criticism and asking himself querulously what Warren and Sagan have that he does not have.

The *Paper-Clip Wheelhorse,* indigenous to all white collar professions, flourishes on every secondary or college English faculty. But there is only one to each staff—he ruthlessly Stalinizes every competitor. Give him a desk with drawers on both sides and a pile of paper clips to push around, and he is happy the livelong day. He speaks and thinks proudly of himself as a *wheel* because the term sounds important, but he is really only a *horse,* a workhorse. Is there a dull, detailed, routine report to be prepared for an administrative factotum? The PCW craves the assignment. Must the autumn teaching schedules be prepared by the middle of the month, time and room assignments included? The PCW requests the job. Are four trouble-packed days of registration facing us? The PCW smiles bravely through the clouds and, like St. Christopher, carries us on his sturdy back over the dark river. He basks in the smile of his department head but orders assistants around in high disdain. He teaches poorly half time and sits at his paper-clip desk dreaming of the day when he will be forced to teach no longer. He tells everybody how, where, when, and what to do but never *why.* He will achieve his highest ambition when he becomes assistant dean or assistant principal, in fact, assistant-anything that is administrative. Then he will have two telephones, a secretary, a chair that leans back when he sits in it, and a much larger and more varied mountain of paper clips to push around over his now glass-topped desk. Truly, he seems "busier than he nas."

The *Old-Time Religionist* believes that if the English curriculum was good enough for Paul and Silas it is good enough for him. He is dedicated to resisting change, but he does not know that the curriculum of the days of Paul and Silas is in his own mind the curriculum of his early years. He speaks glowingly of the old days as if English teaching had been set in one mold for a thousand years.

He regrets the passing of the blue-backed speller—*he* learned to spell there and look at him! He pines for the parsing and the diagramming of his youth, not realizing that such practices are still meritorious provided they do not become the be-all and end-all of grammar teaching. With a morbid illogic he somehow confuses curriculum and methods with other facets of his youthful years—the long walk to school in the snow or mud or rain; the straight-backed benches with three generations of pupils' art and signatures carved in them; the ice which he had to break in the pan before he could wash his face each winter morning. He marinates all his nostalgia with a generous helping of his own failures in life and so degenerates into a pathological apologist for his educational past. Like Miniver Cheevy he was born out of his time and all he can do about it is to think and think—and talk unendingly.

The *Faculty Watchdog*, self-appointed, usually belongs to the English department because, as everyone knows, English teachers write well and are critics—of everything. Sometimes, he is called the "Defender of Faculty Rights." In brief, he watches the administration. He has established liaison, he thinks, with the board of trustees, and he takes every issue to them. If he has an academic complaint (and he never lacks one), his cardinal principle is "Take it to the man higher up." He would no more discuss a disagreement with his department head than he would discuss with a clerk the fact that he had been shortchanged—*he* sees the manager. He writes letters, volumes indeed, to the dean and to the president, and he encourages his accomplices to do the same. He begins his letter with "We" or "All of us here" though he has consulted none of his colleagues and would find them sorely in disagreement with his opinions if he were to approach them. He is convinced that English teachers should form a union, insist on collective bargaining, and strike if their demands are not met. In summary, he is the goon in academe, the sole member of his boss's disloyal opposition. His bite is worse than his bark, and his retirement is awaited eagerly.

The *Nonresident* Pedant is the specialist in writing, grammar, and usage who lives and works off campus. He is a local surveyor, a retired colonel, a physician, a used-car dealer, a professor in a related field, or what-have-you. He avers proudly that during his long career he has found only one good stenographer. He promptly married her, presumably for stenography and not for love. Other girls that have worked for him can scarcely write their names, much less take down correctly the words of wisdom that fall from his lips following "Yours of the 15th instant received and contents noted." He is convinced that every organization of English teachers is affiliated with a teachers' college and dedicated mutually to foul purposes, such as the destruction of discipline, the stultifying of youth, and the weakening of intellectual fortitude. This horrid plot, unknown to parents and to the trusting public, must be ruthlessly exposed and eradicated. He understands that a college professor named John Dewey is to blame for this sad situation. He has read nothing written by this abominable character, but the word *Dewey* is anathema to him. He blames Progressive Education for all instructional woes, not really knowing what it is, or that it is now history. He has never visited an English classroom to find out what is really going on, not even when his own children were in school, but he knows the solution to the problem. He is a master of school curriculum, administration, and finance, not to speak of teaching methods. He votes against local tax rises for new school buildings and for increasing teachers' salaries, and he complains bitterly about the classes now being held in church basements, lodge halls, and warehouses. He writes letters to the local paper and to the metropolitan dailies which in style, diction, coherence, and emphasis give the lie to the fine discipline which he proudly thinks he expounds. He tears his hair at a split infinitive and spends a great deal of time hunting dangling participles which he has trouble recognizing, but he would not flick an eyelash at a blatant solecism or a discreditable piece of illogic.

If this attempt to create twentieth-century characters has resulted in more detestable ones than favorable ones, the reasons are partly historical and partly logical: historical because the same ratio prevailed in the seventeenth century; logical, because we are normally more amused by the frailty of human nature than by its goodness. And it certainly never hurts the teaching profession to laugh at some of its clowns, its absurdities, and its incongruities.

21

LOU LA BRANT

Epilogue
The English Teacher